towards proficiency

student's book

peter may

OXFORD
UNIVERSITY PRESS

contents

Paper	Name	Timing	Content	Test Focus
1	Reading	1 hour 30 mins	Part 1 – three short texts with six four-option multiple choice cloze questions on each Part 2 – four short texts with two four-option multiple choice questions on each Part 3 – gapped text with seven questions Part 4 – long text with seven four-option multiple choice questions	Assessment of candidates' ability to understand the meaning of written English at word, phrase, sentence, paragraph and whole text level.
2	Writing	2 hours	Part 1 – one compulsory question Part 2 – candidates answer one question from a choice of four questions (including the set book option)	Assessment of candidates' ability to write specified text types with a range of functions.
3	Use of English	1 hour 30 mins	Part 1 – modified open cloze with fifteen questions Part 2 – one short text with ten word formation questions Part 3 – six sets of three gapped sentences Part 4 – eight key word transformations Part 5 – two texts with four questions and a summary writing task	Assessment of candidates' ability to demonstrate knowledge and control of the language system by completing various tasks at text and sentence level.
4	Listening	40 mins (approx.)	Part 1 – four short extracts with two three-option multiple choice questions on each Part 2 – one long text with nine sentence completion questions Part 3 – long text with five four-option multiple choice questions Part 4 – one long text with six matching questions	Assessment of candidates' ability to understand the meaning of spoken English, to extract information from a text and to understand speakers' attitudes and opinions.
5	Speaking	19 mins	Part 1 – interview Part 2 – collaborative task Part 3 – individual long turns and follow-up discussion	Assessment of candidates' ability to produce spoken English using a range of functions in a variety of tasks.

Reproduced by permission of the University of Cambridge Local Examinations Syndicate.

unit 1 | money

vocabulary and speaking

1 **a** What were the last three things you paid for? How did you pay for them, e.g. *cash*? Do you think you got value for money?

b Make a list of different ways of paying for something. What are the advantages and disadvantages of each?

2 **a** Look at the people in pictures 1–3 and match them with these adjectives.

> <u>wealthy</u>   penniless   well off   poverty-stricken   <u>prosperous</u>   impoverished
> <u>stingy</u>   badly off   <u>comfortable</u>   loaded   tight-fisted   broke   skint   <u>affluent</u>
> penny-pinching   hard up   miserly

b Discuss where you think each person's money comes from (their *income*, or *earnings*) and where it goes (their *outgoings*, or *expenditure*).

c Which of the words in the box are informal?

d Look at the underlined words. Find their noun forms by looking in a dictionary.

3 Look at the following expressions. Explain the differences between them by giving an example of each.

1 earn money/win money
2 pocket money/easy money
3 save money (two meanings)/waste money
4 have some money on you/be in the money/be made of money
5 get your money's worth/put your money where your mouth is
6 money talks/money doesn't grow on trees

4 Read the paragraph below and study the words in bold. Use the context to work out their meanings.

> **EXAMPLE**   *A loan is money you borrow, often from a bank,*
> *that you have to pay back.*

talking points

1 Why are some countries very rich and others very poor? How can poor countries be helped? What are the main sources of income for your country?
2 What do you enjoy spending money on, and what do you resent having to pay for? Why?
3 How much money do you think you personally need to be happy? What would you do if you suddenly came into a lot of money? Can you think of any disadvantages?
4 Do you agree with the following?
   Money doesn't buy happiness.
   The best things in life are free.
   The love of money is the root of all evil.
5 What books or films do you know in which money plays a significant part? Why is the money so important?

I don't know what the world's coming to these days. All anybody seems to care about is money. My brother's had to take out a **loan** so he can pay for his daughter to go to university, now that **grants** are no longer available. He'll have to pay all her living **expenses**, of course, and the **rent** alone will cost a fortune! My sister wants to get a **mortgage**, but **interest** rates keep going up and all the extras like **taxes** and solicitor's **fees** mean that she might not have enough for the **deposit**. Banks in this country only seem interested in making enormous **profits** and paying huge **salaries** to their fat-cat executives (plus generous **pensions** when they retire early, naturally). Unless you have a job like that, or get a massive **inheritance** from your parents, life can be one long struggle. Bus **fares** keep rising, as do parking **fines** (if you can afford a car). My **wages** at the burger restaurant are as low as ever, and customers never give me a **tip** – no matter how good the service. Meanwhile, ...

reading topic sentences; words from context

1 a Quickly read texts A, B and C to identify what different aspect of money each is about. Where would you expect to read them?

b How much of the texts do you need to read to answer question **a**?

2 a The main subject of a paragraph is often given in the topic sentence. Where would you expect to find this?

b Read the three texts again and use the topic sentence in each paragraph to help answer these questions.

Text A : 1 What was special about this edition of the programme?
2 How long did the tension last?
3 How did the audience and Ms Keppel differ in their reactions?

Text B: 1 What does the bank want to enable customers to do?
2 What facilities are normally available round the clock?
3 Why is it no longer necessary to go to the bank in person?

Text C: 1 What has recently caught the writer's attention?
2 How does he feel about the inventors' attitude to money?
3 What sort of person is best suited to that kind of work?

3 In some texts there may be words that you don't recognise, but the context will nearly always provide enough clues for you to work out what they mean. Work out the meanings of the following words. Text A has questions to help you.

Text A
1 *appeal* (line 2) After two years, how interested will people be in the show?
2 *scooping* (line 6) What verb usually goes with 'prize'?
3 *sound* (line 9) Do you think Judith's judgement was good or bad?
4 *gamble* (line 18) What were the two possible results of answering the question?
5 *intensified* (line 22) Why did the producers have a commercial break at this point? What sort of atmosphere did they want?
6 *tidy sum* (line 31) Why did some of the audience call the newspapers? What were they hoping for?

Text B
1 *account* (line 3)
2 *key* (line 13)
3 *access* (line 18)
4 *secure* (line 27)
5 *excluding* (line 33)

Text C
1 *fortunes* (line 5)
2 *bother* (line 10)
3 *driven* (line 12)
4 *invention* (line 16)

A TV millionaire thanks to Henry II ...

'Anybody can do it' says garden designer who won quiz's top prize

After two years and just as it appeared to be losing its appeal, *Who Wants To Be a Millionaire?* (ITV 8 p.m.) last night turned up its first £1m winner. Judith
5 Keppel, 58, achieved what many had thought impossible by scooping the top prize with a remarkably wide knowledge of history and geography combined with sound judgement and
10 an element of good luck.

Right to the last, the show's host, Chris Tarrant, kept up the pressure on Ms Keppel. Seeing the £1m question 'Which king was married to Eleanor of
15 Aquitaine?' Ms Keppel took the option that no other contestant on the British version of the show had done before – she decided to gamble £468,000 by answering. An incorrect
20 reply would have reduced her winnings to £32,000, and the show's

producers intensified the atmosphere by cutting to a commercial break. It was three minutes before Tarrant
25 revealed what he knew as soon as she had replied: that 'Henry II' was the right answer.

As the audience leapt to its feet in joy (understandable since their
30 presence at the making of television history netted one or two a tidy sum in calls to tabloid newspapers a few minutes later), Ms Keppel remained as cool as she had been since starting out
35 on the journey to £1m. Her daughter Rosie ran down from the audience to hug her, while Tarrant voiced amazement at how calm she was. Ms Keppel replied, 'I can't believe it,
40 that's why.' She then turned to her daughter and joked, 'What do you want for Christmas?'

B MANAGING YOUR FINANCES

As a Barclays customer you can take advantage of the latest technology and banking facilities to keep control of your business finances.

Our aim is to make it as easy as possible for you to get information and use your account when it suits you. As well as the traditional means 5 of using your bank account – cheque books, paying-in books and regular statements – we offer a number of other options.

Most Barclays branches offer 24- 10 hour, automated facilities for cash withdrawals, and balance enquiries. Your Business Barclaybank Card is the key to these services. You can also apply for a charge card for 15 business expenses.

Our latest communications technology also makes it possible for you to access your account directly from home or office. Barclays 20 Businesscall, the telephone banking facility, is available 24 hours a day for most services. This allows you to get information on your account and to carry out various transactions when it 25 suits you, for the cost of a local call.

If you prefer to view information, Barclays Online Banking gives secure 24-hour access to your account from your workplace or home by laptop or 30 PC. This is available free for start-up businesses for the first year and it comes with free Internet access for all customers (excluding call charges). You'll find details on our 35 business website.

C

Who wants to be a teenage millionaire?

Teenagers are earning fortunes overnight, thanks to e-business ideas.

Have you noticed how the newspapers are suddenly full of people who have become overnight millionaires, and I mean not just normal people, but teenagers? These kids don't have a serious thought in their heads, but they are 5 making fortunes from a single brilliant idea that comes to them while they are in the bath or at the launderette. A novel, a film script, an Internet adventure … Why them? Why not me? Why? Why? Why?

Don't get me wrong: I'm not complaining about young 10 people having a bit of good luck, but what does bother me slightly is the way these youngsters don't seem in the slightest bit driven by money. Indeed, they seem perfectly happy to work 100 hours every week in conditions of absolute poverty, wearing the same old Microsoft T-shirt week in, week out, 15 putting together some enormously complicated website invention that they can then casually sell off to some huge organisation that should, of course, have thought of it in the first place.

The truth is, starting your own hi-tech business at home is 20 so much easier when you are barely out of short trousers and you are quite happy to be penniless for months or even years. I mean, you can hardly expect me to live on tins of sardines until Bill Gates gives me a call, can you? ●

4 a Read the texts in more detail to look for specific information. What do the following numbers refer to? 58; £32,000; 24; 100

b Answer these questions.
What was the correct answer to the £1m question?
What's the name of Barclays' telephone banking facility?
Where do the teenage millionaires have their ideas?
What company is mentioned as being on a T-shirt?

5 a • In text A, what was happening during the *three minutes* mentioned in line 24?
• In text B, what kind of customer is the text written for? How do you know?
• In text C, what does the expression *Don't get me wrong* mean? Is it formal or informal? Can you find any more examples like this?

b Apart from making money on the Internet, or by winning TV quiz shows, how else can people 'get rich quick'?

grammar
the infinitive and the *-ing* form

1 a Read the examples then put the verbs in the box into two groups: those that take a *to*-infinitive and those that take *-ing*.
*We sometimes **manage to finish** work early.*
*We always **enjoy finishing** work early.*

> avoid   consider   dislike   expect
> hope   offer   practise   promise

b Add more verbs to each group.

2 a Some verbs can be followed by either the infinitive or *-ing*, but the meaning changes depending on which is used. For each pair, explain the difference in meaning, using the clue to help you.

1   After he had taken my temperature, the doctor *went on* to check my pulse.
    We *went on* discussing the matter until midnight.
    Which one involves a change of activity?

2   I *regret* to have to tell you that there has been an accident.
    Now I *regret* telling her to go away.
    Which refers to what the speaker did in the past?

3   Mariela *stopped* to chat with someone.
    The players *stopped* running when they heard the whistle.
    Which clearly states the purpose of the verb in italics?

4   I won't *forget* spending that wonderful weekend with you.
    I won't *forget* to send you a birthday card, I promise!
    Which refers to a past event?

5   I *meant* to phone you, but I didn't have time.
    Taking the train *meant* getting up at 6.00 a.m.
    Which states the speaker's intention?

6   Pat *likes* to do the housework early in the morning.
    My cousin Luis *likes* racing go-karts.
    Which indicates enjoyment?

7   Charlotte never *remembers* to take her key with her when she goes out.
    He *remembers* seeing a man there, but it was too dark to see his face.
    Which refers to a past event?

8   I *tried* to open the window, but I couldn't because it was stuck.
    I *tried* opening the window, but the room was still hot.
    Which means that the action was difficult?

9   As I passed the window, I *heard* someone playing the violin badly.
    We *heard* the orchestra play all of Mozart's Violin Concerto No. 5.
    Which refers to only part of the action?

    Can you think of other verbs used like *hear* in **9**?

b Choose three of the following subjects and discuss them with a partner.

1   Something you think you should stop doing, and what you could start doing instead.
2   Things you sometimes forget to do, and why you should remember to do them.

3   What you mean to do at the weekend, and what you don't intend to do.
4   Difficult things you've tried to do, but didn't succeed in doing.
5   Interesting things you remember doing as a child, and why you liked doing them.
6   Rock bands you've watched perform live or on TV, and what you heard them play.
7   Sports you've tried doing, but didn't enjoy playing.
8   Things you regret doing, and what made you do them.

3
- Certain verbs followed by the infinitive need an object before *to*:
  We persuaded him to come with us.
- Some cannot have an object in this position:
  Kathy has decided to move house.
- Others may or may not be followed by an object:
  I would like to arrive on time. = I need to arrive on time.
  I would like the message to arrive on time. = <u>The message</u> needs to arrive on time.

a Read the explanation on page 8 and complete 1–7 with the correct form of one of the verbs, plus the object in brackets where given.

> agree   cause   help   hope
> pretend   teach   want   warn

1 A professional musician .... to play the piano beautifully. (my sister)
2 The room was in a terrible mess so I .... tidy it. (her)
3 One player fell to the ground and .... to be injured, but everyone knew he wasn't really hurt.
4 It was becoming clear that he couldn't fix his roof on his own, so reluctantly I .... to help.

5 My father washed his sweater in hot water, which .... to shrink to half its size. (it)

6 At the end of the letter to my penfriend I said I .... to hear from her soon.
7 Julia went into a shop with her boyfriend, and said she .... to buy the most expensive dress they had. (him)

b Which two sentences don't need an object? How does the meaning change if they have one, or don't have one?

This company lets people to work at home if they wish.
The boys were made pay for the damage.
What is wrong with each of these sentences? Why? `

4 Fill in the gaps using the infinitive or *-ing* form of the verbs in brackets. If there is a question in italics, add an object. The first one has been done as an example.

> Joan asked ....*the waiter to bring*.... (bring) the bill after they'd finished ......*eating*...... (eat) their meal. *Who brings the bill in a restaurant?*

1 Our boss encourages .... (work) together because he knows we enjoy .... (share) our ideas. *Who is being encouraged?*
2 You need to practise .... (talk) to each other if you are to learn .... (speak) fluently.
3 I advised .... (think) carefully before she offered .... (look after) three children. *Who is being advised?*
4 Johnson has confessed to .... (set) fire to the building, and most people believe he deserves .... (spend) a long time in prison.
5 My friends reminded .... (take) care, and warned .... (not go) there on my own. *Who is being reminded, and warned?*

5 Read press cuttings 1–5. Rewrite each sentence using the *-ing* or infinitive form of one of the verbs in the box and make any necessary changes.

> advise   can't help   be opposed to   ~~deny~~
> promise   can't afford

EXAMPLE Defence Minister 'did not take bribes from weapons manufacturers'

The Defence Minister has denied taking bribes from weapons manufacturers.

1 Singer Valerie Adams says she finds it impossible to resist the temptation to eat chocolate whenever she feels nervous …

2 On their wedding day, he vowed he would love her forever, but six months later …

3 … many lorry drivers believe it is wrong for oil companies to increase diesel prices again.

4 … a single parent like Jan Selby hasn't enough money for presents for her children …

5 'I think the manager should buy eleven new players …'

listening multiple choice:
types of distractor

1 Do students in your country do part-time jobs to make some extra money? What kind of jobs do they do? Would you like to do any of these jobs?

2 **a** ▣ You will hear two young people – Carl and Joanne – talking about money. For questions **1** and **2**, choose the answer (**A**, **B** or **C**) which fits best according to what you hear.

As you listen, follow the tapescript below.

1 Carl's problem is that
   A he is still at school living on pocket-money.
   B he is a university student without much money.
   C he doesn't earn much delivering food to people's homes.　　□ 1

2 Joanne says that
   A Carl doesn't really need any more money.
   B all young people like Carl get part-time jobs.
   C it will always be impossible to get a good job.　　□ 2

Carl	Yes, I'm enjoying the course but in one way it's as if I was still back at school: I've never got any money in my pocket.
Joanne	Well, what a lot of people in your situation do is find themselves a part-time job.
Carl	What kind of job do you mean?
Joanne	It's usually some kind of evening work; like working in a bar, or delivering pizzas. Something like that.
Carl	Yes, I can ride a motorbike so that might suit me, though I don't imagine it pays very well. Another thing is that I'm in my second year now and the workload is really starting to build up. Most days I end up reading, or writing essays, till late in the evening, and I don't know if I could handle having a job on top of that …
Joanne	So why bother?
Carl	Sorry, I'm not quite with you.
Joanne	What I'm saying is there's not much point in working ridiculously long hours to bring in a bit of extra cash if you've got no time to spend it. Why not wait until you've finished your degree, when you'll easily be able to find yourself a proper job?
Carl	But that's not for years, and I …

b Underline the parts of the tapescript which give the correct answer.

c Look again at the distractors (wrong options) and identify the parts of the text that relate to them.

d Which of the options in questions 1 and 2 is wrong because it
1 exaggerates what the text actually says?
2 uses words from the recording, but about something else?
3 uses words that mean the opposite of those in the text?
4 uses synonyms or equivalents of words in the recording, but about something else?

3 **a** When and where do you think coins were first used? What did people use as money before they were invented?
Check the meanings of these expressions: *counterfeit*, *mint* (verb), *means of exchange*.

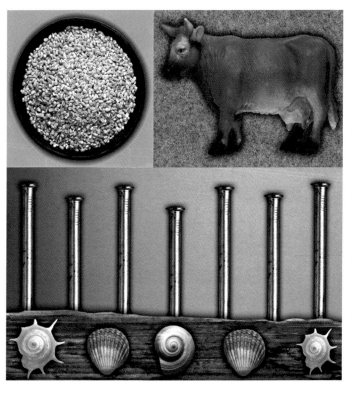

b ▣ You will hear a discussion about the origins of money. For questions **3** and **4**, choose the answer (**A**, **B** or **C**) which fits best according to what you hear.

3 Some kind of money has existed since
   A at least 6000 BC.
   B about 3000 BC.
   C about 1200 BC.　　□ 3

4 The Chinese 'coins'
   A were in fact all shells.
   B were not circular in shape.
   C were made of cheap metal.　　□ 4

speaking explaining; checking understanding

1 Look back at the text in Listening 2. How does Carl ask Joanne to clarify something he doesn't understand? How does she reply?

2 Put two of these expressions under each of the headings below. Then add as many more examples as you can think of.

Do you see what I mean?	I'm sorry, I didn't quite catch that.
Could you say that again, please?	Is everything clear so far?
Let me put it another way.	Yes, that's quite clear.
Right, I've got that.	What I mean is …

Asking for clarification or repetition

....

....

....

....

Checking the listener understands

....

....

....

....

Giving clarification

....

....

....

....

Confirming understanding

....

....

....

....

3 Work in pairs. Student A read the information on page 149. Student B read the information on page 150. Make brief notes.
1 Student A explain the process to Student B in your own words. If necessary, give clarification and check Student B understands using the phrases above. Student B, if necessary, ask for clarification and confirm understanding.
2 Change roles so Student B explains their process.

vocabulary
phrasal verbs

1 The particle (*out*, *up*, etc.) can sometimes help you to work out the meaning of a phrasal verb. Look at these five common particles (in capitals) and decide which sentence, **a** or **b**, has which meaning. The first one has been done as an example.

1 UP (increasing/completing or finishing)
  a The amount of money in her bank account is *building up* nicely. ....*increasing*....
  b I'm glad we've *cleared up* this misunderstanding once and for all. ..*completing or finishing*..

2 ON (continuing or progressing/connecting)
  a I suggest you *read on* to the end of the contract. ....
  b Let's *turn on* the radio and listen to the news. ....

3 OFF (ending or disconnecting/moving away)
  a Twenty athletes *set off* on their 100 km charity run. ....
  b To save money, *switch off* any unnecessary lights. ....

4 DOWN (reducing/failing)
  a Talks between management and unions have *broken down* completely. ....
  b The Government has *scaled down* financial aid to the disaster area. ....

5 IN (moving inwards/participating)
  a It took a while for the good news to *sink in*, then everyone smiled. ....
  b Even if you're not a club member, you're welcome to *join in* the activities. ....

2 Complete sentences 1–10 with one of the five particles above, and write its meaning.

EXAMPLE Sheila rings Australia every day; she must be running ....*up*........ a huge phone bill. (*increasing*)

1 Selling my bike should bring .... some cash, but less than I need.
2 Petrol prices have really shot .... since oil exports were reduced.
3 We couldn't pay the bill so they cut .... our electricity.
4 We'd better drink .... because the bar is closing.
5 The grocer's shop on the corner will have to close .... unless sales improve.
6 We need to cut .... our spending on luxuries if we are to afford a holiday.
7 I hear Cindy's getting .... quite well in her new job.
8 My parents used .... every last penny of their savings on repairs to their house.

9 An angry farmer told the boys on his land to clear .... , and not to come back.
10 The moment he put .... the lights, everyone sang 'Happy Birthday'.

idioms

1 Look at this example sentence and answer the questions.

Before the crisis most people had plenty of cash to spend, but now they've had to <u>tighten their belts</u>.

- What does *tighten their belts* mean literally? What does it mean here?
- Is there a similar idiom in your language? Why do you think we use idioms?

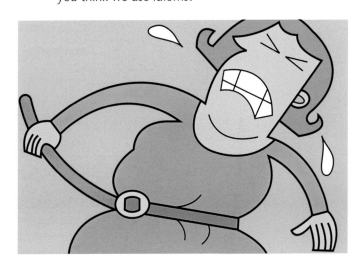

2 Match the six idioms in italics with these meanings. There's one you don't need.

> to pay 50% each
> to not have much money
> to pay for everyone
> to return stolen money to its owner
> to neither gain nor lose money
> to set aside cash for future needs
> to use some money already saved

1 When we got to the restaurant my friends told me they had no money on them, so I had to *foot the bill*.
2 We don't expect to make a profit in our first year; we'll be happy just to *break even*.
3 It's very generous of you to offer to pay, but I think we should *go halves*.
4 Although things are going well now, it's never a bad idea to *save some money for a rainy day*.
5 I might have to *dip into my savings* to buy myself that coat.
6 I used to be able to afford to go out every night, but now I've bought a house I'm *feeling the pinch*.

3 Put these idioms into categories 1–4. There is an example for each one.

> To throw money down the drain.
> He's living on the breadline.
> The company's in the red.
> He's worth a fortune.
> That cost us an arm and a leg.
> They're rolling in it.
> To spend money like water.
> She paid through the nose for that.
> I was ripped off.

1 to be rich
   She's made of money.
2 to waste money
   Throw good money after bad.
3 to have money problems
   They have difficulty making ends meet.
4 to be charged a lot / too much
   He paid over the odds for that.

4 When did you last
  • have to tighten your belt?
  • have to foot the bill?
  • find yourself in the red?
  • go halves with someone?
  • have to dip into your savings?
  • feel glad you'd saved for a rainy day?
  • get ripped off?
  • throw money down the drain?
  • feel you were rolling in it?

EXAM FOCUS

paper 3 part 3 gapped sentences

> In gapped sentences, one word completes three sentences. It is the same part of speech but has a different meaning in each one.
> 1 First decide which part of speech is needed. Look for clues next to the gap such as a phrasal verb particle, which will mean a verb is needed, or a word from an idiomatic expression. Also look at the rest of the sentence for expressions which may have similar or opposite meanings to the missing word.
> 2 Think of as many words as you can for the first sentence, and note them down.
> 3 Repeat stages **1** and **2** above with the second and third sentences.
> 4 If one word appears in your list for all three sentences, you probably have the answer – but check that each sentence makes sense.

1 Read this example. What part of speech is *call*? Which sentence contains
a a contrast? **b** idiomatic language? **c** a synonym?
Trains from London to Brussels ....*call*......... at Lille, but not all stop at Calais.
If you would like to leave your number we will ....*call*......... you back as soon as possible.
Bosses shouldn't ....*call*......... meetings which they may have to cancel later.

What does *call* mean in each sentence?

2 For questions **1–3**, think of **one** word only which can be used appropriately in all three sentences.

Question 1 has clues to help you.

1 It was the first cold, clear .... day in what had been a grey, wet winter. (contrast)
  Lourdes is a very .... pupil who uses her intellectual abilities to the full. (synonym)
  I know you're hard up now, but try to look on the .... side: you'll earn a wonderful salary when you graduate. (idiomatic language)
2 Often, when a girl goes to secondary school, she suddenly .... up very quickly.
  At this time every day, the noise first .... louder, but then it gradually decreases and silence returns.
  He never worries about how much he spends; he seems to think money .... on trees.
3 Our teacher .... us a composition for homework, and asked us to write a summary.
  It only took Colin a few minutes to .... up his new video recorder.
  I'll .... the table if you'll clear away all the dishes afterwards.

writing planning

1 Producing a good piece of writing should involve a series of stages. Complete the words in these suggested stages.

1 Discuss the topic, purpose and st............ of the text you are going to write.
2 Think of as many id............ as you can, and note them down.
3 Choose the best id............ , decide which of them go to............ and make a plan for each pa............ .
4 Decide on a logical or............ for the pa............ .
5 Write a first draft of your te............ .
6 Give your draft to your partner and ask them to write co............ on your work so far. They might write about things they like about your te............ , anything they di............ or think isn't needed, anything that isn't clear, and what they want to read more about.
7 Write your te............ , using a wide range of vo............ and structures, and li............ your ideas together.
8 Check your text is the correct le............ , adding or reducing where necessary.
9 Edit out any repetitions or points that are not re............ to the topic.
10 Correct any er............ in language, pu............ or style.

text structure

1 Different paragraphs usually deal with a different point of the text. Look at the plan and answer these questions. Which paragraph(s):

1 refers back to the beginning of the text?
2 tells you what to expect in the rest of the text?
3 attempts to catch the readers' attention and make them want to read on?
4 probably contain a mixture of reasons, examples and suggestions?

Rapid Riches

Paragraph 1

Give some statistics on the number of 'newly rich' people. Say how much some of them are worth. Suggest it's easy to make a fortune and here are some ways how...

Paragraph 2

Marrying for money - say why it's quite easy and give two ways of meeting rich people.

Paragraph 3

Making money from music - give an example of someone's who's got rich through singing/writing songs.

Paragraph 4

another way of getting rich - as 2 and 3.

Paragraph 5

Reinforce that there are lots of ways of making money, it's easy and it's fun.

paragraph structure

1 Sentences need to be in a logical order and should link well to others in the paragraph. Put the linking expressions in the box under these headings:
a purpose
b addition
c reason
d contrast

> because   as well as   so   in addition   to   as   besides   so that   owing to
> in order to/that   on the other hand   since   seeing that   however   moreover
> apart from   furthermore   so as to   on account of   nevertheless

2 1 Read the second paragraph from *Rapid Riches* below. Identify the idea expressed in the topic sentence, the justification given for it and the two practical suggestions.
2 Underline expressions which link separate sentences and circle those which link clauses within the sentences.
3 Which expression links the paragraph to the rest of the text?

> First of all, marry someone extremely rich. This is not as difficult as it sounds, as among all those thousands of new millionaires we've been hearing about there are bound to be some who, whether they realise it or not, are just waiting to meet somebody like you. One way of improving your chances of meeting them is to invest some of your hard-earned savings in an evening or two at the top nightspots in town. Alternatively, to get to know the more reclusive type of Mr or Ms Super-Rich, register yourself with the most up-market computer dating agency you can afford.

3 The sentences below form the basis of paragraph 3, but many of them are in the wrong order, are too short or are not properly linked. Put them in a more logical order to create a well-structured paragraph, and link them together using a similar style and tone to that in paragraph 2. The first sentence is correct.

> If the idea of wedded wealth doesn't appeal, how about recording or writing a best-selling pop song? The songwriter can make a fortune too. A few years ago singer Ricky Martin was a little-known Puerto Rican actor. He also became very, very rich. When the hit single Livin' La Vida Loca was released he suddenly became internationally famous. He was playing minor roles in soaps like ER.

4 Write paragraph 4 of this text yourself in about 100 words. Use the planning stages on page 14 to help you.

review

1 Match beginnings 1–7 with endings a–g.

1 The bank agreed
2 I really dislike
3 My parents taught
4 The police hope
5 I think I'd advise
6 She obviously enjoys
7 I'm sorry but I don't want

a to catch the thief soon.
b you to buy a cheaper model.
c to lend me what I needed.
d people looking at me like that.
e to stay any longer.
f being highly successful.
g me to save a little every week.

2 Some of these sentences contain mistakes. Correct those that are wrong.

1 Jim tried to take the medicine, but felt no better after he did so.
2 I'm going to say something that I meant to tell you before.
3 I remembered to fall into the river, and how horribly cold it was.
4 When Julia saw her best friend in the street, she smiled and stopped talking to her for ages.
5 I won't forget to see my first child being born.
6 As soon as Carol walked in, they suddenly changed the subject and went on discussing the weather.
7 Please believe me, I deeply regret to have to tell you such terrible lies.

3 Use the clues below to find 18 words from this unit in the wordsquare. The words can read sideways, upwards, downwards or diagonally.

C	M	W	E	A	L	T	H	Y	A	P	I
P	O	R	B	L	O	A	N	N	R	E	D
T	R	U	A	P	M	X	A	I	C	N	U
E	T	S	N	E	V	E	T	N	U	S	Y
R	G	A	K	T	E	S	A	T	E	I	G
A	A	W	N	K	E	T	N	S	Z	O	N
F	G	Y	O	C	I	R	E	E	Y	N	I
I	E	R	T	R	J	G	F	R	E	N	T
N	B	E	E	P	A	S	A	E	C	I	S
E	A	H	S	W	K	L	C	T	I	R	E
C	N	C	E	O	A	Q	U	N	Y	T	S
I	E	V	T	S	P	E	M	I	N	T	A

1 false money
2 what you pay to travel on a bus
3 what you must pay if you break the law
4 money you borrow to buy a house
5 another word for 'penniless'
6 money left to you by a relative
7 payment for private education etc.
8 paper money
9 having a lot of money
10 money you borrow
11 what people pay to the government
12 weekly payment for work done
13 monthly payment for work done
14 to make coins
15 money charged to borrow money
16 money paid to retired people
17 payment for accommodation
18 very mean

4 Complete the sentences with the correct form of these idioms.

> to feel the pinch
> to pour money down the drain
> to spend money like water
> to make ends meet
> to be rolling in it
> to cost an arm and a leg
> to break even
> to pay over the odds

1 I sold the painting for as much as I'd paid for it, so in the end I ....
2 With low incomes and high outgoings, lone parents often find it hard to ....
3 The diamond in Sonia's ring is huge; it must have ....
4 If you buy things in tourist areas like that, don't be surprised if you ....
5 Rock stars like Madonna and Sting, who've been around for years, must be ....
6 Mick had lots of money to spend when he had a job, but now he's ....
7 Buying such useless rubbish as that is like ....
8 Since Jane won the pools she's been out shopping every day; she's ....

unit 2 | *water*

vocabulary and speaking

bait	estuary	reef
bank	explorer	reservoir
bay	gondola	shark
beach	hook	shore
bed	iceberg	spray
canal	mouth	stream
cliffs	pond	tide
coast	port	waterfall
dam	reed	wave

1 **a** Put the words in the box into two categories – those you associate with
  • seas and oceans
  • lakes and rivers.
  Which could go into both?

b In pairs, take it in turns to choose a word from the box and define it, without using the word itself. Your partner must guess which word it is you are defining, and can ask questions if necessary.

2 **a** Which of the verbs in the box below could also be nouns?

sail	bathe	cruise	sink	swim	surface	dive	dampen	float	row
drift	leak	drip	plunge	drown	surf	flood	soak		

b Choose one of the verbs and find at least one other in the same box that is connected to it in some way, explaining what the connection is. Try to use all the verbs at least once.

3 **a** In pairs, take it in turns to choose two of the pictures and compare them. Think about where they were taken and the significance of the water in each one.

b Do any of the pictures resemble scenes in your country? Which picture appeals to you most, and why? Which sounds would you expect to hear in each situation?

talking points

1 Which books, films or TV series are about the water?
  What part does the water play in the story?
2 Do you know any songs about the water?
3 Which jobs or sports do you associate with the sea, lakes and rivers?
  In what ways does the water make them dangerous?
4 Describe a memory you have that is associated with the sea, a lake or a river. It may be happy, amusing, dramatic, etc.

reading multiple choice: rejecting incorrect options

1 **a** Quickly make a list of all the different types of text you can think of, e.g. *letter*, *advertisement*.

b What features usually make them different from each other?

2 **a** Look at the two pictures. How would you describe the water in each one? Quickly read texts A and B, and decide what types of text they are. Which features tell you?

b You are going to read two extracts which are both concerned in some way with water. For questions 1–4, choose the answer (**A**, **B**, **C** or **D**) which you think fits best according to the text.

Why are the other options wrong?
Question 1 has been done as an example.

1 The writer says that Washburn wants to be sure that

A he will arrive at Maverick's on time.
There is no mention of a particular time being important.

B he can survive underwater there. ✓
This is why he's practising holding his breath.

C there will be other surfers there.
Other surfers are mentioned in general but will not necessarily be there at the same time.

D he can find his way there.
There is no suggestion that he won't be able to find his way there. The word 'simply' suggests that it is easy to find.

2 What does the writer say about the sea at Maverick's?

A There are the remains of old buildings in the water.

B There is no shallow water there.

C The waves are particularly strong.

D The water is dangerously polluted.

3 According to the text, you can travel on the *Desert Princess*

A only in the summer.

B at any time of the year.

C only in the evening.

D at any time of the day.

4 On the boat, you can buy

A food.

B photographs of the dam.

C unusual flowers.

D presents.

TEXT A

As Grant Washburn drives along the coast, 40 kilometres south of San Francisco, he begins holding his breath. If he can hold it for two-and-a-half minutes or more he'll be happy. That's the amount of time he thinks he may need if he gets into trouble while surfing one of the most dangerous waves in the world.

He's heading for a secret patch of sea known as 'Maverick's' to a small group of world-class surfers. There are no signs; you simply drive to the nearest place marked on the map – Half Moon Bay – and ask the locals for directions.

What makes Maverick's so scary is not just the size of the waves, which can easily exceed the height of a four-storey building from trough to crest, but the terrifying combination of wave conditions that is found only there. Waves break almost half a kilometre from shore and are therefore bigger and far more powerful than those at most other big-wave spots. Westerly currents pull surfers towards house-sized rocks. Underwater there is a reef that is deep in some places but just below the surface in others, and dotted with arches, caves and crevasses. Then there's the water itself – an uninviting greenish-grey, and cold. Don't bother trying to surf it without a full-length wetsuit, an insulating hood and thick rubber gloves.

And sharks? 'They're definitely around,' says Washburn, 'but there are far too many other things to worry about. There are at least half a dozen nightmare possibilities before you even start thinking about sharks.'

3 Answer these questions about text A.

1 What kinds of conditional sentences are used in paragraph 1? Why?
2 Look at the sentence *What makes Maverick's … is found only there* (line 11). Why doesn't this end with a question mark? How can you rephrase the first clause?
3 Give a synonym for *storey* (line 12).
4 Which parts of a wave do you think the *trough* and the *crest* are (line 13)? How is *trough* pronounced? How else can *-ough* be pronounced?
5 What do you think *arches*, *caves* and *crevasses* are (line 19)? What do you think they look like?
6 What special clothes do surfers at Maverick's have to wear, and why?
7 What do you think the *half a dozen nightmare possibilities* (line 25) could be?

4 Answer these questions about text B.

1 Why is *300-passenger* (line 2) singular, not plural?
2 What part of speech is *pick-up* (line 21)? Rewrite the sentence using *pick up* as a phrasal verb.
3 What do you think a *deck* (lines 8 and 10) is? Look at the context for both uses of the word.
4 Find a word in the text which means the opposite of *aboard* (line 1).
5 What does *take in* (line 18) mean here? What other meanings can it have?
6 Do you think *ample time* (line 19) means insufficient time / only just enough time / as much time as you need?
7 Which other words in the text have similar meanings to *spectacular* (line 11)?
8 What do you think *cliffs*, *coves*, and *gorges* are (lines 11 and 12)? What do adjectives *rocky*, *sheltered*, and *flooded* tell you about them?

5 Think about a stretch of water near where you live and describe its appearance and atmosphere. What is it like at different times of
• the day?
• the year?
What sort of activities do people do there?

TEXT B

LAKE MEAD CRUISE

Enjoy an unforgettable cruise aboard the *Desert Princess*! An authentic 300-passenger paddlewheel steamer, built specially to sail the beautiful, crystal clear waters of Lake Mead.

Lake Mead, America's largest artificial lake, extends almost 200 kilometres upstream towards the mighty Grand Canyon. Covering over 600 square kilometres, the deep blue lake is surrounded by stunning desert vistas.

Whatever the season, travel in comfort on one of the enclosed sun decks, or feel the wind in your hair and the sun on your face up top on the open promenade deck. A delicious but competitively-priced buffet lunch will be served on board. Enjoy the spectacular sights – the rocky cliffs, the sheltered coves, the flooded gorges – and have an outrageously good time!

There will be a full two hours to observe and take pictures of the breathtaking Hoover Dam! Towering 220 metres above the Colorado River, it is still the Western hemisphere's highest concrete dam, providing domestic water and hydroelectric power for nearby Las Vegas, as well as other major cities in Nevada, Arizona and California.

On the voyage back we go ashore to take in the fascinating Botanical Gardens, where you will have ample time to wander and purchase rare plants and gifts from the well-stocked souvenir shop.

Tour time:	Pick-up from your hotel between 9 a.m. and 9.30 p.m.
Length of tour:	Approx. 6 hours. Return to hotel by 3.30 p.m.
Price:	Adults $50 Under 16s $30 All taxes and fees included.
Booking:	Advanced reservations recommended in high season. Contact our secure on-line Reservation Desk up to one year in advance.

grammar

conditionals (0–3 and mixed)

1 a Look at sentences 1–9 and explain the situation by saying what has happened/is happening, etc.

EXAMPLE You'll be sorry if you don't take advantage of our superb spring sale prices.

An advertisement is trying to persuade people to buy things in a sale.

1 It would've been a disaster if he hadn't found the ring!
2 I don't cycle to school if it's raining.
3 If the helicopter hadn't arrived so quickly, we wouldn't be here on dry land now.
4 We would save a lot of money if we cut our staff by half.
5 If I'd known he was going to be here, I wouldn't have come.
6 If you tell us what we want to know, we can finish this and go home.
7 Mobile phones don't work properly if you're this far below ground.
8 If I were ten years younger, I'd buy that!
9 You're probably not going to enjoy this if you've already read the book.

b Study the ten sentences again and find five pairs of conditionals.

EXAMPLE *Sentences 2 and 7 are both zero conditionals.*

2 Complete each sentence using the verb in brackets for the first gap and a suitable verb for the second gap.

1 If we all .... (stay) calm, I'm sure that someone .... us soon.
2 We .... (be) safely on that island now if we .... in the direction I suggested.
3 I .... (not sail) on that ship if I .... what was going to happen.
4 If we .... (have) a radio, we .... the coastguard, but we don't.
5 People .... (not live) very long if they .... fresh water to drink.
6 If I .... (be) a sailor, I .... how to check our position by the stars.
7 It's obvious that we .... (reach) land if we .... sailing in this direction.
8 If we .... (have) more time before we abandoned ship, I .... some food with us.

3 Each of the following conditional sentences are possible, although they might not seem to be. Look at the verb forms in each one and explain the situation. Why don't they appear to be correct?

EXAMPLE If Sarah hadn't been talking to Joe, she would have heard what I said.
Sarah was talking to Joe and, therefore, didn't hear what the speaker said.

1 I would be most grateful if you would reply immediately.
2 I'd get myself a more modern computer if I was you.
3 I'll make the sandwiches if you'll pour the drinks.
4 We always took a short cut across the field if the farmer wasn't there.
5 I should be surprised if we saw him again.
6 We might've got there on time if we hadn't had to wait for your sister.
7 If you will keep on breaking things, we won't give you any more toys.

4 Rewrite four of the sentences in **3** to fit situations 1–4 below, keeping the same verb forms.

conditionals without *if*

1 a In 1–8, underline the alternative expression to *if* and complete the sentence, using the correct form of each of these verbs once.

> take   miss   love   crash   be
> ~~stay~~   rescue   need   own

> **EXAMPLE** <u>Providing that</u> the children ....*stay*............ in the shallow water, they'll be safe.

1 Should you .... any help, you can call us at this phone number.
2 Given the opportunity, I .... to travel around the world.
3 I'll go shopping with you, provided there .... too many people in town.
4 Supposing you .... a very rich football club; which players would you buy?
5 We'll have to hurry; otherwise we .... the six o'clock train.
6 Without the assistance of the lifeboat, they .... the crew from the sinking ship.
7 I won't get bored while I'm at the hotel as long as I .... a good book with me.
8 But for his warning, we .... into a lorry that was parked at the side of the road.

Which of the expressions you have underlined are more common in rather formal contexts?

b Rephrase the sentences in 1–8 using *if*.

> **EXAMPLE** *If the children stay in the shallow water, they'll be safe.*

2 Explain what is necessary in your country if you want to do each of 1–8. Use *provided (that)*, *providing (that)*, *on condition (that)*, *as long as*, *otherwise* or *without*.

> **EXAMPLE** sail a yacht
> *You can sail a yacht providing you have a captain's licence./Without a captain's licence you can't sail a yacht.*

1 drive a car
2 vote in general elections
3 go to university
4 go to the best nightclubs
5 become a dentist
6 get married
7 buy a house
8 get divorced

common errors

If Isabel had have known, I'm sure she would have said something.
What is wrong with with this sentence? Why?

EXAM FOCUS

paper 3 part 4 key word transformations

In Part 4, you study one sentence and complete a second so that the meaning is the same. You are given a 'key word' which you cannot change. It counts as one of the 3–8 words that you are allowed to write.

- Study the first sentence and the key word. Include <u>all</u> the information from the first sentence.
- Ensure that the sequence of tenses matches the meaning of the first sentence.
- Count the number of words used – contracted forms like *isn't* are really two words.
- Check the whole sentence makes sense, and that you haven't made any grammar or spelling mistakes.

1 All the answers to 1–4 require conditional forms. Study the example and the prompts given for each question and follow the instructions and guidelines above.

> **EXAMPLE** I only knew because I heard it on the radio.
> **if**
> I <u>wouldn't have known if I hadn't</u> heard it on the radio.

Which word tells you that there is a cause/effect link which requires a conditional sentence? What do the two past verb forms tell you about the likely conditional type? What happens to positive verb forms in a conditional sentence?

1 They won't play the match unless the weather improves.
   as
   They .... the weather improves.
2 It wasn't cold so we didn't take any warm clothes.
   been
   If it .... warm clothes.
3 Because of that accident, he's afraid of crossing the road now.
   had
   If he .... be afraid of crossing the road now.
4 It was only because of Jennifer that I didn't die in the mountains.
   have
   But .... in the mountains.

1 *What does 'unless' mean? What conditional expression contains 'as'? Does this mean the same as 'unless'? How will you change the sentence?*

2 *What does the use of negative forms in the 1st sentence tell you about the likely form of the verbs in the 2nd sentence? What does the key word 'been' tell you about the kind of conditional required?*

3 *Which verb do we use with 'accident'? When does/did the accident happen and when is/was he afraid? What kind of conditional is needed?*

4 *What conditional expression uses 'but'?*

listening   sentence completion: identifying type of missing information

1 In **2** below, you will hear part of a talk by an expert on water, who is discussing the global water shortage. What do you think he will say about
- how much of the earth is covered in water?
- how much of that is salt water?
- where a lot of the fresh water is?

2 Before you complete 1–4 study the questions carefully and decide what kind of answer you need for each one e.g. *noun, adjective, number, date*, etc.

 You will hear part of a talk by a hydrologist, an expert on water. For questions **1–4**, complete the sentences with a word or short phrase.

The speaker says that there is ice on ⬚ **1** of the Earth's surface.

Very little of the world's water is ⬚ **2** .

Severe water shortage affects the inhabitants of approximately ⬚ **3** countries.

Countries that appear to have plenty of water now have a kind of ⬚ **4** in summer.

3 **a** Read the instructions and answer the question.

You will hear an extract from a radio consumer programme about conserving water supplies. For questions **1–7**, complete the sentences with a word or short phrase.

What suggestions do you think the speaker will make for saving water at home?

b   Think about the kind of words that will go in the spaces then listen to the recording and complete 1–7.

You can lose a lot of water from a tap that is ⬚ **1** .

Placing an object in the toilet cistern can save approximately ⬚ **2** litres monthly.

It is less wasteful if the tap is off when you clean ⬚ **3** .

You can ⬚ **4** or the garden with cold water from the shower.

You waste a lot of water if you wash things like plates in a partly empty ⬚ **5** .

Rinsing dishes wastes less water if you reduce the amount of ⬚ **6** that you use.

Instead of taking water straight from the tap, keep some in a bottle ⬚ **7** for when you want a drink.

c Which of your predictions in **a** were correct? Do you do any of these things? Which ideas were new to you? Would you consider doing any of them?

speaking agreeing and disagreeing

1 **a** Read the expressions in the boxes and add as many as you can to each group.

> **Giving opinions**
> As far as I'm concerned …
> I'm absolutely convinced (that) …
> Well, I reckon (that) …

> **Justifying opinions**
> After all, …
> If you think about it, …
> No matter how unlikely that might seem, …

> **Expressing agreement**
> Well I suppose so, …   I'm not entirely convinced, but …
> Absolutely.   I couldn't agree more.

> **Expressing disagreement**
> I agree to some extent, but …
> I'm afraid I can't agree with you at all.
> I see what you mean about … , but …
> There may be some truth in that, but don't you think (that) …
> You can't be serious!

b Which of them are formal/informal/polite/strong?

2 **a** **🔊** Work in pairs.
Student A Choose one of questions 1–4 to talk about. Under each question there are some ideas which you can use if you want to. Think about the topic for a few seconds before you speak. Give and justify your opinions for about two minutes. Ask Student B if they agree or disagree.
Student B Listen to Student A speaking for two minutes without interrupting. When he or she has finished, say what you agree and disagree with, and why.

b Change roles and choose a different question.

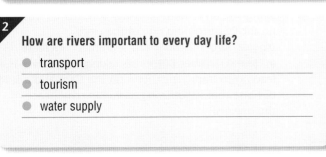

1
What are the likely effects of water shortage in your country?
- natural environment
- daily life
- farming

2
How are rivers important to every day life?
- transport
- tourism
- water supply

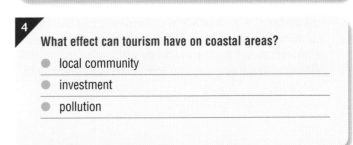

3
What are the attractions of going on a cruise?
- facilities
- destinations
- health

4
What effect can tourism have on coastal areas?
- local community
- investment
- pollution

vocabulary

idioms

1 **a** For each of 1–15, study the context and discuss the meaning of the idiom in italics.

1 As the job's going so well, please don't *rock the boat* by suggesting we change our plans now.

2 He's getting excellent marks in all school subjects, so at the moment he's *on the crest of a wave*.

3 I'm sorry to hear you broke up with your boyfriend, but don't worry, *there are plenty more fish in the sea*.

4 We had a fantastic day out at the seaside; everybody *had a whale of a time*.

5 Emily, dressed in jeans and a T-shirt, *felt like a fish out of water* at the formal dinner.

6 You should take advantage of the opportunity now; otherwise you'll *miss the boat*.

7 Although she could prove he'd told lies, she *let him off the hook* by not saying a word to anyone.

8 Realising she wanted to make me angry, I kept calm and didn't *take the bait*.

9 They'll be *in hot water* if the security guards catch them shoplifting.

10 Sometimes, if you know that everyone else is wrong, you have to *swim against the tide*.

11 As I was only just beginning my physics degree, I felt *out of my depth* when writing my first assignment.

12 Daniel had been thinking about going away for a long time; at last he *took the plunge* and bought a one-way ticket.

13 Before I ask my parents for the money, I'll *test the water* to make sure they're in a good mood.

14 Telling a funny story is a good way of *breaking the ice* when meeting new people.

15 I needed thousands of pounds to buy a motorbike but I'd only earned twenty: it was *a drop in the ocean*.

b Think about recent events and famous people in the news. Tell your partner about them using some of the idioms in 1–15.

EXAMPLE *Everyone had a whale of a time at the MTV Awards party last night.*

collocations

1 Words that frequently go together are called collocations, e.g. dependent prepositions (*on board*), combinations such as adjective + noun (*loud noise*), verb + noun (*catch a fish*), and adverb + adjective (*completely soaked*). How many can you form with *loud*, *catch* and *completely*?

2 Match the words on the left with the words on the right to form collocations, and then put them into the gaps in the text below.

1	heavy	a	ship
2	high	b	attention
3	fully	c	of
4	aware	d	rain
5	headed	e	for
6	at	f	sea
7	abandon	g	winds
8	pay	h	equipped

Survivors of the storm

Few of the passengers had bothered to (1) .... to the weather forecast on the radio before they boarded the car ferry for the short trip from the mainland to the island. Minutes after they left port, though, the ship was hit by (2) .... and huge waves. Then the ship came to a terrifyingly sudden stop. It had run aground on a sandbank, and it would soon break up. The captain ordered everyone to (3) .... immediately. The lifeboats, full of frightened passengers, (4) .... the coast, which was several kilometres away and invisible owing to the (5) .... that was falling. Everybody was (6) .... the danger, but they also knew that the boats they were in were solidly-built and (7) .... There was a ship-to-shore radio, as well as plenty of drinking water and food in case they had to spend some time (8) ....

3 **a** Quickly read texts 1–3 below. Where do you think each one comes from?

b Read the texts more carefully and underline the correct collocations.

1 As we arrived in the village, the summer sun was *dropping / setting* behind the towering peaks of the country's highest mountain range, casting enormous shadows *right / completely* across the lake. There was a *light / small* breeze, but the water remained *considerably / perfectly* still, as if it were made *of / by* the finest glass.

2 In *rural / natural* areas, you'll find that many of the *local / regional* people don't trust the tap water – and you shouldn't, either. Follow their example and drink *bottled / contained* water only. Remember to use it when brushing your teeth, and for cleaning fresh fruit and salads. Many a holiday has been *extremely / totally* ruined by just a few *drops / spots* of contaminated water.

3 One of the most charming and enduring images of the *ancient / antique* city of Cambridge – punting along the River Cam on a lazy summer afternoon – is quickly becoming one of the city's *biggest / largest* headaches. A dramatic increase *in / of* the number of tourists taking to the river is leading to traffic *lines / jams* on the Cam and a level of noise that is *bothering / disturbing* the peace of the university.

multiple-choice cloze

1 Discuss these questions:

1 What should you do <u>before</u> you start to fill in any of the gaps in a multiple-choice cloze?
2 To fill in a gap, which words should you look at first to find clues?
3 When you have filled in all the gaps, what should you check?

2 **a** You are going to read a text about exploring the Mariana Trench, the deepest point in the world. Where do you think it is? What do you think conditions would be like there? What life forms would you expect to find? Read the text quickly and find the answers.

b For questions 1–6, read the text below and decide which answer (**A**, **B**, **C** or **D**) best fits each gap.

exam factfile

In Reading Part 1 (multiple-choice cloze) you will answer 18 questions in total. There will be three texts with six questions each.

VOYAGE TO THE BOTTOM OF THE OCEAN

I've often wondered why it is that humans have started to explore (1) .... planets, while we still know so little about the oceans here on Earth. So it was something of a (2) .... come true when I was invited to join researchers filming the Mariana Trench for the first time.

Fascinated, I watched on the TV (3) .... as the ten-foot submarine descended to 10,898 metres, the deepest point in the world. All of us above on the mother ship were (4) .... excited as the tiny vessel's video camera showed it was approaching the bottom of the Pacific, at what seemed like a (5) .... pace.

At last it touched the ocean bed, which the submarine's lamp revealed to be like a smooth, brown-red desert. The water was totally still, and at first nothing seemed to be moving, but suddenly we spotted a sea slug, and then a shrimp. The scientists were over the (6) .... , and I shared their delight.

1 **A** outer	**B** distant	**C** foreign	**D** far
2 **A** vision	**B** fantasy	**C** thought	**D** dream
3 **A** screen	**B** face	**C** mask	**D** surface
4 **A** utterly	**B** completely	**C** absolutely	**D** tremendously
5 **A** snail's	**B** tortoise's	**C** worm's	**D** oyster's
6 **A** moon	**B** sky	**C** heaven	**D** stars

3 **a** Look again at options 1–6, and say what part of speech they are.

b Can you form collocations with any of the incorrect answers in 1–6?

writing articles

1 Where do you usually see articles? Tell your partner about an article you have read and enjoyed recently. What did you like about it?

2 Look at these six suggestions for writing an article. Five of them give useful advice. Which one doesn't and why?
1 Your first paragraph should attract the reader's attention and make them want to carry on reading.
2 Each paragraph should deal with a different aspect of the topic.
3 Hold the reader's attention by informing, persuading or entertaining them, and by not repeating expressions.
4 Any facts that you give should be true, but often you can also write your own ideas and opinions.
5 Always write your article in a very formal style.
6 Your last paragraph should make the article feel complete, for instance with a conclusion or brief summary.

3 a 1–5 below suggest different ways of beginning an article. Can you match them with introductory paragraphs A–C?
1 A well-known phrase or saying, such as a quotation, proverb or idiom. It could be from a famous song, poem or book. The rest of the paragraph puts it into context.
2 An interesting, possibly surprising, fact. This is often followed by an explanation, sometimes using figures or other factual details as evidence.
3 A question that indicates the topic of the article. It also encourages the reader to think about the subject, and want to read on to find out the answer.
4 A description of an event or situation that illustrates the topic of the article.
5 A surprising, strange or controversial opinion. The reader wonders how the writer can possibly explain or justify this, and so continues reading.

A travel magazine has asked readers to send in articles with the title *The River*. Write an article describing a river and its effects on the people who live near it. It could be a river in your own country or abroad.

 A

People in my country often say 'Rivers never sleep'. What they mean is that rivers are active 24 hours a day. They can quickly change from being slow-moving stretches of calm water, almost like lakes, and suddenly become raging torrents that can flood and destroy. This can happen at any time of night or day, so if you live on or near the river banks you never know what to expect when you wake up in the morning.

 B

What does a river add to a great city? That may be an easy question to answer if you live, for example, in Paris or Moscow, but in my city the river is very small. It is little more than a stream that has been diverted under the city into a concrete tunnel, and which dries up in summer.

 C

The River Danube is by far the most important waterway in the world. Rising in Germany, it flows 1,700 kilometres to the Black Sea, linking eight countries and major cities such as Vienna, Budapest and Belgrade on its way. It is also connected by canal to other great rivers like the Rhine, so that you can travel by river boat all the way from Holland to Bulgaria.

b Of the two ways from 1–5 not used to begin an article, choose one and write your own introductory paragraph for the same article.

4 **a** Read the instructions and article below.

A college magazine has asked students for articles about the present-day importance of the sea to their country. Write an article for this magazine, with the title *My country and the sea*.

My country and the sea

Satellite pictures of Spain show it to be a peninsula shared with Portugal, yet to many of its inhabitants it somehow feels like an island, with ocean and seas to the north, west, south and east.

My country's virtual isolation has created a unique, powerful culture which has many links with the sea. From Galicia to Andalucia, fishing villages live from it. Spain has the largest fishing fleet in Europe; we consume far more fish than our neighbours – and live longer.

Spain's sunny coastline also attracts tens of millions of visitors from abroad, bringing in foreign currency and providing employment for many local people. Much of Spain's population also heads for the seaside at the beginning of July or August.

The sea at the southernmost tip of Spain forms the dividing line between prosperous Europe, typified by the enormous wealth of the nearby Costa del Sol, and the terrible poverty in much of Africa. Every year, thousands of desperate people attempt to cross the treacherous waters separating the two continents, often in unseaworthy boats. Tragically, many drown in the attempt.

To Spain, then, the sea brings sadness as well as happiness and prosperity. This is a country with a long and proud seafaring tradition, despite the fact that its capital – unlike that of other maritime nations such as Portugal, England or Greece – is hundreds of kilometres inland.

b Does the example article follow all the instructions in the question? Think about key words such as *my country* (not 'my town') and *present-day* (not 'traditional'), plus the appropriate style, format and length.

c Which verb tense does the writer use throughout most of the article? Why?

5 **a** Choose one of these to write about.

1 *The River*, as in **3**. You could begin with your introductory paragraph from **3**. When you plan your article, think first about the river itself: where it starts, where it ends; the towns and countryside it passes through and how it links them. Then consider its effects on where people live, their jobs, their leisure activities and so on, as well as the dangers that can come from living next to it.

2 *My country and the sea*, as in **4**. Decide what kind of introductory paragraph you will use. You could refer to aspects of the topic similar to those in the sample text, and use some of the same vocabulary.

b Write your article in about 200 words. As you write, check that you are following the useful advice in **2**.

THERE IS ANOTHER MODEL ARTICLE ON PAGE 160 IN THE WRITING BANK

review

1 In 1–6, circle the word that collocates with the underlined expression.

1 Overnight, there have been storms *fully / right / just* <u>across</u> the country.
2 Please *give / pay / spend* <u>attention</u> while we explain essential safety precautions.
3 Welcome *in / to / on* <u>board</u> our flight to Rome's Fiumicino Airport.
4 The captain ordered everyone to *leave / abandon / jump* <u>ship</u>.
5 The spectacular <u>mountain</u> *range / chain / series* splits the country into two parts.
6 There was a *light / low / little* <u>breeze</u> blowing as we set off from the mainland.

2 Complete 1–5 to form conditional sentences.

1 People shouldn't park their cars on the pavement, otherwise …
2 But for that warning you gave me, …
3 Given the choice of meeting any film star in the world, …
4 Without the help of my friends, …
5 I'd travel alone in another country, providing …

3 Complete 1–6 with the correct form of one of these idioms. There is one you don't need to use.

> out of his depth   in hot water
> swim against the tide   take the plunge
> let him off the hook   like a fish out of water
> miss the boat

1 Jane is a city girl, so she felt ……………… living in that small, quiet village.
2 He was terrified she would say 'no' but at last he ……………… and asked her out.
3 They found themselves ……………… when they were caught cheating in the exam.
4 Simon felt ……………… when he realised he had to race against professionals.
5 There's always someone who disagrees with everyone else and has to ……………… .
6 A well-known politician was caught shoplifting but the manager ……………… by not calling the police.

4 What's the difference between

1 *cliffs* and *banks*?
2 *to float* and *to drift*?
3 *to dive* and *to plunge*?
4 *a beach* and *a shore*?
5 *an arch* and *a trough*?
6 *to drip* and *to leak*?
7 *a tide* and *a flood*?

5 Complete the crossword with words from this unit.

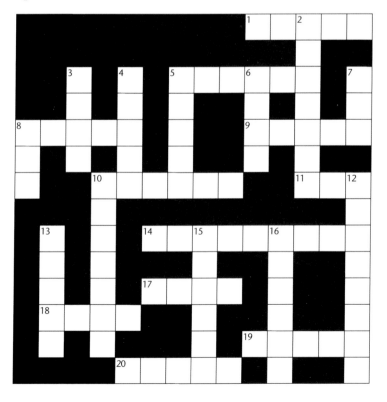

across

1 small sailing boat
5 to go from place to place
8 to remove dirt or soap with water
9 top of a wave
10 small river
11 water comes out of this
14 artificial lake
17 food used to attract fish
18 piece of metal for fishing
19 pointed tops of mountains
20 informal word for 'frightening'

down

2 faster-moving water in sea or river
3 side of a river
4 group of boats or ships together
5 huge marine mammal
6 a floor of a ship
7 (of the sun) go down below the horizon
8 to make a boat move through the water
10 opposite of 'deep'
12 formal word for 'buy'
13 another word for 'swim'
15 person who works on a ship
16 formal word for 'boat' or 'ship'

unit 3 | film and tv

vocabulary and speaking

1
a Write a list of ten things you consider to be 'entertainment'. Do you think there are any negative aspects to the things on your list?

b Which of the types of entertainment in the picture would you choose for
• a night in with friends?
• a relaxing evening on your own?
• keeping up with the news?
Is there anything you don't like about any of these forms of entertainment?

2 What are the characteristics of these types of programme? Can you think of an example of each? Which do/don't you watch regularly? Why/Why not?

serial   quiz show   consumer programme   sitcom   soap   panel game
documentary   current affairs programme   costume drama

3 Match each of these adjectives to a film you have seen. What kind of film was it (e.g. *action*)? Can you summarise the plot in one sentence?

action-packed   gripping   convincing   far-fetched   moving   slow-moving
breathtaking   mediocre   unforgettable   hilarious   spine-chilling   atmospheric
corny   bloodthirsty   pretentious

4 Read what these six people say about their work in films and match them with these jobs.

producer   designer   director   editor   agent   casting director

1 'I decide how a film is performed and shot.'
2 'I find the script, the director and the finance for the film.'
3 'I cut the film and put it together in the way that the director wants.'
4 'I find work for actors.'
5 'I decide what the set looks like, and decide on the actors' costumes and make-up.'
6 'I choose the actors to play the characters in the film.'

5 Imagine that you do any three of these different jobs in television. With a partner, take it in turns to say what you do, and what you like or dislike about your job.

news reader   presenter   interviewer   scriptwriter   chat-show host
foreign correspondent   understudy   stuntman/woman   critic

talking points

1 What, for you, are the ingredients of a good film?
2 Which film would you most like to have been in, and which part would you have played?
3 Are there any films that you would like to remake? What changes would you make (e.g. to the setting, the characters, the ending) and who would you cast in it?
4 What is censorship? Are there any circumstances in which it can be justified?

reading understanding content;
figurative language

1 **a** Look at the title of the text and the two lines below
it. What do you think is the purpose of the text?

b Do you think you would be suited to the kind of
work it discusses? Why/Why not?

2 The eight headings are in the wrong places. Read the
text quickly and put them at the beginning of the
correct paragraphs.

EXAMPLE *The shooting – paragraph 6*

Extra!

READ ALL ABOUT IT

Time on your hands? Always wanted to be in the movies? Then it's an
extra's life for you. Old hand Henry Rupert tells how it works.

1 The shooting Agents usually want experience (which, of
course, you can't get unless you've already got an agent). They
5 will ask about your details, so know all your sizes. Don't fib: you
will find costumes don't fit and you'll be very unpopular. Your
special skills are noted down – whether you can drive, swim, tap
dance.

2 The fame Some agents say 'Don't ring us – we'll ring you',
10 which may mean three times a year. With others it's worth
phoning at least once a week. 'We need you the fifth, sixth and
seventh,' you might be told. 'You will be a Victorian passer-by.
There's a costume fit Thursday 10.30 a.m.' Ring the agent late
afternoon the day before. He or she is under real pressure at
15 this point – production rang late, altered the requirements – and
you aren't going to get much help, so you need a street map
and an up-to-date road atlas.

3 The fee Don't wear rings or a watch if it's not present-day,
take nothing you mind leaving in a bus for a while, and

20 remember it's cold sitting about in winter. When you get there,
sign on with the third AD (assistant director) and then get on
the extras' bus – usually a tired converted double-decker with
every other row of seats reversed and small Formica tables
between them. After the crew and cast have had their turn, it's
25 breakfast, which is usually wide in choice and plentiful.

4 The questions Wardrobe check next – 'Change his tie for
something plainer'; 'She can't wear those shoes' – then hair and
make-up and back to the bus. Experienced extras doze or read a
book; first-timers, like patients in a dentist's waiting room, flick
30 through newspapers and magazines. Eventually the second AD
arrives: 'We want you.' Into a minibus, and before too long you
will at last be performing.

5 The arrival Keep quiet: you wouldn't be the first person to be
thrown off set after 'Quiet, please' is called. Watch, listen, do just
35 what you are asked, no more. Know where the camera or
cameras are but never look at them during a take. This is it: you

may now be right there with a superstar, or at least a well-known
TV face. Don't watch them or talk to them. Above all, don't ask
for an autograph. Come rehearsal time, you are told when and
40 where to move, so just keep going until somebody says, 'Cut!'
There may be several tries.

6 The booking 'Let's go for a take. Final checks!' That's a cue
for everybody from wardrobe and make-up to leap in and brush
every coat, comb every hair, straighten every tie. The stars
45 remove their quilted jackets and you wait for the 747 to pass
out of earshot. 'Roll sound – background action – action!' Off
you go. Don't rush it, and if a cast member is going to walk into
you, move out of their way. 'Cut!' You may do that again and
again. I was on 17 takes last week. 'Okay, guys' is what we all
50 want to hear – that means the director is happy, unless a hair
from the cameraman's toupee has got inside the camera and it
will look as if somebody has been waving a palm tree in front of
the lens.

7 The wait You'll get £64 for a flat day, overtime before seven
55 in the morning and after nine hours, occasionally £20 – £40
extra for a spoken line or close-up. So, after your agent's 10 per
cent, travel and lunch if you're at a studio, you'll make between
£50 and £100 for a really long day. You'll be lucky to get 100
days a year, so don't give up a regular job.

60 **8 The studio** Never tell anybody to watch anything you think
you are in unless you have seen it. Chances are, you are just out
of shot, they use the bit that shows the back of your head, or
the whole scene is cut. It's all about hope: hope that you will get
work on an advertising shoot, hope that you will address a line
65 to a huge star, hope that you will end up as one of those TV
names who started as an extra. You can do it from eight to 80.
Your responsibility ends the moment you sign off, and even if
today was boring and cold and dashed your hopes, there's
always the next booking, when you just might get your break. ●

3 **a** Read the first three paragraphs and decide whether
these statements are true or false. Give reasons.
1 You should always say what your true size is.
2 Your agent will tell you exactly how to get to the
studio or location.
3 Jewellery must be removed for historical films.
4 Your belongings will be safe on the bus during the
filming.
5 Extras are given a good breakfast after everyone
else has eaten.

b Choose at least four details in paragraphs 4–8. For
each one, write a short statement about it in your
own words. Give your statements to your partner,
who must decide whether they are true or false. Be
prepared to justify your answers.

4 For 1–5, use the context to decide on the meaning of
the word in the text. Say what other common meaning
the word has.
1 *fit* (line 6)
2 *take* (line 36 and 42)
3 *cut* (line 40 and 48)
4 *shoot* (line 64)
5 *break* (line 69)

5 Look at these types of figurative language and match
them with 1–4.
- **idioms** (an expression with a meaning that you
cannot guess from the meanings of the separate
words)
- **metaphors** (words not normally applied to those
people or objects)
- **similes** (a comparison between two things, generally
beginning with *like* or *as*)
1 *time on your hands* (line 1)
2 *tired* (line 22)
3 *like patients in a dentist's waiting room* (line 29)
4 *as if somebody has been waving a palm tree in front of
the lens* (line 52)

Explain their meaning as used in the text.

6 Use the context to work out the meanings of 1–6.
1 *old hand* (line 2)   4 *cue* (line 42)
2 *fib* (line 5)   5 *out of earshot* (line 46)
3 *doze* (line 28)   6 *dashed* (line 68)

7 After reading the text, does the idea of working as an
extra appeal to you more, or less? Why?

grammar
question forms

1 **a** Complete the gaps in these notes about different question forms using the examples to help you.

1 **(1)** .... *Yes/No* .... *questions* .... where a
(2) .... or **(3)** .... answer is expected:
Do you live with your family?
These questions may also be negative:
Don't you usually walk to school?

2 .... *'Alternative'* .... *questions* .... where one of two answers is expected:
Do you have a job or are you a student?

3 .... *Wh-questions* .... which begin with the word
(4) .... , **(5)** .... , **(6)** .... , **(7)** .... ,
(8) .... , **(9)** .... or **(10)** ....
We don't use the verb **(11)** .... if *Who, What*, etc. is the subject, but it is necessary if this question word is the object.
Who directed the film? Who did you like best in the film?
Negative forms are also possible:
Why didn't you enjoy the concert?

4 **(12)** .... *questions* .... which can combine any of 1–3 above with an *if* clause:
If you had time, would you learn another foreign language?
If your parents give you all that money, will you save it or spend it?
If you'd gone home early, who would've noticed?

5 **(13)** .... *questions* .... in which the auxiliary does not go before the subject. To report a yes/no, alternative or conditional sentence, we can use *if* or *whether* (without a **(14)** .... at the end):
I asked Laura whether she was having fun.
Paula wanted to know if she was first or second on the list.
I asked Ray if he would still work there if he didn't need the money.
To report a wh-question, we don't use *do*, unless the question is negative:
Sam asked me where I went on Friday evenings.
The police wanted to know why I didn't have a licence.
If there is no important change of time between the action and the reporting, the original tense may be used.
I asked Laura whether she is having fun.

b Which of these types of question do you normally find easy to form, and which are difficult? Why?

2 **a** Identify the types of question in 1–10, and correct the mistakes in eight of them.

1 Who did give you those lovely flowers?
2 Will you let me know if do you hear any news tomorrow?
3 Do you want to come out with us or you are going to stay at home?
4 How you found out about the job?
5 Would you dance with her if she would ask you to?
6 Weren't you able to get tickets?
7 What you saw last night on TV?
8 If had they offered you a role in the film, would you have accepted it?
9 She asked me if I had heard about Nicholas.
10 I asked Carol what time had she arrived home.

b Match 1–10 in **a** with responses a–i. One answer can be matched with two questions.

a Unfortunately, they were all sold out.
b Well, we watched the news and then a documentary.
c There was an ad in the paper for extras.
d Just after midnight, she said.
e I'm staying in this evening.
f I certainly would.
g I said I hadn't, so she told me.
h John did; he brought them round this morning.
i Yes, of course, I'll tell you straightaway.

3 Re-order the words in 1–6 to form accurate sentences.

1 walked the ever of out finished cinema have you film before the?
2 affairs keep you with how current do up?
3 famous who you choose if would interview could somebody you?
4 TV you has effect people on do a negative think some?
5 saw the film teacher us was what last our asked we.
6 prefer the or do to watching you videos going cinema?

4 Work in pairs. Look at the picture for one minute.

1 Student A prepare six questions about what is happening to ask Student B.

2 Close your books. Student A ask Student B the six questions. (e.g. *Who is holding the …?*)

3 When Student B has answered as many questions as possible, change pairs so that Student B works with a different Student A.

4 Student B reports the questions they were asked for new Student A to try to answer. (e.g. *He asked me who is/was holding the …*)

5 a Which of a–c is the best answer to these questions? What might be a suitable question for the wrong answers?

1 What will you study if you go to university?
   a Yes, it's likely I'll go to university.
   b I'll probably do engineering.
   c No, I don't like studying at all.

2 What kind of music do you like most?
   a I don't like jazz very much.
   b I listen to music all the time.
   c I think folk music is my favourite.

common errors

Have they left yet or they are still here?
What is wrong with this sentence? Why?

b You'll hear eight questions similar to those in **a**. For each one, two of the answers (a–c) reflect typical misunderstandings of the question. Which one is correct?

1 **a** I work in a travel agency.
   b Do you mean after work?
   c I'm trying to find my pen.

2 **a** My favourite lessons are geography and history.
   b I love playing rock CDs really loudly.
   c I enjoy going for walks in the country.

3 **a** I've just got my first job.
   b No, I don't work on Saturdays.
   c We have to work very hard at school.

4 **a** I think I'll probably get through them.
   b Yes, I really want to do a degree.
   c I haven't decided where I'll go yet.

5 **a** I do rather a lot of work at home.
   b I'd prefer a job I could do at home.
   c I wouldn't like to work at weekends.

6 **a** The easiest way to learn it is to live in the UK or US.
   b We find some things, like the spelling, very difficult.
   c It's easy for me because I started when I was eight.

7 **a** I'd have to think about it.
   b I'm going there next month.
   c I didn't want the job.

8 **a** Ever since I was a child.
   b Until I was about thirteen.
   c Before I started studying medicine.

listening   multiple choice: focusing on stems (1)

1 a Read the instructions and questions 1–4. While you listen, follow the tapescript on page 158 and highlight the parts of the text that answer each question.

You will hear an interview in which Suzie Molina, a foreign correspondent for a well-known international TV news organisation, talks about her work.

1 What does Suzie like most about doing interviews?
2 When does reporting make her feel nervous?
3 When does she worry about her own safety?
4 How is her job affecting her relationship with her boyfriend?

b Write your own answers to 1–4.
c Look at the multiple-choice questions on page 149. For each of 1–4, choose the option (A–D) closest in meaning to your answer.

2 Listen again, without looking at the tapescript, to confirm your choices.

speaking introducing yourself

EXAM FOCUS

paper 5 part 1

Part 1 lasts about three minutes. There will be two examiners in the room: the interlocutor, who asks the questions, and the assessor, who takes no part in the conversation after the introductions. In this part, you will be encouraged to give information about yourself and express personal opinions. One of the aims of Part 1 is to help you relax and this should be quite easy as the topic is a familiar one: yourself.

In Part 1 it's important to
- use tenses accurately;
- make your answers as interesting as possible and expand on the information you give;
- include natural expressions, e.g. *Actually* ..., *Well* ..., etc. and idioms where appropriate;
- use more advanced lexical items where possible, e.g. *odd* rather than *unusual*.

1 **a** Look at the following possible responses to questions in Part 1. What question do you think was asked?
  1 I do actually, just round the corner. I've been in the same flat ever since I moved to the UK.
  2 With friends. The arrangement is ideal really because we've known each other for ages and get on very well.
  3 My girlfriend's parents come from Newcastle and they have really strong accents! I'm hoping a better command of the language will make it easier to chat to them.
  4 I've been working at an electronics company for a few months now, just trying to get as much experience as possible. It's quite hectic there, but never dull.
  5 Looking back on them, rather idyllic really. We lived in a small village and there were only three classes at the local school so everybody knew each other. It was a very secure environment and nobody thought of playing truant.
  6 Well, more than anything I suppose it's vital to be adaptable and have a broad range of general skills. People move companies and careers so regularly nowadays that knowledge in just one area isn't always enough.

  b Underline words in the answers that mean
  busy; extremely important; safe; boring; wide; perfect.

  c How many different tenses are used in **a**? Why are they used?

2 **a** Look at 1–5 below and write notes about yourself using the advice in this section.
  1 where you live and who with
  2 why you are learning English
  3 your work and study
  4 your schooldays
  5 important skills for the future

  b 🔊 In pairs, take it in turns to interview each other. Use the questions from **1a** and your notes from **2a** to help you.
  - If you need to, ask for clarification or repetition.
  - Don't worry about getting every detail (such as the precise date you started school or work) exactly right.
  - Don't say you 'don't know anything' about a topic and then fall silent.
  - Give reasons and examples to justify your opinions.

vocabulary

prefixes

1 What is the difference between a prefix and a suffix? What is the function of a prefix? Write down all the English prefixes you know, together with an example word for each one. Which of these prefixes do you recognise from your own language?

2 **a** Which prefixes from **1** can be added to words to give them the opposite meaning?

b Complete these groups of words with the correct negative prefixes, and write more examples. The first one has been done as an example.

1 ...*un*...dress, ...*un*...well, ...*un*...easily
  untie, unfashionable, unhappily

2 ....obey, ...satisfied, ...respectfully, ...honesty

3 ....efficient, ...consistently, ...competence

4 ....mature, ...patiently, ...balance

5 ....logical, ...legally, ...literacy

6 ....regular, ...responsibly, ...relevance

7 ....-existent, ...-stop, ...-fiction

3 Underline the prefix in each word then write more words with that meaning of the prefix. Can you define the meaning of the prefix?

EXAMPLE *foreground – forehead, foretaste, forehand, foreword, foreshore. Meaning = front*

> ~~foreground~~ rebuild semicircle undercooked
> subheading pre-university pro-democracy malfunction
> multicultural overeat autobiography postwar
> transatlantic bilingual ex-boyfriend co-star
> microcomputer megaphone defrost anti-hunting

4 **a** Which of these words have a prefix, and which don't?

> insist hyperactive biscuit forest counteract
> present monologue existence innovation

b What do these words mean? Why might they be confusing?

> invaluable inhabited infamous inflammable

c What can make these words difficult to say or spell?

> re-educate misspell forehead cooperate amoral

phrasal verbs

1 Underline the words that help you to work out the meaning of the phrasal verbs in italics.

1 I hear they are *bringing out* 'Devastation II' just six months after 'Devastation' was released.

2 The debate on Channel 2 used to *deal with* quite serious topics, but nowadays they only appear to be concerned with trivial matters.

3 A good director can *build up* tension throughout a film, gradually increasing the excitement for the audience.

4 Let's quickly *run through* the points we're going to discuss at tomorrow's meeting.

5 They showed the first episode at 9.30 last week, but I don't know what time tonight the second one *is on*.

6 Big film stars can *turn down* roles that don't appeal to them, only accepting offers in major productions.

7 On TV she *comes across* as highly self-confident, but in real life she seems a bit shy and unsure of herself.

8 The film crew spent hours *setting up* all the equipment, only to have to put everything away when it started to rain.

2 Use the correct form of all the phrasal verbs in **1** to complete 1–8.

1 Many bands .... a new single just before Christmas in the hope that people will buy it as a present.

2 It took our teacher some time to .... the overhead projector, but it made the activity much more interesting.

3 It's a pity that he .... as unintelligent, because he's really quite clever.

4 I've no plans for this evening beyond watching my favourite soap, the volleyball match and whatever .... after that.

5 Tension had been .... up for some time before the riots broke out.

6 We hope the town council will not .... our request for more spending on facilities for young people.

7 Why don't we .... the agenda before we finalise it?

8 The first part of Professor Jordan's talk .... the causes of homelessness; she then went on to discuss its effects.

EXAM FOCUS

paper 3 part 2 word formation

In Part 2 you are given a short text with gaps for ten missing words. Alongside the text are the stems of these words. This is a vocabulary test, and for many of the answers you need to add a prefix or suffix.

1 Skim through the text to get the gist.
2 Pencil in any obvious answers.
3 For each gap, decide what part of speech (e.g. *adjective*) is missing.
4 Study the context to see whether a negative is needed.
5 Note down all the e.g. *adjectives* that can be formed from the stem.
6 Choose the most likely one and write it in.
7 Read through the completed text to check everything makes sense.

1 All the answers to 1–5 require prefixes. Study the example and prompts given below the text. For each question decide which part of speech is needed.

The Filming of *Railway*

Central Station, ...disused.... since the last   **USE**
train left over twenty years

Adjective needed, context indicates
negative. Possibilities: misused ✗,
unused ✗, useless ✗, overused ✗,
underused ✗, disused ✓.

ago, was the main location chosen for
Railway. This new film, in many ways a
(1) .... of the 1970s classic of the   **MAKE**
same name, was shot almost entirely in
or around the station. Compared to the
enormous cost of the original, therefore,
it was quite an **(2)** .... film to   **EXPENSE**
make. Money was saved by using
technology in ways that were
(3) .... back in 1975. For   **IMAGINE**
instance, instead of hiring thousands of
extras, they used computers to give the
impression of huge crowds, when in fact
for some big scenes the film crew
probably **(4)** .... the actors by   **NUMBER**
two to one. They also avoided using
(5) .... superstars, some of whom   **PAY**
charge millions of dollars for just a few
minutes' appearance on screen.

1 Which prefix means 'again'?
2 Was the new film cheaper to make than the original? Therefore, is the word likely to be positive or negative? What does the use of 'an' tell you?
3 In 1975 could they imagine the technology of the future? Therefore, is the word likely to be positive or negative?
4 Which prefix means 'more than'? What tense is required?
5 Which prefix means 'too much'? What spelling change is needed?

37

writing
summary

1 What is the point of writing a summary? Which of these do you think help to make a good summary?

a copying long extracts from the original text
b rewriting information in your own words where possible
c writing the summary in note form
d using appropriate linking words to join sentences
e putting the points in a logical order
f keeping the information in the same order as in the text
g adding in your own opinions
h only using information from the text
i including only the relevant information
j including as much information as possible

exam factfile

A very long summary probably includes irrelevant information; a very short summary is probably missing something important. In the exam you must write between 50 and 70 words.

2 a Read the text and say what two main topics it deals with.

b Read notes 1–7 and say which parts of the text they refer to.

1 There may be money from sales abroad.
2 Foreign companies have invested in Indian TV.
3 Zee Television is broadcast at home and abroad.
4 Indian singers perform in the US.
5 Some fans are non-Asian.
6 Foreign businesses are promoting Indian singers.
7 Many Indians have more money to spend.

On a Mediterranean yacht two years ago, a group of South Asian businessmen decided to develop the overseas Indian television market. Why not use satellite technology to launch a 24-hour digital channel? Last autumn, B4U was launched in Britain and the Arab Gulf, and then in the United States.

B4U has competition. Zee Television is now making TV shows, movies, music and Internet sites. Received in 23 million Indian homes, the channel reaches 30 million viewers in 120 other countries, too. Attracted by the growing buying power of India's middle class and possible foreign sales, foreign money has poured into the TV industry.

Foreign companies are chasing Indian

musicians, too. The country's pop-music industry sold 300 million records last year, making it the world's second largest after the United States. 20 'People here are able to buy things like music,' says one local expert. 'Before, the middle class was small and didn't have any spare money.'

With an eye on the global market, companies like Sony are backing Indian singers. MTV and 25 other Western media giants are showing Indian videos across Asia; over the past decade, Indi-pop, a mixture of South Asian folk and Western beats, has become hugely popular. Indian music stars appear on stages in New Jersey, California 30 and even Chicago. Many of the fans are Asian, but they bring non-Asian friends with them – the beginnings of a new market. ■

3 **a** Underline the key words in these instructions.

In a paragraph of between **30–50** words, summarise **in your own words as far as possible**, the reasons given in the text for the success of Indian television.

b Which of the notes in **2b** are relevant?

c Read these three summaries. Which is the best one? Why? What is wrong with the others?

A

Indian television used satellite technology to launch a 24-hour digital channel. Received in 23 million homes, the channel reaches 30 million viewers in 120 other countries, too. Attracted by the growing buying power of India's middle class and possible foreign sales, foreign money has poured into the TV industry.

B

Indian television uses satellite technology. It is now seen in over 100 countries. Foreign companies are making huge investments in Indian television. There is the potential for sales abroad. Many Indians are increasingly wealthy.

C

Indian television is now seen in over 100 countries because of satellite technology. Moreover, foreign companies are making huge investments in Indian television owing to the potential for sales abroad, as well as the increasing wealth of many Indians.

4 Underline the linking words in summary C. Which words could you use instead?

5 Underline the key words in these instructions. Which of the notes from **2b** are relevant? Use them to write your summary, linking the notes appropriately.

In a paragraph of between **30–50** words, summarise **in your own words as far as possible**, the reasons given in the text for the success of Indian pop music.

review

1 Put the words in the correct order to form questions.
1 you job have most which like to would ?
2 asked Angela who was man he the
3 not letter why arrive the did ?
4 whether the had asked he Richard film I seen
5 have it different would had enjoyed more ending if the you been ?
6 on he Joe say asked would I if what TV were he

2 Write suitable questions for these answers.
1 Because I need to be able to speak it at work.
2 They were showing a basketball match and an old film.
3 I don't know; I didn't see last night's episode.
4 On 8 August, 1985, at La Paz Maternity Hospital.
5 Yes, I am. I've got two years left of my course.
6 No thanks, I'm too busy.
7 Single, and I'm planning to stay that way!

3 Write three questions that you might need to ask in each of these situations.

1 airport enquiries

....
....
....

2 hotel reception

....
....
....

3 tourist information office

....
....
....

4 cinema box office

....
....
....

4 Add particles from B to verbs from A to form twelve phrasal verbs. Then match them with the meanings in C.

EXAMPLE *be + on = be broadcast*

A
~~be~~ give build run come set deal end turn flick

B
across ~~on~~ down through up with

C
appear to be   prepare for use   reject
slowly increase   resign from   rehearse briefly
skim the pages of   finally become   ~~be broadcast~~
have as its subject

5 **a** Write the adjective (with prefix) for someone who
1 is in poor health
2 used to be your boyfriend
3 can speak two languages
4 earns too much
5 is unable to read or write
6 is very easily upset
7 is unable to relax or stay still
8 is not very grown up
9 is extremely famous
10 works at the same place as you do

b Write the adjective (with prefix) for something that
1 is made up of many cultures
2 is not in fashion
3 has not been cooked enough
4 can catch fire
5 is millions of years old
6 is worth a lot
7 is against the law
8 makes no sense
9 cannot be imagined
10 cannot be explained

vocabulary and speaking

1 What are the people in the pictures doing and why?

talking points

1 Which of these issues do you think people should feel passionate about?
racial and sexual equality; protection of animals; government spending; plight of 3rd world countries; euthanasia. Give some examples of typical areas of concern for each one.

2 How might people raise awareness of these issues, and what activities might they be involved in and why?

3 Can you think of any other things which people might feel passionate about? What might cause them to feel like this? Are these passions a good or bad thing? Do you feel passionate about anything?

2 a Match each picture with one of the dictionary definitions in the box below.

> **pas·sion** /ˈpæʃn/ *noun* **1** [C, U] a very strong feeling of love, hatred, anger, enthusiasm, etc: *He's a man of violent passions.* ◇ *a **crime of passion*** ◇ *She argued her case with considerable passion.* ◇ *Passions were running high* (= people were angry and emotional) *at the meeting.* **2** [sing.] (*formal*) a state of being very angry: *She **flies into a passion** if anyone even mentions his name.* **3** [U] ~ **(for sb)** a very strong feeling of sexual love: *His passion for her made him blind to everything else.* **4** [sing.] ~ **(for sth)** a very strong feeling of liking sth; a hobby, an activity, etc. that you like very much: *The English have a passion for gardens.* ◇ *Music is a passion with him.* **5** (**the Passion**) [sing.] (in Christianity) the suffering and death of Jesus Christ

Extract from the *Oxford Advanced Learner's Dictionary*, sixth edition

b Look at these abbreviations from the definition box. What do they mean?
C, U, sing., sb, sth

3 a In your opinion, which of these emotions and attitudes are positive, and which are negative? Give reasons and/or examples in each case.

> indifference jealousy idealism joy aggression jubilation bitterness
> enthusiasm restraint fanaticism devotion infatuation single-mindedness
> bias vindictiveness prejudice narrow-mindedness hysteria spitefulness

b What are the adjective forms of the nouns from **a**? Which would you use to describe the people in the pictures?

reading multiple choice:
recognising incorrect options

1 a Before you read the extract from the novel *Fever Pitch* check that you know the meanings of these sports expressions:

division	*season*
promotion	*extra time*
equalise	*cup-tie*
linesman	*lead*

b Look at the cover of the book and read the extract quickly to answer these questions.

- In what way is the picture on the cover relevant to the content of this chapter?
- Which of the five paragraphs deal with the past, and which with the present?

exam factfile

Some Proficiency Reading texts may be over 1,000 words long, so the first thing you need to be able to do is read them quickly for overall meaning.

2 Read the text more carefully, and use the context to work out the meaning of these expressions.

1 *popped* (line 21) – what is the direct object of this verb?
2 *unwillingness* (line 35) – there is a phrase in the next sentence which has a similar meaning.
3 *inability* (line 35) – which expression in the next sentence has a similar meaning?
4 *my partner* (line 42) – his previous partner is mentioned in line 11.
5 *she keels over* (line 43) – which other *she* is mentioned in the text, and what did she do?
6 *physical robustness* (line 66) – this contrasts with an adjective at the start of this paragraph.
7 *went into labour* (line 68) – what does he say about Cup Final day?
8 *retardant* (line 73) – how old do you think the author is? What age does he say he 'becomes' during football matches?

3 a Before you answer the multiple-choice questions, match options A–D with the highlighted text for each question. Question 6 is a global question.

FEVER PITCH

'Funny, wise and true'
Roddy Doyle

NICK HORNBY

My arrival in Cambridge provoked the best seasons in United's short history. In my first year they won the Fourth Division by a mile; in my second, they found life a bit tougher in the Third, and had to wait
5 until the final week of the season before clinching promotion. They had two games in a week at the Abbey*: one on the Tuesday night against Wrexham, the best team in the division, which they won 1–0, and one on the Saturday against Exeter, which they
10 needed to win to be sure of going up.

With twenty minutes to go, Exeter went into the lead, and my girlfriend (who together with her girlfriend and her girlfriend's boyfriend had wanted to experience at first hand the dizzy glory of
15 promotion) promptly did what I had always presumed women were apt to do at moments of
Q1 crisis: she fainted. Her girlfriend took her off to see the St John's Ambulancemen; I, meanwhile, did nothing, apart from pray for an equaliser, which
20 came, followed minutes later by a winner. It was only after the players had popped the last champagne cork at the jubilant crowd that I started to feel bad about my earlier indifference.

I had recently read *The Female Eunuch*, a book

25 which made a deep and lasting impression on me. And yet how was I supposed to get excited about the oppression of females if they couldn't be trusted to stay upright during the final minutes of a desperately close promotion campaign? And what 30 was to be done about a male who was more concerned about being a goal down to Exeter City of the Third Division than he was about somebody he loved very much? It all looked hopeless. **Q2**

Thirteen years later I am still ashamed of my 35 unwillingness, my *inability*, to help, and the reason I feel ashamed is partly to do with the awareness that I haven't changed a bit. I don't want to look after anybody when I'm at a match; I am not *capable* of looking after anybody at a match. I am writing 40 some nine hours before Arsenal* play Benfica* in the European Cup, the most important match at Highbury* for years, and my partner will be with me: what happens if *she* keels over? Would I have the decency, the maturity, the common sense, to 45 make sure that she was properly looked after? Or would I shove her limp body to one side, carry on screaming at the linesman, and hope that she is still breathing at the end of ninety minutes, always presuming, of course, that extra time and penalties 50 are not required? **Q3**

I know that these worries are prompted by the little boy in me, who is allowed to run riot when it comes to football: this little boy feels that women are *always* going to faint at football matches, that 55 they are weak, that their presence at games will inevitably result in distraction and disaster, even though my present partner has been to Highbury probably forty or fifty times and has shown no signs of fainting whatsoever. (In fact it is I who have come 60 closest to fainting on occasions, when the tension of the last five minutes of a cup-tie constricts my chest and forces all the blood out of my head, if that is biologically possible; and sometimes, when Arsenal score, I see stars, literally – well, little splodges of 65 light, literally – which cannot be a sign of great physical robustness.) But then, that is what football has done to me. It has turned me into someone who would not help if my girlfriend went into labour at an impossible moment (I have often wondered 70 about what would happen if I was due to become a father on an Arsenal Cup Final day); and for the duration of the games I am an eleven-year-old. When I described football as a retardant, I meant it. **Q4 Q5**

---

* the Abbey: Cambridge United's football ground

* *The Female Eunuch*: well-known feminist book

* Arsenal: English football team

* Benfica: Portuguese football team

* Highbury: Arsenal's football ground

b You are going to read an extract from a novel about the author's love of football. For questions **1–6**, choose the answer (**A**, **B**, **C** or **D**) which you think fits best according to the text.

1 The writer did not care about the incident involving his girlfriend until
   A Cambridge had scored their second goal.
   B Cambridge had scored their first goal.
   C the team had celebrated their success.
   D Exeter had scored a goal.

2 What does the writer say about himself in the third paragraph?
   A He didn't really love his girlfriend.
   B He found nothing of any interest in *The Female Eunuch*.
   C His girlfriend mattered to him less than the football score.
   D He was extremely angry about the way society treated women.

3 Before the Benfica match, the writer is afraid that he might
   A have to miss the end of the game.
   B have to go on his own.
   C upset one of the match officials.
   D do nothing to help his girlfriend.

4 The idea that women should not attend football matches comes from
   A the writer's current girlfriend.
   B the writer's young son.
   C people who cause trouble at football matches.
   D a childish part of the writer's personality.

5 What does the writer imply in the sentence beginning *In fact …* in the last paragraph?
   A He knows a lot about how the human body works.
   B He has sometimes fainted at football matches.
   C He is weaker than his girlfriend.
   D He only watches Arsenal play at night.

6 Overall, how does the writer feel about his passion for football?
   A proud
   B worried
   C unconcerned
   D optimistic

4 The following expressions all appear in the text. Without looking back, try to fill in the dependent preposition in each case.
*be sure …   be ashamed …   be capable …
result …   show signs …*

5 Do you feel passionate about any sports team, or individual player? If not, do you understand why some people do? Which sports do people feel very strongly about in your country? Is it good or bad to be passionate about sport?

grammar
relative clauses

1 Read these examples and answer questions 1–7 below.

a The people who work in this office are very friendly.

b Steven, who is rarely late for school, didn't arrive until 9.30.

c The dress which she bought yesterday is lovely.

d My cousin Hannah, whose brother you've met, is coming to stay with us.

e The forest was suddenly lit up by a bright light, which surprised all of us.

1 Which of a–e have defining, and which non-defining, relative clauses?
What is the difference between a defining and a non-defining relative clause?
Which of them is separated from the rest of the sentence by commas?

2 In which of a–e could we leave out the relative pronoun? Why?

3 In which of them could we use a different relative pronoun?

4 In which does the relative pronoun refer back to all of the previous clause?

5 Which has a relative pronoun that can only be used before a noun?

6 Why can't we use 'that' instead of 'who' in **b**?

7 Why can't we use 'what' instead of any of these relative pronouns?

2 a Match 1–6 with a–f and join the sentences using a relative pronoun.

1 That's the house.
2 There are professional Olympic athletes.
3 Tennis is a sport.
4 At my school there's a new teacher.
5 It's often after 2 a.m.
6 I once met a man in a pub.

a People usually play it in summer.
b She comes from Canada.
c My brother arrives home.
d Their salaries are enormous.
e I used to live there.
f He had tattoos all over his head.

b Do the sentences you have formed contain defining, or non-defining relative clauses?

3 Use a relative pronoun plus information from the picture to add a relative clause to sentences 1–4.

1 James rescued someone from the sea.
2 At 6.30 in the morning it's still dark.
3 The bar is open all night in summer.
4 You can use this mobile phone anywhere in the world.

Have you written defining, or non-defining, relative clauses?

reduced relative clauses

1 Read the information, then say which words have been left out of sentences 1–5. What has changed in 3?

In defining relative clauses, we sometimes leave out *which*, *that* or *who* and *is*, *was* or *were* by using
- **passive sentences**: The person who was given the job had little experience.
  The person given the job had little experience.
- **adjectival clauses**: Florence is a city that is famous for its works of art.
  Florence is a city famous for its works of art.
- **continuous forms**: The people who were standing at the back couldn't see a thing.
  The people standing at the back couldn't see a thing.

  Notice that we can also do this with verbs not normally used in the continuous:
  We scored eight points, which meant we were the winners.
  We scored eight points, meaning we were the winners.

1 All money received will go to charity.
2 Students taking the exam should register today.
3 Equipment belonging to the Club must not be removed.
4 Everything necessary is being done.
5 A man swimming off the beach spotted the shark.

2 Cross out the words that can be left out in 1–4 and make any necessary changes.

1 A man who is capable of such cruelty should never go free.
2 People who were arriving at the station saw the train leave 10 minutes early.
3 Those of you who want tickets can buy them here.
4 Items which are bought in the sales cannot be returned.

3 Complete these sentences with a participle and your own ideas.

EXAMPLE People *found guilty of* shoplifting should *be prosecuted.*
1 Children .... to read or write must ....
2 Countries .... by natural disasters are ....
3 Families .... in poverty can ....
4 Students .... to travel round the world should ....

common errors

An ambulance, arrived within just 10 minutes, took the injured to hospital. What is wrong with this sentence? Why?

EXAM FOCUS

paper 3 part 1 open cloze

In an open cloze, you fill in fifteen gaps in a text of approximately 200–250 words. Missing grammatical words, which include prepositions, conjunctions, articles, relative pronouns, etc., are almost certainly words you already know; while vocabulary words , which combine with others to form phrasal verbs, collocations and so on, are also tested. In some cases, where, for example, either *this* or *that* fits the text, two answers are possible, but you must only put one. Contracted forms, marked by an apostrophe in words like *isn't*, count as two words, so cannot be the correct answer.

1 **a** Read the text and answer these questions.
1 Where does the information in the text come from?
2 Where do people usually have their first kiss?
3 What remains a mystery?

b For questions 1–15, read the text below and think of the word which best fits each space. Use only **one** word in each space. There is an example at the beginning (**0**).

FIRST KISS

The first kiss, (**0**) _whether_ between Romeo and Juliet in Renaissance Italy or today's teenagers at a bus stop, is the most memorable experience in life. It is (**1**)........... powerful that it will be recalled more accurately (**2**)........... any joys and tragedies occurring years later. Couples remember up (**3**)........... 90% of the details surrounding the first kiss, (**4**)........... the colour of a shirt or blouse to the first words said after their lips parted, according to nearly 300 interviews with people (**5**)........... first kiss happened between 1977 and the past six months. Sarah Fisher, (**6**)........... co-authored the study, said that researchers had also asked (**7**)........... first kisses happened – and found that the rules of the game had hardly changed at (**8**)........... over the past 50 years. 'The first kiss is usually in a semi-public place, (**9**)........... as saying goodnight outside the girl's house.' Yet the team admits it is not sure (**10**)........... the kiss is so significant. They know that the average kiss (**11**)........... 45 seconds and involves 34 muscles; that it creates chemical changes in a part of the brain associated (**12**)........... strong emotions; and that it was first recorded (**13**)........... an expression of affection by the Romans 2,000 years (**14**)........... . William Shakespeare praised it – but the scientists still do not know why it gives so (**15**)........... pleasure.

listening three-way matching:
ways of agreeing and disagreeing (1)

1 **a** What are these examples of?
*life imprisonment   community service   a caution
electronic tagging*
Can you think of more?

b Check the meaning of these expressions:
*bail   convict (v)   trial   criminal record
compensation   curfew   probation   re-offend*

2 Quickly read through statements 1–12 below. Which do you agree with?

1 A prison sentence reforms most criminals.
2 It is very expensive to imprison someone for a long time.
3 Life in modern prisons is not hard enough.
4 People accused of a crime should stay in prison until they go to court.
5 Young people who commit minor offences should only be cautioned.
6 Some people should never be released from prison.
7 Prisoners should be educated and trained, rather than punished.
8 Convicted criminals should pay compensation to their victims.
9 We should build more prisons.
10 Prisoners should go to prisons near their family and friends.
11 Released prisoners should have to wear electronic tags.
12 There are too many people in prison.

3 **a** Look at the example, and the extract from the recording. Is Sandy's response type **a**, **b**, **c** or **d**?

You will hear part of a radio discussion in which two people, Giles McKay and Sandy Carter, talk about the prison system. For questions **1–6**, decide whether the opinions are expressed by only one of the speakers, or whether the speakers agree. Write **G** for Giles, **S** for Sandy or **B** for Both, where they agree.

EXAMPLE It is wrong to put so many people in prison. ....G.....

Giles: We lock up more of our citizens than they do in any comparable country, with the sole exception of the United States. What on earth are we doing? This policy is a disaster for all concerned, whether they be prisoners, their dependants or their victims!

Sandy: Well, not entirely. You may think so but …

a **stating agreement** i.e. directly
b **indicating agreement** i.e. indirectly
c **stating disagreement**
d **indicating disagreement**

b Listen to the recording and answer questions 1–6.
1 Imprisoning young people for lesser crimes is a mistake.
2 Privately-run prisons are starting to improve.
3 It is wrong that innocent people are imprisoned.
4 Prisoners should earn quite good wages.
5 We must make jails less unpleasant places.
6 The current prison system is a failure.

4 Check your answers, then study the tapescript on pages 151 and 152 and label the underlined language types **a**, **b** or **d**.

speaking giving and justifying opinions

1 When you are trying to persuade someone to agree with you or to accept a particular point of view, which of these are good ideas, and which are not?

1 Talk in a much louder voice than the other person.
2 Contradict them by simply saying things like 'No it isn't'.
3 Listen carefully to their point of view, and reply to each point.
4 Interrupt a lot.
5 Give reasons and examples to reinforce your arguments.
6 Be polite, even if you feel the other person is being unreasonable.
7 If they reject your ideas, question their intelligence, motives or sanity.

2 Which of the following expressions can be used to debate in favour of something and which against?

1 But isn't it a fact that …?
2 There cannot be any doubt that …
3 All the evidence would indicate that …
4 Yes, that's one way of looking at it, but …
5 There is obviously no alternative to …
6 You claim/say that … but surely …?
7 Something else to bear in mind is …
8 Another factor to be taken into consideration is …
9 Well it seems logical/sensible/reasonable, but …

3 a Look at the picture. What do you know about genetically modified food? How much of an issue is it in your country?

b 1 Divide into Side A and Side B.
Side A: You are in favour of GM foods. Read the text *Some say YES!* on page 157 and make notes. Choose five or six arguments, with reasons to justify them. Add some points of your own if you can.
Side B: You are against GM foods. Read the text *Some say NO!* on page 150 and make notes. Choose five or six arguments, with reasons to justify them. Add some points of your own if you can.
2 Choose a spokesperson.
   A: Present the arguments for GM foods in about two minutes, using expressions from **2**.
   B: Listen carefully, take notes and prepare counter-arguments.
3 B: Present the arguments against GM foods in about two minutes, using expressions from **2**.
   A: Listen carefully, take notes and prepare counter-arguments.
4 Choose a second speaker.
   A: Criticise each of B's arguments, using expressions from **2**.
   B: Criticise each of A's arguments, using expressions from **2**.
5 If you are working with others, choose a third speaker.
   A: Sum up your arguments, and criticisms of B's arguments.
   B: Sum up your arguments, and criticisms of A's arguments.

vocabulary

idioms

1 **a** For each of 1–9, underline the idiom, look at the context and discuss its meaning.

1 When my dad saw the huge phone bill he hit the roof, blaming me for it.

2 Watching people dance Flamenco is great, but I'm dying to try it for myself.

3 Kira loves motorbikes, so when she won a new one in a competition she was over the moon.

4 Being beaten by United always makes me angry, but losing so unfairly makes my blood boil.

5 When the police started arresting people, the demonstration got out of hand and serious damage was caused.

6 Sam and his brother never agree; in fact, they fight like cat and dog all the time.

7 We'll stop at nothing to prevent them building a factory in this beautiful valley.

8 Carol and Derek hate being apart even for an hour: they're mad about each other.

9 Ron is a good manager, but he's bitten off more than he can chew by promising that we'll win the next World Cup.

b Which of the above idioms do pictures 1–3 illustrate?

2 Rewrite the following paragraphs more informally using as many idioms from **1a** as possible.

> Are you fascinated by all things Spanish? Desperate to experience 'authentic' Spain? Why not visit our new website? You'll be delighted when you see what's on offer!

> 'It infuriates me to see finance companies offering such huge loans. The number of people I know whose spending on credit cards has escalated beyond control – then they realise they can't deal with it and have to take out more loans to pay off what they owe.'

collocations: adjective + noun

1 Study the adjectives in 1–6 and decide which of these nouns can form collocations with all five of them.

love	hatred	excitement	hope	instinct	emotion(s)

1 strong	4 faint
deep	vain
powerful	desperate ....
raw	slight
pent-up	only

2 human	5 growing
natural	great
gut	considerable ....
basic	mounting
maternal	tremendous

3 true	6 bitter
young	pure
everlasting	absolute ....
first	blind
unrequited	intense

2 Complete 1–7 with an adjective + noun collocation from **1**. More than one adjective may be possible.

1 Jealousy is a(n) .... that can make people do terrible things.

2 At the end of the trial all her .... came out as she broke down in tears.

3 The week before she was going to marry Joe, Sergio told Pam of his .... for her.

4 Although the climber has been missing for a week, there is still a .... that he might be alive.

5 There was .... as first Lazio scored, then Barcelona, and then Lazio again.

6 It is one of man's most .... to protect his offspring.

7 When Sylvia saw her ex-boyfriend laughing at her, she gave him a look of ....

3 Use some of the collocations from **1** to describe what is happening and the background to this event.

EXAM FOCUS

paper 3 part 5 comprehension questions

In this part of the exam you read two related texts and answer two questions on each. The questions test your understanding of the use of language.

Question types include
- explaining the meaning of specific words or phrases;
- identifying words with a similar or contrasting meaning within the text;
- understanding general ideas in the text;
- understanding why the author has used a particular word or phrase;
- focusing on specific information in the text.

1 Read the advice on tackling comprehension questions, then match suggestions 1–8 with reasons a–h.

1 Begin by quickly reading both texts.
2 For each text, study the two questions and then read the text again carefully.
3 If you can't do a question, go on to the next one.
4 Give short, concise answers.
5 Don't repeat the question in your answer.
6 Where you can, answer in your own words.
7 Check that your answer makes sense.
8 Don't spend <u>too</u> long on these questions.

a You will lose marks if you copy too much from the text.
b You won't get any marks if the meaning isn't clear.
c There are more marks for the summary section of Part 5.
d You don't need to write complete sentences.
e This will give your reading a specific purpose.
f The question order is the same as the information in the text, so it may help you find the answer to the one before.
g This will give you a general impression of the topic.
h There are no marks for doing so, it takes time and you could make mistakes!

2 Read the text below and decide which of these is the best title:
- How pop stars set a bad example.
- Stop your children idolising the famous.
- The dangers of hero-worship.

Obsession with pop stars may be innocent enough when you're 14 years old. Carry the fixation into your twenties, however, and your teen idol can become bad for your health.
5 Worshipping famous singers, supermodels or footballers into adulthood increases your chance of psychological problems, eating disorders and difficulties forming relationships.

Psychologist Dr Tony Cassidy looked at 163
10 adults in a recent study. During adolescence, three-quarters of men and women in the group – now aged between 20 and 28 – said they had hero-worshipped someone. Most people throw off their fixation by their twenties, but half of those who
15 had idols could not let their feelings go.

'Another aspect of teen idols is that they serve as role models,' said Dr Cassidy. 'Many young girls develop distorted body images of themselves, and ultimately eating disorders, as a result of the media
20 portrayal of supermodels with ideal bodies.'

The obsessive tended to be less satisfied with their relationships and were more likely to have short-term affairs. The most extreme fantasised about having a relationship with their adored one
25 or becoming jealous of their idol's partners. There were even cases, after one boy band split up, of attempted suicides among fans.

But parents should not rush to the bedroom to rip down their children's posters. There was one
30 bright spot for fans who did have a teen idol but who gave it up when they reached adulthood: they were subsequently better at problem-solving.

3 Look at example questions a–c and match them with possible answers 1–3.
a Which word in paragraph 4 echoes *adored one*? (line 24)
b Explain *let their feelings go* (line 15) in your own words.
c What is the first thing that often happens to girls who idolise supermodels?
1 *Stop hero-worshipping a famous person.*
2 *They get the wrong idea of how they really look.*
3 *idol*

4 Answer questions 1 and 2.
1 What is the significance of *even* in line 26?
2 Explain in your own words what the *bright spot* is (line 30).

writing set books

1. Imagine you are directing a film version of your chosen book. Decide:
   1 where you would film it and which actors you would cast in which roles
   2 which parts of the book you would change or leave out, and what you would add
   3 what music you would use for the soundtrack, and what special visual effects
   4 who you would expect to watch it, in terms of age and type of audience
   5 which role in the film you would like to play, and why.

2. Discuss how studying the set book can help you with your English generally, and in the exam specifically.

3. Fill in the missing words in these suggestions for preparing for the set book question.
   1 Build up a list of useful q............ about people, places, events, etc.
   2 Watch a film or TV version of the book to consider the d............ in the presentation.
   3 Write down what you notice about society in the time and p............ in which the book is set. For instance, the attitudes shown towards women and marriage, education and poverty.
   4 Imagine the places where events happen, and draw m............ or d............ . If you are good at sketching, you might want to draw pictures of some of the characters, and see if other students who are reading the same book agree with your impressions.
   5 Make notes about the main characters and their r............ with each other. Try drawing diagrams of their r............ if this helps.
   6 Think about the minor c............ and their importance to the story.
   7 Make a list of the k............ events in the story, who is involved and where they happen.
   8 Write a s............ of the main events in each chapter.

4 a Look at the pictures from *Jane Eyre*. What do they tell you about the book? If you have read it, or seen a film or TV version, briefly tell your partner about it.

b Read the instructions and underline the key words.

In 250–300 words write an essay for your tutor describing how Jane and Rochester's relationship develops and finally succeeds.

c Quickly read the model essay and decide whether it follows the instructions. Think particularly about the words you underlined in **b**.

d Read the text again. Which paragraph describes
- the break-up of their relationship?
- various social obstacles to the relationship?
- the reasons for their reconciliation?
- personal characteristics that make a relationship unlikely?
- a practical reason why they cannot marry?
- how they first become close to each other?

5 a A good writer uses various ways of describing character. Find examples of 1–5 in the essay.
1 direct description of character
2 describing actions that illustrate character
3 saying what a person is actually thinking
4 mentioning what one person says about another
5 linking physical appearance to character
6 referring to his or her background.

b Why does the writer use quotations? What should you be careful about when using them?

6 Follow the instructions and the advice which follows.

Think of a relationship in your set book or in any book you have read in English or your own language. In 250–300 words, write an essay for your teacher describing the development of the relationship and the reasons for its success or failure.

- Underline the key words in the instructions.
- Plan separate paragraphs for different stages of the relationship. (see **4d**)
- Justify your statements by referring to the text. Notice how paragraphs in the sample essay use short topic sentences backed up by evidence and examples from the book.
- Use different ways of presenting character. (see **5a**)
- If you use extracts/quotations from the text, make sure they are short, correctly quoted and have a clear purpose.

The differences that exist between Jane and Rochester at first seem insurmountable. Not only do they come from social worlds which are completely different, Rochester has a terrible secret – his marriage to Bertha.

Jane is at a disadvantage in many ways. As well as being her 'master', Rochester is much older and more worldly than she is. He is rich and from an established and respected family. She on the other hand is young and innocent. She is poor, an orphan who has relied on benefactors all her life. Socially they are far apart. 'He is not of your order: keep to your caste', Jane tells herself.

Neither of them seem candidates for romantic love. Rochester is stern and cynical, 'very changeful and abrupt'. Jane is still affected by the restraints of Lowood School and her own position as governess. She is not traditionally beautiful, any more than Rochester is handsome.

However, they both have different sides to their personalities. Rochester speaks gently to Jane when she cries. He speaks with passion when he proposes. He ignores good sense as he refuses to consider the consequences of bigamy. Rochester compares Jane to a bird. 'A vivid, restless, resolute captive is there' he tells her; 'were it but free, it would soar cloud-high.' Jane's 'flight', however, is when she takes the agonising decision to leave Thornfield Hall after Rochester's secret is revealed.

It is only after Jane has discovered she is an heiress and has affectionate and respectable relatives that she is able to return. Then she finds that Bertha is dead, but that Rochester has suffered the ruin of Thornfield and the loss of his own sight and arm. At last, with such a high price paid for freedom, Jane and Rochester may find happiness together.

⊙ THERE IS A MODEL ARTICLE FOR A SET BOOK ON PAGE 161 IN THE WRITING BANK

review

1 Some of 1–8 contain an unnecessary word. Cross out this word, or put a tick if the sentence is correct.
1 The woman who standing there is my boss.
2 They were playing a song that it was familiar.
3 It was the neighbour's dog that barking last night.
4 The film what I saw ended quite differently.
5 We want to find someone is keen to work long hours.
6 The police were looking for a man was carrying an umbrella.
7 The person who explained this to me is an expert.
8 The total number of tickets which sold is now over a million.

2 Join the sentences using *who, which, whose, where* and *when* once each.

EXAMPLE I love watching basketball on TV. (It's very popular in my country.)
I love watching basketball, which is very popular in my country, on TV.
1 Raul plays for Spain. (He's my favourite footballer.)
2 That island is a special place for my girlfriend and I. (We first met there.)
3 At 5.30 the noise in the stadium will be deafening. (The match starts then.)
4 Love is an extremely powerful emotion. (Nobody can fully explain it.)
5 Danielle is coming with us, I hope. (Her boyfriend is very good-looking.)

3 Complete 1–6 with one of these collocations.

> faint hope   great excitement   first love   pent-up emotion
> blind hatred   natural instinct

1 Some say that competing with others is a
....
2 I had a .... of seeing her at the disco, but I didn't really expect her to be there.
3 The relationship between the fans of the two teams is one of .... rather than sporting rivalry.
4 England winning the cricket resulted in .... among the spectators.
5 At the rally there was a lot of .... , which burst out when their leader began to speak.
6 Many people remember their .... as the most intense relationship they've ever had.

4 Five of 1–6 contain the wrong idiom. Rewrite them with the correct one.
1 I hit the roof when my favourite team at last won the Cup.
2 My aunt and uncle were mad about each other so they got divorced.
3 It makes my blood boil to see children behaving badly.
4 He got out of hand to ensure their first wedding anniversary would be unforgettable.
5 My boyfriend and I are going skiing next month because it makes our blood boil.
6 My elder sister was over the moon when she found out I'd ruined her dress.

5 Use clues 1–15 to complete the puzzle with words from this unit. Which saying do the letters down spell?

1 two people who are in a relationship
2 a permanent picture or pattern made on the skin
3 the reason somebody has for doing something
4 great love, affection or admiration for someone
5 something that prevents concentration
6 a large group of people
7 to say that something another person says is not true
8 to make the number of goals scored by both teams the same
9 the length of time something lasts or continues
10 to refuse to accept something that is offered
11 a way of referring to someone in a relationship if you don't know their marital status
12 a show of affection
13 one of the four parts of the year
14 to greatly admire someone famous
15 something in the way that makes progress difficult

unit 5 | *privacy*

vocabulary and speaking

THE RIGHT TO
PRIVACY

Everyone has a basic right to the following:

- Solitude: the right to be left alone when they wish, without being observed.
- Confidentiality of data: personal details such as medical records, credit information and school records to be kept secret.
- Privacy of communications: security of mail, e-mail, faxes and telephone calls.
- Freedom from intrusion: respect for individuals' property or personal space, such as their house, room, office, desk or locker.
- No unfair reporting: protection from false stories in newspapers, television or other media, including the Internet.

talking points

1 In which of these public places do you think CCTV (closed-circuit television) is justified? Give reasons for your answers.
   banks   motorways   shops
   schools   nightclubs   hospitals
   metro stations   airports
   football grounds
2 What kind of information do you think should – and should not – be held on you by
   1 the government?
   2 employers?
   3 businesses, including shops?
   4 schools and universities?

1 **a** Read this extract from a Right to Privacy statement. Which of these rights are important to you? Why? Which of them are sometimes not respected?

b Are there any other kinds of privacy you think should be protected?

2 **a** What do these people do?

> intruder   informer   eavesdropper   hacker
> spy   paparazzo   stalker   trespasser   private investigator

b Which of these adjectives do people often apply to them?

> sneaky   threatening   inquisitive   sly   sinister   despicable
> alarming   glamorous   sleazy   nosy   cunning

c Can you give examples of recent events which involved these people?

d Find four pairs of words below with similar meanings. Which of the people above do you associate them with?

> taping   observing   tracking   bugging   recording
> trailing   tapping   monitoring

What equipment might they use in each of these activities?

3 **a** Match pictures A–E with 1–5 below.

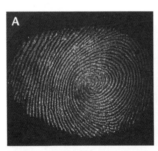
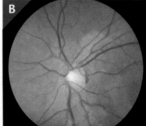
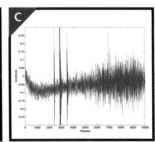
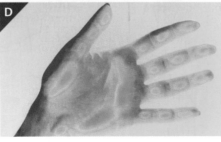
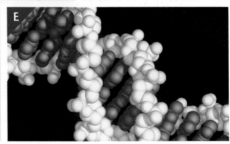

1 Hand geometry.
2 Fingerprints.
3 Retina scan.
4 DNA samples.
5 Voice recognition.

b Discuss how these methods of identifying people work. In what situations might they be used?

4 What kind of information should be carried on identity cards and passports, and what should not? Why?

reading gapped text:
lexical and grammatical links (1)

1 Quickly read the text and paragraphs A–H and make a list of the ways companies spy on their employees.

2 Read the information on how to do gapped texts, then do a–c.

> In a gapped text task you have to fit paragraphs into a text. When you are doing one, these types of words are often excellent clues.
> - **reference words** like *this* and *us*. For example, in line 7 of the text, *It* refers back to *book* in line 5.
> - **conjunctions** such as *in addition* and *though*. In line 20, *since* links *they can get your address and date of birth* to *voter registration forms are a matter of public record in most states*.
> - **lexical links**, for example the use of synonyms, contrasts and repetition of the same word. In line 22, the word *days* contrasts with *minutes* in line 24.

a Which words, within the same paragraph, do these words refer to?
her (line 32)   *that* (line 40)   *This* (line 84)
them (line 91)

b Identify the clauses and / or sentences that these expressions link and think of another way of saying the same thing:
thus (line 60)   *in short* (line 63)   *even though* (line 74)
not only … but (line 77)

c Find lexical links with these in the same paragraph.
company (line 25)   *employees* (line 27)
badge (line 56)   *most* (line 67)

3 a You are going to read an article about how some American companies treat their employees. Choose from the paragraphs **A–H** the one which fits each gap (**1–7**). There is one extra paragraph which you do not need to use.

b These questions will help you decide if you have put the paragraphs in the right places.

What do these words refer to?
this (line 22)   *they* (line 48)   *that* (line 55)
this (line 87)

What do these conjunctions link?
Conversely (line 25)   *Still other* (line 30)
However (line 42)   *For instance* (line 72)

What are the lexical links with these?
Internet (line 17)   *pharmaceutical* (line 26)
these two bits of information (line 47)   *court* (line 77)
methods (line 80)   *these two firms* (line 96)

How Corporate America destroys privacy

Now here is something to remember should you ever fir yourself using a changing cubicle in an American departmer store. It is perfectly legal – indeed, it is evidently routine – f the store to spy on you while you are trying on their clothe

> refers to last sentence, previous paragraph

> links to next paragraph

5 **1** **C** I know this because I have just been reading a book b Ellen Alderman and Caroline Kennedy called *The Right Privacy*. It is full of alarming stories of ways that shops an employers can – and do – intrude into what would normal be considered private affairs.

> links to previous paragraph

10 As the authors point out, nearly everyone is being spied on some way in America these days. A combination technological advances, employer paranoia and commerci greed means that many millions of Americans are having the lives delved into in ways that would not have been possible
15 dozen years ago.

2

Worse still, there are now electronic private investigators wh make a living going through the Internet finding person information on people. If you are an American resident an have ever registered to vote they can get your address and da
20 of birth, since voter registration forms are a matter of publ record in most states.

3

Most of this was possible before, but it would take days inquiries and visits to various government offices. Now it ca be done in minutes, in anonymity, through the Internet.

4

25 Conversely, one large, well-known company joined up with pharmaceutical firm to go through the health records employees to see who might benefit from a dose antidepressants. The idea was that the company would ge more serene workers, the drug company more customers.

5

30 Still other companies are secretly watching their employees work. A secretary at a school in Massachusetts discovered tha a hidden video camera was filming her office 24 hours a da She is suing and will probably get lots of money. But elsewher courts have upheld companies' right to spy on their workers

6

35 Many large companies now prohibit employees from usin tobacco or alcohol at any time, including at home. There ar companies, if you can believe it, that forbid their employee to drink or smoke at any time – even one beer, even on Saturday night – and enforce the rules by making thei
40 workers give urine samples. That is outrageous, but if peopl want a job, they must accept it.

7

However, there is one development, I am pleased to report which makes all this worthwhile. A company in New Jerse has invented a device to determine whether restaurar
45 employees have washed their hands after using the lavatory Now that I can support.

A With these two bits of basic personal information, they can (and for as little as $8 will) provide almost any information about anyone: court records, medical records, driving records, credit history, hobbies, buying habits, income, telephone numbers (including ex-directory ones). You name it: they'll find it.

B But company control gets even more sinister than that. Two big electronics firms working together have invented something called an 'active badge', which tracks the movements of any worker told to wear one. This little device sends out an infra-red signal every 15 seconds. The signal is picked up by a central computer, which is thus able to keep a record of where every employee is and has been, how many times they have been to the toilet or water-cooler – in short, to follow every single action of their working day. If that isn't ominous, I don't know what is.

C *I know this because I have just been reading a book by Ellen Alderman and Caroline Kennedy called* The Right to Privacy. *It is full of alarming stories of ways that shops and employers can – and do – intrude into what would normally be considered private affairs.*

D On the contrary, he said that very few employees had complained. Most, he believed, were completely in favour of any such security system which helped the company prevent these types of crime occurring. Those few who criticised it, he seemed to be saying, were either naïve – or else had something to hide.

E For instance, when an employee of a large firm discovered it was routinely reading employees' e-mail, even though it had assured the employees that it was not, she blew the whistle and was promptly fired. She sued for unfair dismissal and lost the case. A court upheld the right of companies not only to review employees' private communications, but to lie to them about doing it. Whoa!

F One of the simplest methods of finding out about you, of course, is by checking where you go on the Internet. Log on and nearly every website you go to will make a record of what you looked at and how long you stayed there. This can, and usually will, then be sold on to mail order and marketing companies.

G Many countries are taking advantage of this to make their businesses more profitable. In Maryland, according to Time magazine, a bank searched through the medical records of its borrowers – apparently quite legally – to find out which of them had life-threatening illnesses, and used this information to cancel their loans. Other companies have focused on their own employees – for example, to check what prescription drugs they are taking.

H These two firms are not alone. In fact, according to the American Management Association, two-thirds of companies in the US spy on their employees in some way. Thirty-five per cent track phone calls and ten per cent even tape telephone conversations to review later. About a quarter of companies admit to going through their employees' computer files and reading their e-mail.

c Which linking expressions – reference, conjunction and / or lexical – made it impossible to fit the extra paragraph into any of the gaps?

4 1 In what way are *focus on* (line 94) and *spy on* (line 34) similar in meaning?
2 Find a verb and a noun in paragraph E that both mean 'losing her job'.
3 Identify two verbs in the paragraph from lines 35–41 that both mean 'ban'.
4 Which two phrasal verbs in paragraph B have contrasting meanings?
5 Use the context to work out the meanings of these words.
  cubicle (line 2)   *delve into* (line 14)
  sue (line 33 and 76)   *enforce* (line 39)
  upheld (line 77)   *log on* (line 82)
6 What do you think is the origin of the idiom *blow the whistle?* (line 75)
7 Which verb in line 8 does *do* refer to? Find other examples of this in paragraphs A and F.

5 Do you agree or disagree with the writer's opinion? Why? In what circumstances do you think people change their behaviour when they think they are being watched, and when does it probably make no difference?

grammar
the passive

1 Write all the passive forms – simple and continuous, past and future, etc. – of *we watch* that you know.

EXAMPLE present simple passive – *we are watched*

Which forms are <u>not</u> normally possible? Why?

2 Discuss these questions.
1 How do we form the passive?
2 Why might somebody choose to use a passive sentence rather than an active one?
3 Why do we often leave out the agent (e.g. *he was arrested* ~~by the police~~)?
4 In what kinds of writing is the passive **a** common **b** rare?
5 How can we rewrite *the pictures were shown to us* using a different passive structure? Which other verbs work like this?
6 Do we use intransitive verbs like *fall* and *smile* in the passive? Why/Why not?
7 What verb do we often use instead of *let* in the passive?

3 Explain why the passive is used in each of these sentences.

EXAMPLE I was brought up in a small village.
(someone has asked you about your childhood)
The emphasis is on me, and the agent is obviously my parents.
1 The radio's been stolen. (you've just returned to your car and found the door open)
2 The Prime Minister was met at the airport by his French counterpart.
(report on British television)
3 It can't be done that quickly. (your boss has asked you to do a job in 15 minutes)
4 I'm sorry but I think your tickets have been lost. (travel agent to customer)
5 She was taken to hospital by a man who happened to be driving past the building at the time of the explosion. (news report of an accident)
6 Patrons are reminded that the use of portable telephones is not permitted. (sign in expensive restaurant)

4 a Match 1–6 with a–f and complete the rules with the words below. The first one has been done as an example.

to be	past participle	be	adjective
being	to-infinitive	have been	

1 She doesn't enjoy being treated like that.
2 All employees were made to work hard.
3 Young Michael looks upset to be left on his own.
4 That picture might have been painted by Dali.
5 Tourists often expect to be looked after like children.
6 Library books must be returned within 14 days.

a Present modals: modal + ...be.... + past participle ....(6)....
b Past modals: modal + ... + ...
c Verb + -ing: verb + ... + ...
d Verb + infinitive: verb + ... + ...
e *hear/see/make/help*: be + ... + ...
f Verb + adjective: verb + ... + ... + ...

b Complete 1–8 with the passive form of one of these verbs. There's one you don't need.

develop	see	hear	kill	film	meet
prevent	make	thank			

1 Accidents can .... by following the safety advice.
2 Someone in the audience .... to call the speaker a liar.
3 We have arranged .... at the station by a taxi.
4 We .... to wait in a queue for over two hours.
5 Most of us are pleased .... when we help someone.
6 If we'd crossed the road a moment later, we might .... by that car.
7 The thieves managed to avoid .... by the security cameras.
8 An angry player .... to make a rude gesture to the crowd.

common errors

We were explained the reasons for the delay.
What is wrong with this sentence? Why?

5 Rewrite the sentences using the passive form of the underlined verbs. If the passive is impossible with the verb given, use a different one.

EXAMPLE Many brave soldiers <u>died</u> on that hill.
Many brave soldiers were killed on that hill.

1 At the airport, I asked them to <u>give</u> me a window seat on the plane.
2 Philip can't stand people <u>laughing</u> at him.
3 The lights <u>go out</u> at 11 o'clock at night.
4 They <u>heard</u> Dominic complain about the food.
5 Nicola prefers people to <u>use</u> the name 'Nicky'.
6 People <u>saw</u> a man fall into the sea.
7 Somebody should have <u>warned</u> us of the danger.
8 They don't <u>let</u> anyone smoke in this office.
9 A salesman <u>said I could have</u> some cut-price CDs.
10 A big parcel <u>arrived at</u> my house yesterday.

6 Think about changes in your town or city that are taking place now, or have occurred since you were a child. Using the passive and including some of the verbs below, tell your partner about them.

> pull down improve widen modernise rebuild
> knock down spoil turn into

EXAMPLE *The old houses near the station have been pulled down.*

7 Read the explanation and rewrite 1–6 using one of the two forms.

> Media reports often use the form subject + passive verb + infinitive:
> *All the passengers are believed to be safe.*
>
> Reports about the past use the perfect infinitive:
> *The band are thought to have arrived an hour ago.*

1 Everyone expects Ferrari to win tomorrow's Monaco Grand Prix.
2 Newspapers report that Jennifer has bought a house near Rome.
3 Scientists know that sea levels are rising.
4 Experts reckon that this company has lost $100 million in six months.
5 They say that those walls were built 3,000 years ago.
6 Detectives think the gang have left the country.

key word transformations

1 **a** Read the example and the instructions for questions 1–5. Use the passive and make one other change.

EXAMPLE Some people are saying that the Prime Minister told a lie.
accused
The Prime Minister ...*is being accused of telling*... a lie.

1 the verb changes from active to passive
2 correct structure after *accused*, which is *of + -ing*.

For questions **1–5**, complete the second sentence so that it has a similar meaning to the first sentence, using the word given. **Do not change the word given.** You must use between **three** and **eight** words, including the word given.

1 I spoke very softly so that nobody would hear me.
avoided
I .... very softly.
2 The school doesn't usually let students eat in class.
are
Students .... eat in class.

3 We have received no information about this matter.
been
We .... about this matter.
4 Scientists believe that a huge meteorite hit the Gulf of Mexico.
have
A huge .... Gulf of Mexico.
5 The lights aren't on so the bar must be closed.
switched
The lights have .... be closed.

b Match your answers to 1–5 with these changes a–e.
a completing a phrasal verb
b changing to a verb that you can use in the passive
c using the *-ing* form after the verb
d using the perfect infinitive
e changing a noun to a verb

listening multiple choice: predicting content

1 Read the advice and the example, then do the same with the other two situations below.

> Before you do a listening task, study the instructions and questions as these may help you to try to predict what you will hear. Think about
> 1 the number of speakers
> 2 the relationship between the speakers (if more than one), e.g. *workmates, lecturer/students*
> 3 vocabulary associated with the topic
> 4 likely grammatical forms, e.g. *verb tenses, active or passive, comparatives*
> 5 possible functions, e.g. *giving directions, asking for opinions, clarifying*
> 6 expected style, e.g. *formal, neutral, informal.*

EXAMPLE

- You are going to hear two students talking during the break between lessons about their favourite kinds of motorbike.
  1 *two*
  2 *classmates*
  3 *names (types of motorbike, etc); technical words like* cylinders, gears *and* brakes; *adjectives such as* fast, powerful *and* reliable.
  4 *present simple forms like* looks, goes *and* has; *superlatives*
  5 *describing, giving opinions, showing enthusiasm, agreeing, disagreeing*
  6 *very informal, possibly with slang expressions*

- You are going to hear a speech by a politician hoping to be elected.

- You are going to hear a technician helping a telephone caller who is having problems with their computer.

2 a 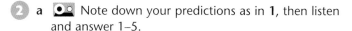 Note down your predictions as in **1**, then listen and answer 1–5.

You will hear an interview with Gary Slade, whose work involves secretly photographing famous people. For questions **1–5**, choose the answer (**A, B, C** or **D**) which fits best according to what you hear.

1 Slade works for
  A himself.
  B the police.
  C the secret service.
  D a security firm.

2 He sometimes has to
  A ride motorbikes very fast.
  B fly helicopters.
  C drive very quickly.
  D sail on ferries.

3 He says he would not photograph people if they were
  A on a public beach.
  B unwell.
  C swimming in the sea.
  D eating in a restaurant.

4 It costs him a lot to
  A buy a car or a boat.
  B hire a private aeroplane.
  C pay for accommodation.
  D buy photographs of famous people.

5 He claims that some famous individuals
  A try to stop people giving him information.
  B pay him to photograph them.
  C want him to photograph them.
  D prefer to be in the newspapers than on TV.

b Were your predictions in **a** correct?

speaking

giving examples; developing the topic

1 **a** In each of these extracts from the Listening text, there is an expression that **a** introduces an example or **b** develops the topic. Underline it and say whether it is type **a** or **b**.

1 'Such as fast cars. Some of these celebrities tear round like maniacs in their Ferraris … '
2 'How do you know where they're going, by the way?'
3 'A typical situation is when someone jets off to the Caribbean …'
4 'Why should they want to do that?'

b Sort these expressions into types **a** and **b**.

> for instance … and what is more … as well as that, there's …
> a case in point is … furthermore, … and it's not only …
> …, say, … more importantly, … to illustrate this point, … take …
> and then … worse still, … additionally, … look at … moreover, …
> and what about … even better is … …, among others, …

2  Look at the three pictures and discuss the following:
• whether the subject knew the photo was being taken or not;
• how the subject was probably feeling when the photos were taken;
• what you think might have happened just before they were taken;
• how the photographer could have obtained the photos;
• for which photo magazines would be likely to pay the most.

3 Look at the following questions which develop the topic. Discuss them using the language from **1**.

EXAMPLE What other methods of obtaining secret photos have you heard of?

*One journalist specialises in actually becoming an employee of the celebrities he wants to photograph, **for instance** by becoming their gardener, driver or bodyguard. **And it's not only** professional reporters who do things like this. **Take the case of** …*

1 What do you think of photographers like Slade?
2 Do you think celebrities invite media attention, and therefore shouldn't complain?
3 What effects can the activities of the paparazzi have on the lives on famous people?
4 If you were a celebrity, how would you react to being photographed secretly?

vocabulary
phrasal verbs

1 Look at the following passage and work out the meanings of the phrasal verbs in italics.

Did you hear what happened here last week? They're trying to keep it quiet but somehow the story's *leaked out*. Rather embarrassingly, the security guard on duty last Wednesday was *fooled into* letting a tabloid reporter into the building. He had loads of time to *snoop around* and even managed to *dig up* some rather harmful information. He'd left the building before anyone realised what had happened and they're still trying to *track* him *down*. The police are *looking into* it now as well, but apparently there's very little they can do because he didn't *break in*. One thing's for sure though, security around here is going to be *tightened up*.

2 Rewrite the sentences using forms of all the phrasal verbs from **1** once each.

1 We're going to investigate the causes of the accident and find out what really happened.
2 The college has decided to make the rules on cheating stricter.
3 The truth about the prince's relationship became generally known at Christmas.
4 Someone used force to enter the art gallery and steal several paintings.
5 While I was working on my school project, I discovered some interesting facts about the history of my home town.
6 The Navy eventually managed to find the missing submarine by studying satellite pictures and the captain's last messages.
7 I don't trust her, she always seems to be in places she shouldn't be.
8 One salesman lied to make people think that his cars were almost new.

dependent prepositions

1 a Decide which of these prepositions follow each group of words and expressions in 1–6. There's one you don't need to use.

down	for	from	of	on	to	with

1 sensitive/to object/to consent/an obstacle
2 dependent/to insist/to concentrate/hooked
3 satisfied/to associate/to have links/crowded
4 responsible/to long/a substitute/to have respect
5 safe/to differ/to discourage someone/freedom
6 critical/to accuse someone/to consist/aware

b Which of the six prepositions complete 1–12?
1 Are you <u>familiar</u> .... this game?
2 Are you <u>keen</u> .... that colour?
3 She has <u>confessed</u> .... the crime.
4 She doesn't <u>approve</u> .... my boyfriend.
5 That book made a big <u>impression</u> .... me.
6 The group is <u>opposed</u> .... hunting.
7 Scotland is <u>famous</u> .... whisky.
8 If found <u>guilty</u> .... murder, he will be executed.
9 We've a good <u>chance</u> .... winning.
10 There's something <u>missing</u> .... my bag.
11 Her <u>relationship</u> .... him was destructive.
12 Dark glass <u>prevents</u> anyone .... seeing inside.

2 Complete each caption with an expression from **1**. Use each preposition once only.

1 He wasn't .... the reporter following him.

2 The narrow street was .... photographers.

3 They thought they were .... the press.

4 Some people have no .... other people's privacy.

5 She .... people taking her picture without asking.

3 Complete these questions with an appropriate preposition, noun, adjective or verb, then discuss each question with a partner.

1 Have you ever been prevented .... doing something you wanted to?
2 What is your town / country particularly .... for?
3 Do you find it difficult to .... on your homework if the TV is on?
4 Are you .... of current affairs in other countries?
5 Would you .... to parts of your body being used for medical research after your death?
6 Are you satisfied .... the way the government is running your country?
7 What qualities do you associate .... true friendship?
8 Does the north of your country differ .... the south in any way?
9 Do you .... of the enormous wealth that some celebrities have?
10 Do you think you have a(n) .... of becoming famous one day?

EXAM FOCUS

paper 1 part 1 multiple-choice cloze

In the first part of Reading, you read three short texts from which a total of eighteen words have been removed, and replace them by choosing the correct one from four options. This is a vocabulary test, so a missing word may form part of a phrasal verb, idiom, collocation or fixed expression.

1 Begin by reading through the text for gist, without attempting to fill in any gaps. Think about the source of the text and its style.
2 Look for clues in the words next to the gap (particularly for collocations, phrasal verbs and idioms), but also in the rest of the sentence and in the text as a whole.
3 You may have to choose between options with very similar meanings, so look at the surrounding text very carefully.
4 When you have filled in <u>all</u> the gaps check that each text makes sense overall.

exam factfile

In Reading Part 1 the texts are not connected in any way, so there is no advantage in reading all three before you begin.

1 Read the text quickly. What is a *bug*?

2 For questions 1–6, read the text below and decide which answer (A, B, C or D) best fits each gap.

Use these clues to help you.

Questions 1, 3, 5, 6: Which dependent preposition can follow each of A, B, C and D?
Question 2: Which word used with *up* forms a phrasal verb that means 'buy'?
Question 4: Which verb forms a collocation with the noun *order*?

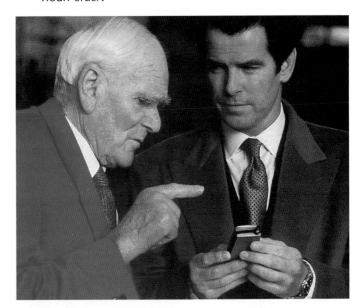

Shopping for bugs

Anyone, nowadays, can buy themselves a whole range of sophisticated bugging devices. Stores with names like *Superspy* and *Spies-R-Us* are openly selling the kind of equipment that until recently was more often **(1)**............ with the likes of James Bond. For little more than the price of a compact disc, you can **(2)**............ up a microphone and transmitter disguised as a packet of cigarettes. Internet websites that **(3)**............ in surveillance equipment will happily sell you bugs hidden in calculators, pens or watches, and ask no questions if you **(4)**............ an order for a micro-transmitter that looks like a credit card. For those **(5)**............ about their privacy, the same suppliers also stock bug detectors. The shop *Counter Spy*, for instance, sells a handy little device **(6)**............ of locating most bugs within a radius of 30 metres.

1	A limited	B associated	C famous	D typical
2	A pull	B hold	C draw	D pick
3	A profit	B specialise	C focus	D concentrate
4	A put	B set	C place	D arrange
5	A concerned	B keen	C obsessed	D dissatisfied
6	A able	B likely	C suitable	D capable

61

writing reports

1. When do people need to write or read reports? What kinds have you written, or read? Have reports ever been written about you?

2. **a** Underline the key words in these instructions, and note down four threats and four measures you think might be included in the report.

   An international human rights organisation has asked you to write a report about privacy in the home in your country. Write your report, outlining the threats to privacy that worry people most, and the measures they are taking to protect it. (250–300 words)

   b Read the model report. Are your ideas included?

PRIVACY IN THE HOME

INTRODUCTION

This report, which is based on information gathered from local people, researches the question of how privacy in the home is being threatened.

THREATS

Among those interviewed, it was generally agreed that telephone sales were a major annoyance to householders, together with nuisance phone calls. The former apparently happened fairly regularly with the main callers being mobile phone companies and health clubs or gyms. Some feared that the growing availability of specialist equipment could lead to further invasions of privacy, either by secret filming or telephone tapping. For people who used the Internet, unwanted e-mail was also seen as an intrusion into what should be personal correspondence. Furthermore, those in the public eye such as TV presenters, film and pop stars, football professionals, and so on, are under growing threat from stalkers.

MEASURES

There was a consensus of opinion regarding the necessity for greater personal protection: many local residents had dogs; computer-users recommended only giving out e-mail addresses to trusted friends or business contacts, and young people were being warned about the dangers of giving out confidential information over the Net. People were also beginning to use a number-identification service for victims of nuisance phone calls.

CONCLUSION

It is very clear that the interviewees are concerned that personal privacy is being threatened. They believe that the state needs to act on this. They recommend the introduction of greater controls on the use of technology that can endanger privacy, and stricter laws against harassment of public figures.

3 Read the report more carefully, and choose the correct alternative in 1–10.

The purpose of a report is to (1) *entertain/inform* the reader. It does this by presenting mainly (2) *abstract ideas/facts* ideas in a fairly (3) *formal/informal* and impersonal style, which may include the use of (4) *contracted/passive* forms of verbs. It often begins with (5) *a greeting such as 'Dear Sir'/a short, clear title*, and the text is normally divided into (6) *paragraphs with headings/a list of numbered sentences*. In the first paragraph the (7) *aims/conclusions* of the report are stated. The main body of the text deals with (8) *facts/the writer's own opinions*, often with (9) *direct speech/reported opinions*, and usually ends with (10) *questions the writer cannot answer/a summing up of the content and its significance*.

4 Which of A–D would be a suitable alternative last paragraph? What is wrong with the other three?

A

It is obvious from the above that much of the population is becoming ever more concerned about threats to their privacy. This is particularly the case in areas such as telephoning and other forms of electronic communication. A certain number of people also appear to be uneasy about the proliferation of electronic surveillance devices, and stalkers would seem to pose an increasing security risk to celebrities.

B

- The public in general believe their privacy is under threat.
- Government action on this issue is necessary.
- Surveillance technology should be subjected to stricter controls.
- Further legal measures to protect the famous are required.

C

It's clear from all this that people are fed up with what's happening to their privacy. Their message to MPs is: 'wake up and do something about it'. They're saying they want to see less bugs and stuff in the shops, too. And they reckon that anyone stalking celebrities ought to be locked up.

D

In this report I have explained that many people are concerned that their privacy is under threat. I believe that the authorities need to become aware of this problem and I urge them to do something practical about it. I recommend the introduction of further restrictions on the use of surveillance equipment, and I suggest there should be new and stronger legislation to protect the privacy of famous individuals.

5 How do you feel about the threats to privacy mentioned in this report, and the measures taken (and proposed) against them?

6 a Read these instructions and decide what your four paragraph headings will be.

Imagine you are a security adviser to a famous person. Your job is to protect them from the media. Write a report for this person, explaining the problems you have faced over the last month and what you have done about them. (250–300 words)

b Make notes on:
- high risk places and situations
- the methods the press, radio and television might use to try to photograph or speak to him or her
- the steps that could be taken to deal with each of the above risks.

c Look through your notes, crossing out any less useful ideas and those you won't have room for. Divide the 'steps' into those you have already taken and those you will recommend for the future. Then decide on a logical order for all of your points.

d As you write your report, think about who will be reading it, why, and what they will do with the information you are providing. Follow the guidelines in **3** and use expressions from the model text, as well as some of those in the box.

This report aims / is intended to …
The aim / purpose of this report is to …
It is obvious / apparent / would appear / is felt that …
It has been suggested / found / revealed that …
There would seem / appear to be / to have been …
The opinion / view has been expressed that …
Another cause for concern / disturbing feature is …
Action has / Steps have already been taken to …
In conclusion / To sum up …
Consideration should be given to …

● **THERE IS ANOTHER MODEL REPORT ON PAGE 162 IN THE WRITING BANK**

review

1 Use the infinitive or passive infinitive to rewrite these headlines as complete passive sentences.

EXAMPLE

MANY CONSIDER MOBILE PHONES ESSENTIAL
Mobile phones are considered by many to be essential.

1 MISSING EXPLORER REPORTED ALIVE AND WELL

2 FRIENDS EXPECT LIZ AND JIM TO MARRY SOON

3 SHOPPERS CONSIDER POP CDS TOO EXPENSIVE

4 FISHING BOAT FEARED SUNK IN STORM

5 DIAMONDS STOLEN LAST WEEK, POLICE BELIEVE

2 Choose the correct alternative.
1 Britain is not *familiar / safe / famous* for good weather.
2 We should *prevent / object / accuse* them from listening in on our conversation.
3 There's no *chance / obstacle / substitute* of him changing his mind.
4 The King refused to *approve / consent / associate* to his daughter's marriage.
5 My boss is never *aware / critical / satisfied* with the amount of work I do.
6 I've got no *respect / links / relationship* for the people who did that.

3 Work out the phrasal verb from the anagram, and use it to complete the sentence.
1 The name of the Oscar winner may ...   AUTOELK
2 To prevent another escape, the prison governor ...   INEPTTHUG
3 The thieves left lots of clues, so the police ...   CROWDTANK
4 My twin sister is going to borrow my clothes and ...   TONOFOIL
5 Our car doesn't have an alarm so it's easy ...   TAKENBIRO
6 The Olympic Committee knows about the problem, so ...   OINKTOOL
7 Our nosy neighbour loves to ...   PRONOUNSODA

4 Complete the crossword with words from this unit.

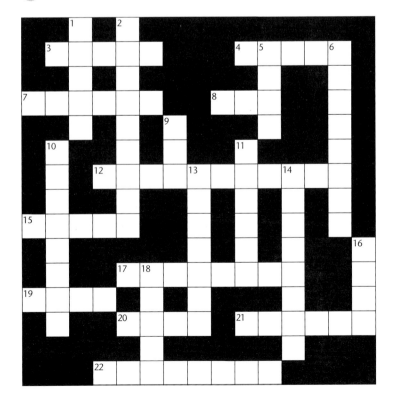

across
3 a wish to have more than is necessary
4 series of actions taken to achieve an aim
7 person who breaks into computer programmes
8 to attach a device to a telephone to listen in
12 mark made when someone touches something
15 convenient to use
17 person in a place they are not supposed to be
19 person who does not tell the truth
20 dismiss someone from their job
21 person or place that is not respectable
22 to enter someone's property without permission

down
1 to follow someone's movements
2 famous person
5 to make a recording of
6 evil or dangerous
9 small electronic listening device
10 belief that everyone is trying to harm you
11 to support or confirm a decision
13 to ensure that a law or rule is obeyed
14 person who gives information to the authorities
16 someone who is over-curious about others
18 having little experience of the realities of life

unit 6 | *on the move*

vocabulary and speaking

1 **a** Look at pictures 1–4. What is the reason for being 'on the move' in each?

b What difficulties / dangers might some of the people face?

c What are the benefits of activities such as the one shown in picture 2?

d What would you miss most about your home if you lived on the road?

2 **a** What activity or situation do you associate with each of the verbs below? Which ones imply moving slowly and which mean moving quickly?

> flee   stroll   stride   ramble   trot   trudge
> accelerate   gallop   brake   trek   roam

Which two words are not usually applied to people or animals?

b Look at the map below and describe the route taken, including as many of the words in the box as possible.

> marshy   rural   rugged   inhospitable   rough   plateau   muddy   hilly
> rocky   steep   remote   scenic   urban   arable   arid

talking points

1   Increasingly, people nowadays
   • don't stay in the same job for life
   • don't stay in the same town for life
   • travel more than ever before.
   Discuss each statement, saying why you think this is the case.

2   Do you see yourself staying in the same house or flat / city / country for the rest of your life?

3 In pairs or groups, discuss the differences between these pairs of words.
   1   a *fugitive* and a *refugee*
   2   an *itinerant* and an *itinerary*
   3   to *evict* and to *expel*
   4   a *nomad* and a *vagrant*
   5   to *subsist* and to *shelter*

reading multiple choice: types of distractor

1 **a** Write down all the purposes of written texts that you can think of, e.g. *to entertain, to ask for information.*

b Quickly read the three texts. What is the common theme? What kind of text is each one, and what is its purpose?

2 For questions **1–6**, choose the answer (**A**, **B**, **C** or **D**) which you think fits best according to the text.

A

H-C TRAVEL MOTORCYCLE TOURS to India, Bhutan, Nepal and Tibet offer something for everyone: from the beauty of Sikkim, the challenging Ladakh High Roads and the mysteries of Tibet to the splendour of Rajasthan. Our Lost Horizon Run takes you
5 to Sikkim, until 1975 an independent remote mountain kingdom and unsurpassed for scenic beauty. With more spectacular mountain terrain, more mountains higher than 7,300 metres per square kilometre, and a greater variety of flora and fauna, including over 4,000 species of rare plants, than anywhere else
10 in the world, Sikkim has long been regarded as one of the last Himalayan Shangri-Las. To enhance your experience, you will be riding India's finest machine, the Royal Enfield Bullet 500, nearly new and thoroughly maintained.

Ladakh is one of the only places left on the planet where the
15 Tibetan Buddhist faith still flourishes as it has for thousands of years. Situated in the northernmost part of India, bordering the Karakoram Range and Tibet, it is surely one of the last unspoiled ultimate destinations. Closed to outsiders until 1974, Ladakh also contains the world's highest motorable pass,
20 Khardung-La (5,605 m). If you want just one reason to take this tour, then riding the world's highest road is surely good enough.

Our motorcycle expedition takes us from the plains of Delhi, through the valleys and foothills of the Himalaya, over the military road first opened to foreign travel in 1992, crossing the
25 Tibetan Plateau and finally to the Indus River Valley and Ladakh. We cross five major passes en route, including the world's highest and second highest, traversing three distinct Himalayan ranges. The ultimate mountain motorcycle tour!

1 Among the attractions of Sikkim is
  A its unusually mild climate for such a mountainous area.
  B the fact it has most of the world's mountains of over 7,300 metres.
  C the huge number of unusual plants found there.
  D its uniquely wide range of types of plant and animal.

2 According to the text, the region of Ladakh has
  A successfully maintained its religious tradition.
  B begun to suffer the negative effects of tourism.
  C a road that was closed to visitors from abroad until 1992.
  D the five highest mountain passes in the world.

B

Traditional rollerskates have been around for many years, but inline skates have several advantages over the older kind of design. Rollerskates have inside and outside wheels, which makes turning inconsistent and often
5 unstable. By contrast, inline skates offer precise and accurate turns similar to ice-skating or skiing on snow, and many rollerskaters have adopted inline skates for their improved performance, speed and manoeuvrability.

Inline skates were first invented by a Dutchman in the
10 1700s in an attempt to simulate ice-skating in the summer. Over two hundred years later, inline skating has really come of age, thanks to the availability of sophisticated modern materials and the use of new manufacturing technologies.

Inline skating can help you get fit whatever your choice
15 of sport. For cross-trainers, inline skating tones a variety of different muscle groups, complementing other forms of exercise. Inline skating is a great way to practise skiing technique, to dance, to race, or just to get around. All human beings need some degree of physical exertion to keep fit,
20 and inline skating is a great all-round source of exercise.

3 The writer claims that inline skating

    A can be practised on ice and snow surfaces.

    B has been very popular for at least two centuries.

    C enables skaters to change direction more easily.

    D is now practised by all rollerskaters.

4 What benefit of inline skating does the writer mention?

    A You can become an expert at other sports without practising them.

    B You can improve your ability at other activities.

    C You can get fit without having to make an effort.

    D You can become much slimmer if you are overweight.

C

If J. Ralston of Manchester (Letters, July 16) genuinely believes that offroaders do no harm to the countryside, then clearly he has not visited a National Park recently.
5 Should he take the trouble to do so, he will find that vast areas of outstanding beauty have been cut to pieces by convoys of four-wheel-drive vehicles, many of them organised on a commercial basis for
10 tourists and company entertainment. Hillsides that used to be covered in lush vegetation now have ruts two metres deep, with enormous bald patches where offroaders' wheels have torn up the soil,
15 destroying plantlife and animal habitats. Paths have been turned into impassable quagmires, with mud so deep that farmers have been unable to reach livestock. Horseriders and ramblers have had enough,
20 and many local residents are up in arms about the noise, the fumes and the disruption. Codes of conduct drawn up by offroaders associations are widely ignored and therefore wholly ineffective. The only
25 action that will suffice, Mr Ralston, is a total ban on these vehicles in National Parks.

P. Wilson, Cumbria

5 The writer says that Ralston

    A does not know the facts.

    B has angered farmers.

    C deliberately damages the land.

    D last went to a National Park a long time ago.

6 Who, according to the text, is angry about the harm done by offroaders?

    A environmental organisations

    B people who live in the countryside

    C those who walk, ride or live in the countryside

    D countryside residents and users, including most drivers of offroaders

3 Look again at the distractors in 1–6 and choose from these reasons why they are wrong.

    1 It contains words from the text (or words with similar meanings) but about something else.

    2 You may expect the information to be true but it is not actually stated in the text.

    3 The answer may only be partly true or does not give the whole answer.

    4 The information is the opposite of what the text says.

    5 The answer exaggerates what the text says.

EXAMPLE

    1 A: *not in text (2)*

    B: *words from text with a different meaning (1)*

    C: *does not give the whole answer (3)*

    D: *correct*

4 Answer these questions about text A.

    1 Which two words are used in the text with the same meaning as *run* (line 4)?

    2 Why does the writer use the present simple form of *cross* (line 26)? Which word in the same sentence has a similar meaning?

    3 Bearing in mind the purpose of this text, choose the likely meanings.

    unsurpassed (line 6):

    a not very special

    b better than any other

    enhance (line 11):

    a make even better

    b make less boring

    ultimate (lines 18 and 28):

    a very worst

    b very best

5 Answer these questions about text B.

    1 What does *the older kind of design* (line 3) refer to?

    2 Which word in the 2nd and 3rd sentences of the same paragraph is a clue to the meaning of *manoeuvrability* (line 8)?

    3 What does *come of age* (line 11) mean when used about a young person? What does it mean here?

    4 Find a phrasal verb in the last paragraph which means 'to go from place to place'.

6 Answer these questions about text C.

    1 Rewrite the first sentence so that it begins 'If J Ralston of Manchester had recently visited …'

    2 What does *them* (line 8) refer to?

    3 Find words in the text that have similar meanings to these: *offroaders* (line 2), *cut* (line 7), *vegetation* (line 12), *animal* (line 15), *quagmires* (line 17).

7 Text C is concerned with damage to the environment. How could the activities mentioned in text A damage the environment?

grammar   present perfect, present perfect continuous and past simple

1 Read each pair of sentences and answer the question.
1 a Ben has done very well at school.
   b Ben has been doing very well at school.
      Which should you use if you think he will continue to do well?
2 a Has Kathryn been here all morning?
   b Was Kathryn here all morning?
      Which is correct if she is there now?
3 a I've tidied my room.
   b I've been tidying my room.
      Which is better if you want to say it is now tidy?
4 a How long have you had that old bicycle?
   b How long did you have that old bicycle?
      Which is right if the person still has the bicycle?
5 a I waited here for you for two hours!
   b I've been waiting here for you for two hours!
      Which would you say to someone who has at last arrived?
6 a I lost my key.
   b I've lost my key.
      Which would you say when you first discover it is missing?
7 a I've lived with my grandmother.
   b I've been living with my grandmother.
      Which would you use if you expected to be there temporarily?

2 Decide which of statements 1–10 are true then match them with examples a–g below.

EXAMPLE We can use the present perfect when something started in the past and is still going on. *T*
Samantha has liked folk music from childhood.
  1 We use the present perfect for something that has been repeated several times up to now.
  2 If we want to mention something that happened in the past without saying when, we can use the present perfect.
  3 We can use the present perfect with expressions like 'ten minutes ago' because the events are very recent.
  4 The present perfect is used when you can see the results of something that happened in the recent past.
  5 We can use the present perfect to mean 'at any time in someone's life'.
  6 The present perfect continuous can be used with any verb except 'to be'.
  7 We use the present perfect continuous for something that started in the past, and is still continuing.
  8 The past simple is used for something that happened in finished time periods, for example 'last Friday'.
  9 We use the past simple to talk about longer unfinished actions.
 10 To talk about situations that lasted for some time in the past, but are not continuing now, we can use the past simple.

  a Eva bought a new dress yesterday afternoon.
  b Chrissie's been sleeping all morning and it's impossible to wake her up.
  c I know the girl you mean; I've seen her standing at the bus stop.
  d In those days, we lived in a small flat near the stadium.
  e The neighbours have often complained about the noise.
  f Be careful where you tread because someone's broken a glass on the floor.
  g Have you ever been to Parc Asterix, near Paris?

3 Complete the sentences with the present perfect, present perfect continuous, or past simple form of the verbs in brackets.

1 Since James .... (buy) that moped, he .... (have) two accidents.
2 We .... (stand) here for 20 minutes because the others .... (not arrive) yet.
3 Keith and Sonia .... (be) in love ever since they .... (meet) six months ago.
4 I .... (write) for an hour now and I .... (nearly finish) my essay.
5 The blue car in front .... (try) to overtake that lorry, but it still .... (not manage).
6 Melissa .... (study) even harder since she .... (fail) her exam last month.
7 I still .... (not receive) the book I .... (order) on the Internet last month.
8 Ever since I .... (go) there in 1992, I .... (look forward) to going back.

4 **a** Look at pictures 1–3 and complete the dialogue using the correct form of suitable verbs.

1 'Hi Joey, I .... you for ages. What .... recently?'
'Well a few weeks ago I .... myself this bike, and ever since then I .... around the countryside, up and down the motorway – everywhere, in fact.'
2 'Hey, ... we .... the top yet? We .... for hours and my feet are killing me.'
'No. I'm afraid not. We .... at about 9.30 so probably we .... only .... about three quarters of the way up so far.'
3 'Jane! I thought you .... still away on holiday! When .... you .... ?'
'Very late last night. I .... to bed until 5 this morning, so as you can probably tell I .... much sleep.'

b Think of similar dialogues for these situations:
• two colleagues talking about a project at work
• two friends who haven't seen each other for a while
• two people talking at a party.

other uses of the present perfect

1 Most of these sentences are correct. In those cases, explain the use of the present perfect as in the example. If a sentence is wrong, say why and correct it.

 EXAMPLE This is the worst comedy film I've ever seen.
To compare the present film with all the others you've seen in your life.

1 He's caused trouble ever since I've known him.
2 I've known Nora since we've played tennis together.
3 After I've finished playing, I'll have a shower and meet you outside.
4 At first I feared the worse, but I've since heard that everyone is safe.
5 I've been born in this village and I've lived here all my life.
6 I've always wondered why she suddenly left school.
7 I won't go until I've found out the truth.
8 This is the first time I've been to Warsaw.

listening sentence completion: focusing on clues (1)

1 **a** You are going to hear someone talking about long distance footpaths. Look at question 1 and the relevant extract from the recording.

    1 <u>Walking routes</u> form a .... <u>across the continent</u>.

    '... not many people realise that there's a network of <u>footpaths criss-crossing Europe</u>, too.'

      a What kind of answer (e.g. *adjective*, *number*) is needed?

      b What is the correct answer?

      c Do the language clues come before or after the answer?

      d Which key words in the question correspond to which language clues?

    The key words in the question and the clues in the extract are underlined.

  b **●●** Listen and complete 2–6, thinking about a–d above.

    2 The ERA has been <u>working</u> for <u>more than</u> .... on the paths.

    3 The routes <u>do not stop</u> at .... <u>between countries</u>.

    4 Along the <u>Spanish</u> route, there is <u>inexpensive</u> ....

    5 It is said you can have a <u>drink</u> of .... at one fountain <u>without having to pay</u>.

    6 There are <u>some</u> .... in the network, especially where there have been <u>recent wars</u>.

c Check your answers and then look at the tapescript on page 154. For each question, underline the language clue(s). Did it / they come before or after the answer, or both?

2 **●●** You will hear a walker describing part of her journey along a section of E-path in Crete. For questions 1–8, complete the sentences with a word or short phrase.

Remember to listen out for language clues both before and after the words you need to write down.

No other European island is as [**1**] as Crete.

Sonia has always considered herself to be quite [**2**] .

At first she suffered a lot of pain in her [**3**] .

There was a lovely smell from the [**4**] .

Because of the recent weather, the [**5**] was moving very fast.

She was nearly hurt when she was walking in [**6**] on the mountains.

As she reached lower ground, she heard the sound of [**7**] .

She was surprised by her rapid progress with the [**8**] .

KASTELLI

KATO ZAK

CRETE

	MOUNTAIN HUT		PREHISTORIC SITE
	ARCHAEOLOGICAL SITE		MEDIEVAL SITE
	CAMPSITE		CAVE

speaking organising speech

EXAM FOCUS

paper 5 part 3

In the third part of Speaking, each candidate is given a written question to respond to. Prompts are also provided to help with ideas for answering the question. This is followed by a discussion between both candidates to explore the topic further. You will be speaking on your own for approximately two minutes, so you need to use these different language functions:

- giving your opinions;
- expressing preferences;
- comparing and contrasting;
- developing the topic and giving examples.

exam factfile

In Part 3 of Speaking, you will have a few seconds to think about what you are going to say.

1 Add further examples to 1–4.

1
Saying what you would or wouldn't do
Assuming …, I would …
I'd be a bit reluctant to …
I'd have serious reservations about …
Nothing would induce me to …

2
Stating purpose
In order not to … I'd …
So as to … I'd …
I'd … just in case …
I wouldn't … or else …

3
Giving reasons for doing something
I've always wanted to … ever since …
… has always intrigued/fascinated me on account of …
… would leave me cold/bore me stiff, I'm afraid, especially if …
… just isn't my cup of tea.

4
Introducing and sequencing reasons
Well, the thing/the basic reason is …
In the first place …
And on top of that, …
And last but not least …

2 🔊 Work in pairs. Study the map of Crete showing a possible walking route. Choose a question from 1–4. Talk for about two minutes, using the prompts and language from **1**. Ask your partner to comment on what you have said.

1
Which part of the route would be the most enjoyable?
- the countryside
- the terrain
- culture, historic buildings, etc.

2
When would be the best/worst time to go?
- the weather
- few/too many people
- cost

3
What would you need to take?
- weather
- food
- emergencies

4
Who would you like to go with?
- company
- expert or local knowledge
- security

3 🔊 Choose three of these related topics and discuss them with your partner.

1 What differences did it make to society when the only way to travel between towns and villages was on foot, or on horseback?
2 How would our lives change if we had to walk everywhere? Would it be for the better?
3 Does the opening of new footpaths for walkers help protect the countryside, or damage it?
4 What would be the most exciting walk in the world?
5 Many young people take time off from work or studies to go travelling. What do you think they gain from their experiences?

vocabulary
idioms

1 Replace the missing word in each of the idioms, using the picture of its <u>literal</u> meaning as a clue. What do the complete idioms mean?

| brake uphill crow lane U-turn short cut snail's |
| track gear nowhere |

1 It was a(n) .... struggle, but in the end she succeeded.

2 The queue for tickets was moving at a(n) .... pace, and then it stopped completely.

3 The company needs to put a(n) .... on spending to avoid running out of money.

4 It's only two kilometres across the valley as the .... flies, but a lot further on foot.

5 There is no .... to success in this profession; you'll just have to work very hard.

6 The Government had promised to cut all taxes, but then they did a(n) .... and started to put them up.

7 After his first film came out, it was life in the fast .... for Tom, with endless parties and TV appearances.

8 There's a great little picnic spot near a quiet beach out of town: it's right off the beaten ....

9 As the exams drew nearer, Katie knew it was time to move up a(n) .... and started studying late into the evening.

10 When the pilot had to crash-land the plane he found himself in the middle of ....

2 Look at the following newspaper headlines and re-word them using an idiom from **1**.

1
Security increased for star's visit

2
Difficulties for teachers as pupils' results worsen

3
Ministers to stop spending on new rail network

4
PROGRESS SLOWS AS PROTESTS ESCALATE

5
PM changes mind about election date

collocations: verb + noun

1 a In 1–8, all the verbs except one can go with the noun. Cross out the one that does not collocate.
1 *pick up / maintain / reduce / lower* speed
2 *run / take / have / miss* a chance
3 *break / set / win / hold* a record (speed, time, etc.)
4 *sustain / inflict / cure / treat* an injury
5 *cause / feel / repair / assess* (the) damage
6 *obstruct / impede / hamper / brake* progress
7 *ensure / guarantee / assure / jeopardise* someone's safety
8 *save / use / conserve / spend* your energy

b Which collocations in **a** describe the following situations?
1 going faster in a car
2 not taking an opportunity
3 working out what repairs need to be done to your car after an accident
4 doing more sit-ups in one minute than anyone else in the world
5 drinking and then driving a friend home

gapped sentences

1 a Look at these sentences. Which part of speech is needed for all three?
A sports car came racing down the road and then .... into a side street.
His face .... red when he realised that everyone knew what he had done.
I'm sure I .... off all the lights when I left the classroom.

b Here are some example words for the first sentence; how many can you think of for the second and third?
went, raced, shot, turned, accelerated, sped
Is one of your words possible in all three sentences?

2 There are no marks for a word that fits only one sentence, or even two. It must fit all three sentences. For this question, decide which of *chance, luck, opportunity* or *risk* fits **a** none of the sentences **b** one sentence **c** two sentences **d** all three sentences.

If you are prepared to take a .... , you may make a lot of money.
Despite the weather forecast, I think there's a definite .... that it might snow tonight.
I'm sure he won't make the same mistake again, so please give him a second ....

3 For questions **1–3**, think of **one** word only which can be used appropriately in all three sentences.

1 If we're very .... we may see some deer, but the slightest sound will scare them off.
I've never seen the roads so .... as they were during the petrol crisis.
You can tell everyone next week, but for now I'd like you to keep it .... , please.

2 Louise had to push her scooter to start it because the battery was completely ....
After reaching the top of the last hill, Jeremy lay .... on his back, exhausted.
One cyclist stopped to change a wheel because he had a .... tyre, probably caused by broken glass on the road.

3 We saw a .... next to the gate that said the land was private property.
Unfortunately, nobody takes any .... of warnings to slow down, so there are often accidents here.
The boss has given me a month's .... but where I am I supposed to find a new job in just four weeks?

writing summary

1 Quickly read the text. In two columns list the positive and negative aspects of riding a mountain bike in the Pyrenees in the summer.

positive	negative
....	....
....	....
....	....
....	....

DOWNHILL RACER

Increasing numbers of ski resorts in both the Alps and the Pyrenees now allow mountain bikers to use their lifts in the summer to enjoy the fun of descending without the agony of climbing. And you don't even have to be a particularly brilliant or committed mountain biker to enjoy the high life.

5 For instance, there are more than 70 km of marked trails running down from the Pyrenees resort of Superbagnères, south-west of Toulouse. These are graded in a similar fashion to ski runs, from 'easy' green – some are used by family and novice groups – to the progressively harder blue, red and black runs, which may involve some climbing.

10 There's nothing comparable in many countries – the size of the mountains, the summer climate allowing you to ride at altitudes of almost 2,000 m on a good day in shorts and T-shirt, and descents that seem to go on forever.

Swooping through pine-scented forests, scraping around hairpin dirt tracks in a cloud of dust, splashing through streams and even stopping occasionally 15 to admire the peaks and glaciers on the Spanish border. One experienced mountain biker described it as 'like being on a huge fairground ride – only better, and cheaper'.

Typical route distances are from 14 km–21 km, 90% or more of which will be downhill. Do enough of this and you will be aching the next day if you're not 20 used to it. Forearms and shoulders in particular take a hammering, soaking up the bumps and bounces.

For this reason, a good-quality mountain bike with full suspension is essential. You'll also need a helmet, cycling gloves to prevent cuts if you fall, and a waterproof/windproof top – even in summer the weather can be cold and 25 wet in the mountains.

You'll need to carry plenty to drink, especially if you choose to ascend as well as descend the mountains. In summer, it can be hot and you need to ensure you don't suffer from dehydration. A tool kit, puncture repair kit and spare inner tubes are also vital as punctures are common in this terrain. It's also worth 30 taking a basic first-aid kit and sun cream. ●

2 Use the clues from the text to work out the meanings of these words.
agony (line 3) *novice* (line 8) *hammering* (line 20) *ascend* (line 26) *kit* (line 30)

3 **a** Read these instructions and underline the key words.

In a paragraph of between **50–70** words, summarise **in your own words as far as possible** the attractions of mountain biking in the Pyrenees, as described in the text.

b Which parts of the text are relevant to the question?

c Study these three possible answers. Which is the best, and why? What is wrong with the other two?

A

Many ski resorts now allow mountain bikers to use their lifts in summer, so they can descend without the agony of climbing. Marked trails are graded from easy to harder. The size of the mountains, the summer climate, the descents: many countries have nothing comparable. You can swoop through forests, scrape round hairpins, splash through streams and admire the peaks and glaciers. It's better than a fairground ride, and cheaper.

B

By taking ski lifts in summer, it is now possible to cycle down without the pain of first having to ride up. These mountain bikers are mostly beginners, and there are special tracks for them to follow. In many countries there aren't any mountains and it always rains. Here you can ride through trees and water, race along twisting trails, enjoy the views and visit fairgrounds without spending much.

C

In summer, many ski lifts are now open to mountain bikers seeking the thrill of cycling down without first having to ride up. All levels are catered for, with tracks of varying degrees of difficulty. Unlike in many countries, the mountains are high, the weather often good and the slopes long. There is the inexpensive excitement of racing through woodland and streams, riding round tight bends and enjoying spectacular scenery.

d Look in the original text for the equivalents to these expressions in text C.
1 *All levels are catered for*
2 *Unlike (in many countries)*
3 *inexpensive excitement*
4 *racing through woodland*
5 *riding round tight bends*
6 *enjoying spectacular scenery*

4 **a** Underline the key words in the instructions. Which parts of the text are relevant?

In a paragraph of between **50–70** words, summarise **in your own words as far as possible**, the dangers and discomforts of mountain biking in the Pyrenees, as described in the text.

b Make notes in your own words <u>where you can</u>. Whenever you write a summary, you will have to use <u>some</u> expressions from the text, and the instructions allow for this. How might the following changes actually weaken a summary?
1 Rewriting *Pyrenees* as *mountain range between Spain and France*.
2 Changing *mountain* to *hill*.
3 Referring to a *ski elevator* instead of a *ski lift*.
4 Using *owing to the fact that* instead of *as*.

c When you have finished, ask your partner to check for phrases from the text that could still be rewritten.

review

1 Correct the mistakes in five of these six sentences.
1 I didn't hear Pauline come in last night because she's been out very late.
2 Uncle Ray has been ill so he's been staying with us since two weeks.
3 There was trouble early this morning, but since then there have been no further incidents.
4 Last year I often went out in the evenings, but nowadays I haven't had time to go anywhere.
5 They left this afternoon but I don't think they arrived yet.
6 When he was alive, has Shakespeare ever written anything similar to this?

2 Complete the sentences with the present perfect, present perfect continuous or past simple form of the verb in brackets, plus *for*, *since*, *yet* or *still* where possible and/or necessary.
1 Ricky (try) to start his motorbike .... at least half an hour, but he (not manage) to ....
2 I (not go) to the fairground .... ages, though I don't suppose it (change) very much .... my parents (take) me there back in the 1980s.
3 Sam and I (play) tennis twice at the new courts .... they (open) them last month, and we're going again when we (finish) all our exams.
4 It's the third time I (be) to this festival and .... the last six hours I (enjoy) myself even more than when I first (come) here two summers ago.
5 I (look for) a dress like that ever .... I (see) that model wearing one last spring, but I .... (not find) a shop that sells them.
6 I don't know how long we (watch) this film, but it seems like hours .... it (begin), and not much (happen) ....

3 Each of 1–9 contains one word that belongs to another idiom. Rewrite them correctly and then match them with meanings a–i.
1 as the snail flies
2 life in the middle lane
3 put a U-turn on
4 a beaten struggle

5 move up a brake
6 at a crow's pace
7 make a gear
8 in the uphill of nowhere
9 off the fast track

a quiet and isolated
b very slowly
c requiring a great effort
d have a complete change of policy
e in a straight line
f a very busy lifestyle
g slow something down
h increase rate of progress
i a long way from civilisation

4 Complete each sentence to make the meaning of the collocation clear.
1 She sustained a slight injury but …
2 The record for the 100 metres is held by …
3 Conserve your energy by …
4 I think I'll take a chance and …
5 It is impossible to guarantee the safety of …
6 The best way to treat a minor leg injury is to …

5 Use the clues below to find 19 words from this unit in the wordsquare. The words can read in any direction, including backwards.

B	R	A	B	C	A	J	T	A	T	I	B	A	H
A	N	P	U	I	E	E	R	U	T	C	N	U	P
R	E	O	M	T	N	O	I	E	Y	A	E	R	G
E	B	T	O	H	A	P	V	O	L	S	W	E	N
T	Y	M	A	D	Z	A	I	L	E	B	I	L	I
A	E	N	C	G	O	R	G	E	P	S	M	B	H
R	C	G	O	S	E	D	A	N	I	T	E	A	C
E	H	O	B	G	H	I	N	D	E	R	V	S	R
L	A	M	L	R	A	S	T	E	P	I	A	S	O
E	S	D	I	S	R	E	G	A	R	D	W	A	C
C	U	D	S	N	I	W	Y	V	K	E	T	P	S
C	X	H	T	A	P	T	O	O	F	B	A	M	E
A	O	L	E	N	U	A	S	U	A	T	E	I	P
M	T	I	R	E	G	N	A	R	B	L	H	N	O

1 very deep and narrow valley
2 to put something at risk
3 painful sore on feet or hands
4 hole in the tyre of a vehicle
5 extreme pain
6 to walk with long steps
7 series of mountains
8 far from anywhere else
9 extremely hot
10 natural environment of plants or animals
11 person who walks in the countryside
12 to increase speed
13 narrow track where people walk
14 to try to do something
15 someone who is new, has little experience
16 impossible to travel along, due to blockage or bad condition
17 to improve the value or attractiveness of something
18 period of hot weather
19 to obstruct progress

unit 7 | *living spaces*

vocabulary and speaking

1 What do the words in each group have in common? How do they differ?

1 guest / lodger / tenant / squatter
2 inner city / outskirts / suburb
3 landlord or landlady / landowner / proprietor / manager
4 villa / terraced house / semi-detached house / bedsit / cottage

2 Who would you expect to find in these places and what would they be doing?

> cell   darkroom   workshop   waiting room   greenhouse
> staffroom   canteen   hostel   fitting room   ward

3 **a** Which of these words would you use for décor that is really
1 beautiful   2 attractive
3 unattractive   4 extremely ugly?

> elegant   tasteless   stylish   repulsive   ghastly   classy
> gorgeous   tasteful   tacky   grotesque   exquisite   hideous

b Are there any things in your house which you would use these words to describe?

4 **a** Look at the three rooms. What are the main differences between them? What is each room used for? What sort of person do you think lives there? Which style do you prefer? Why?

talking points

1 What does your home or room say about you, and how could you make it reflect your personality even more?
2 Tell your partner about the first house you can remember living in as a child. Describe the colours, any special objects that were there, and any sounds, smells, etc. that you associate with it.
3 In what ways does climate affect the way people build houses? What other factors can affect architecture?

b Now choose one of the rooms and describe it in more detail to your partner.

reading reading for specific information

1 In the town where you live, are there any buildings that have been converted into something else? What did they use to be like? What are they like now? Do you prefer them as they were or as they are now?

2 **a** Look quickly at text A and without reading in detail decide in which part – the main text or the details in italics – you are likely to find these.
1 telephone numbers
2 a description of the rooms
3 prices of rooms
4 the history of the hotel
5 quotes from hotel staff
6 the exact location of the hotel
7 the nearest well-known places
8 guests' reactions to the hotel

b Now read the introduction and A–E more carefully and check your answers.

3 **a** Choose three of the texts A–E and underline two facts about the hotel in each. Then write six short questions, beginning *In which hotel …*, as in the example, for your partner to answer. Put your questions in jumbled order.

b After answering your partner's questions, check the answers in pairs.

EXAMPLE *In which hotel …*
are all the rooms different? D
can guests get married? A

4 Answer these questions about each hotel.
1 Why might the angel fish be *staring curiously* (text A line 5)? Explain the use of the phrase *inner space* (line 16).
2 What do you think the *extra body in the picture* (text B line 31) is? Explain the following words: *untimely* (line 25), *B&B* (line 26), *dodge* (line 28), *encounter* (line 30).
3 Find all the expressions in text C that mean 'place where people are imprisoned'. Which two expressions mean 'in prison'? What do you notice about the sound of the word *clang*? What do we call this kind of word?
4 Find two expressions in text D that mean 'must be booked some time before arrival'.
5 Explain the meaning of *reaches new heights* (line 70) and *peckish* (line 73) in text E.

5 • If you could stay in a room named after any actor, which would you choose? What would you expect to find in it?
• What features do you think the jungle, grotto and French rooms in text D have?
• There is often background music in hotels. What kinds, and what particular songs, would be most suitable for each of hotels A–E? What pictures might you see on the walls of each one? Can you think of any other features that could be added?

Checking in at the weirdest hotels in America

An underwater hotel, a haunted house – America offers some crazy places to spend a night.
Helen Foster picks some of the best.

A ▶ THE UNDERWATER HOTEL

JULES'S UNDERSEA LODGE, KEY LARGO, FLORIDA

When you wake up in the morning at Jules's, the first thing you're likely to see when you look through your metre-wide round window is an angel
5 fish staring curiously back at you.

Named after Jules Verne, author of *Twenty Thousand Leagues Under the Sea*, this former research laboratory is reached by diving 10 metres down into the Emerald Lagoon off Key Largo. Entering through an opening beneath the structure, guests arrive in the world's only underwater
10 hotel, where their air-conditioned rooms are equipped with TV, video and stereo sound system. They also find a 'well-stocked kitchen', complete with refrigerator and microwave, and a chef will dive down to the hotel and prepare and serve a gourmet dinner.

The Lodge is available for underwater weddings, and exclusive use can
15 be arranged for couples who want to be the only lovers in the world spending the night alone in inner space – a pretty romantic thought!

Jules's Undersea Lodge, 51 Shoreland Drive, Key Largo, Florida 33037 (001 305 451 2353). The hotel is a good stopping-off point between Miami and Key West. Cost of rooms starts from $250–$350 per person
20 *per night; the 'ultimate romantic package' costs $1050 per night.* ●

B ▶ THE HAUNTED HOTEL

THE MYRTLES PLANTATION, ST FRANCISVILLE, LOUISIANA

THE Myrtles earned the title of 'Most Haunted House in America' in the 1830s, when the owner's mistress poisoned his wife and children. Since
25 then, there have been 12 untimely deaths in this old plantation house-turned-B&B. In spite of its gruesome history, every weekend the six French antique-furnished rooms fill with guests hoping to hear ghostly footsteps, spot shadowy figures or dodge the balls of light that shoot from room to room.

30 Some people don't realise they've had an encounter until their photos return with an extra body in the picture; others know immediately. 'We lose a lot of guests in the night,' says manager Fern Aldridge. 'Something happens and they pack up and run. We take payment in advance.'

The Myrtles Plantation, PO Box 1100, St Francisville, Louisiana, 70775
35 *(225 635 6277). Cost $140–$180 per room per night in the house or $90 to stay in the motel-style rooms in the grounds. Both rates include breakfast.* ●

C ▶ THE JAIL HOTEL

THE JAILHOUSE INN, PRESTON, MINNESOTA

40 FOR 102 years, this Italian-style property housed some unpleasant types as the courthouse and jail of the village of Preston. Now it's a stop for travellers who want to taste life behind bars.

The attraction is the Cellblock, a suite of rooms that used to be the jail's lock-ups. Set in 20 tons of steel and concrete, painted sterile white and
45 with the regulation bars on the door, they offer sleeping space for up to four.

'When the door clangs shut it can get claustrophobic,' says Marc Sather, owner of the hotel. 'But we're good to our prisoners here, we don't lock the bars.' Doing time is also made easier with the hotel's double
50 whirlpool bath.

The Jailhouse Inn, PO Box 422, 109 Houston Street NW, Preston, Minnesota, 55965 (507 765 2181). A night in the Cellblock costs $120 per party. ●

D ▶ THE THEME HOTEL

55 THE MADONNA INN, SAN LUIS OBISPO, CALIFORNIA

FORGET the singer, this Californian institution is named after owners Alex and Phyllis Madonna who, over the last 40 years, have let their fantasies go wild in its 109 rooms. Each is themed, no two are the same – and most are painted a shade of rose named Madonna Pink.

60 A night in the Caveman room (solid-rock floor, ceiling and walls, leopard-print bed and waterfall shower) requires a reservation at least six months in advance. Most others (jungle, grotto, French room, etc.) need four weeks' notice – but if you can't get a reservation you can still have a Madonna experience, as the amazing restaurant is open to the public.

65 *The Madonna Inn, 100 Madonna Road, San Luis Obispo, California, 93405 (805 543 3000). The Inn is perfect for drivers travelling between San Francisco and Los Angeles. Room rates start at $110.* ●

E ▶ THE CINEMA HOTEL

BEST WESTERN MOVIE MANOR MOTOR INN, MONTE VISTA, COLORADO

70 PAY per view reaches new heights at Movie Manor: it's built in the middle of a drive-in movie theatre. Rooms with huge picture windows give a front-row view of the screen, with sound through wall-mounted speakers. And there's popcorn if you're peckish. Rooms aren't numbered, they're named after actors, with Tom Cruise being the favourite for tired
75 travellers.

Movie Manor Motor Inn, 28–30 West Highway 160, Monte Vista, Colorado 81144 (719 852 5921). Monte Vista is about halfway between Durango and Pueblo, close to Rio Grande National Park. Rooms cost $65–$80 per night. Movies only shown May–September. ●

grammar
participle clauses

1 Read the explanation then do 1–6 below.

> Particularly in written English, we often use present participles instead of adverbial expressions of reason, time, result and contrast.
>
> Feeling tired, we stopped for the night at a hotel. (= *As we felt tired …*)
> Before leaving the house, I had a quick look in the mirror. (= *Before I left …*)
> The Irish song scored 180 points, winning the contest. (= *… so it won the contest.*)
> Despite knowing little Arabic, I managed to communicate. (= *Although I knew …*)

For each of 1–6, state the meaning (reason, time, result or contrast) and rewrite the sentence using the linking expression in brackets.

EXAMPLE We switched on the TV, expecting to see the news headlines. (because)
Reason. We switched on the TV because we expected to see the news headlines.

1 Seeing the flames, people began to run. (when)
2 Breaking through the police barrier, the car disappeared into the distance. (after)
3 Being Australian, Ruth is used to travelling very long distances. (so)
4 We left the house at 6.30 a.m., arriving at the airport in good time. (so that)
5 Karl eventually won the match, in spite of losing the first set. (even though)
6 Talking in low voices, the gang planned their next move. (while)

2 Read the explanation then do 1–4.

> Negative forms use *not* before the participle:
> Not wanting to upset her, I said nothing.
> (= *Because I didn't want to …*)
>
> To stress that one action followed another, we can begin *Having* + past participle.
> Having won the 200 metres final, Simone prepared for the 100 metres.
> (= *After she had won …*)
> We form the negative like this:
> Not having been to the north before, I was surprised how poor it was.
> (= *As I hadn't been to …*)

Rewrite these sentences using a participle.
1 Because people don't want to appear rude, they buy things they don't really want.
2 As she didn't have any experience, Carrie had to learn the job fast.

3 Muldoon didn't see the men in the shadows, so he walked into their trap.
4 Despite the fact that our team played well, they lost.

3 **a** Read quickly through this text, then use participle clauses to replace the underlined verbs. Remember to make any other necessary changes.

b Continue the story, using participle clauses. Describe the arrival of their belongings, what they found when they unpacked, and what they had to do then.

Moving experiences

I'll never forget that hot summer's day when we moved house. We (**1**) <u>had got up</u> at 6 a.m. and spent the whole morning packing, but by lunchtime we still had an enormous amount to do. We (**2**) <u>didn't want</u> to risk any breakages, so we had to wrap up fragile items individually, and carefully (**3**) <u>place</u> each one in protective containers. I (**4**) <u>realised</u> that we were running short of time, so I phoned my best friend for help, but she was out. I (**5**) <u>had told</u> the removal company to come at 2 p.m., and I expected them to appear any time.

As it happened, the traffic was heavy and they turned up half an hour late, so that (**6**) <u>gave</u> us a little more time, but once they'd started work they quickly moved everything we'd packed into the van. We (**7**) <u>started</u> to panic a bit and, with the temperature

4 **a** Read the explanation then do 1–4.

> We can use past participles instead of conditionals with a passive meaning.
> Played quietly, music like that is boring. (= *If it is played quietly ...*)
> Past participles can also replace adverbial expressions.
> Watched by billions, the World Cup Final was a huge success. (= *As it was watched by billions ...*)

rising all the time, we worked even faster. We still had everything from the kitchen to pack, as we (**8**) <u>had left</u> that until last: we had to eat, after all! Foolishly, we threw everything together into boxes. We (**9**) <u>didn't bother</u> to wrap them, or keep jars, bottles and packets apart, and we ended up with fresh fruit and vegetables buried under piles of heavy tins. We (**10**) <u>emptied</u> the fridge and put the contents – butter, yoghurt, fish, meat and milk – straight into a big box, but without anything to keep them cool.

At last we had finished. After the removal people (**11**) <u>had loaded</u> the last of the boxes into the van, they set off, and we left our house for the very last time. Eight hours later we (**12**) <u>arrived</u> at our new flat, and waited for our belongings to get there.

Rewrite these sentences using a present or past participle.

1 As she was worried about her young son, Mrs Fowler rang the school.
2 If these plants are left to grow naturally, they reach tremendous heights.
3 I slept for 12 hours because I was exhausted by the long journey.
4 If we took the results on their own, they wouldn't prove much.

b A present or past participle at the beginning of the sentence refers to the subject of the main clause. What is wrong with these sentences? How could you improve them?

Washed at 90°C, my boyfriend found his underwear had turned pink.
Covered in thick mayonnaise, I love fresh asparagus.

5 **a** Participle clauses are particularly common in the types of text shown below. Say where you would expect to read 1–10, then rephrase the sentences adding linking expressions (including *if*), or relative pronouns, where necessary.

1 Made of pure lamb's wool, this garment should be hand washed.
2 Dial number before inserting coins.
3 Dissolved in water, the tablets act quickly to relieve symptoms.
4 Investigating the disappearance of a local businessman, Detective Hamilton uncovers more than he bargains for.
5 On hearing the alarm, please leave the building via exit D on the diagram.
6 Mixed with a little lemonade, this is the ideal drink for warm summer nights!
7 Stirring constantly, bring the sauce to the boil, and serve.
8 The Empire State Building, built in 1931, was the tallest building in the world.
9 Guests requiring an early breakfast are requested to inform Reception.
10 Having inserted a blank cassette, press 'record' on the remote control.

common errors

Having died, the plants had not been watered.
What is wrong with this sentence? Why?

b Why are participles so common in short texts like those above?

listening three-way matching

1  Listen to this introduction to a talk about Feng Shui. Decide whether each of 1–14 has a positive (+) or a negative (–) effect, according to the speaker.

1 straight lines ....
2 cleanliness ....
3 tidiness ....
4 the bed facing a wall ....
5 the bed facing a door ....
6 windows always closed ....
7 mirrors ....
8 lighting above the bed ....
9 the colour green ....
10 small rocks ....
11 wearing shoes indoors ....
12 leaving plugs in plugholes ....
13 live fish ....
14 flowers in a vase ....

EXAM FOCUS

paper 4 part 4 three-way matching

In three-way matching you read a series of statements which you match to two main speakers, deciding who expresses each opinion, or whether they agree. There may also be a presenter or interviewer who introduces the conversation.

- The two main speakers will be a man and a woman, so you will always know who is speaking.
- Use the 30 second pause before the conversation starts to familiarise yourself with the questions.
- Listen out for both stated and non-stated agreement and disagreement.
- The questions will be in the same order as the text.
- As you have to listen to <u>two</u> people's opinions, use the second listening to check your answers carefully.

2 You will hear two people, Fay and Milo, talking about Feng Shui. For questions **1–6**, decide whether the opinions are expressed by only one of the speakers, or whether the speakers agree. Write **F** for Fay, **M** for Milo or **B** for Both, where they agree.

1 Most people say they feel better after using Feng Shui. [ ] **1**
2 The effect of real Feng Shui is obvious straightaway. [ ] **2**
3 There is no need to prove the existence of *chi*. [ ] **3**
4 In Europe, we don't know enough about the philosophy of Feng Shui. [ ] **4**
5 The football match story makes a useful point. [ ] **5**
6 Feng Shui hasn't been discredited by the football match story. [ ] **6**

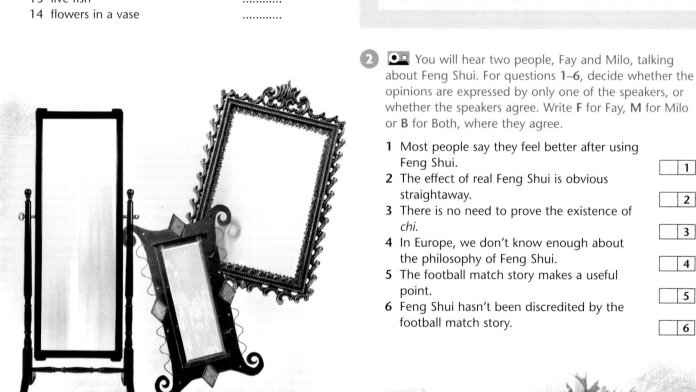

speaking emphasising

1 a Look at these examples and underline the emphasising expressions.

1 'Surely the point is that people's lives are being improved by their belief in something they can't actually see but can definitely feel ...'

2 'It certainly doesn't do anyone any harm, after all. It doesn't even need to cost anything.'

3 ... if people really believe that Feng Shui will help them, it almost certainly will ...

4 '... the vast majority *do* report definite improvements.'

5 'It's not only the colour that matters, but also the lighting.'

b Underline the emphasising expressions in these negative statements.

1 We've no time left at all.

2 There has been no improvement whatsoever.

3 The noise doesn't bother me in the least.

4 Her opinion hasn't changed in the slightest.

Can you think of any other ways of emphasising a negative point?

2 ◁)) Choose four of the following statements to discuss with a partner. Try to use emphatic forms to help to get your point across.

Children should not be allowed to own mobile phones.

Society is becoming more materialistic.

The car is the curse of the 21st century.

Left-handed people should be made to write with their right hand.

Higher education should be free to everyone.

Cities are more important than the countryside.

Unemployed people should be supported by their families.

Exams are not a fair method of assessment.

Smoking should be banned in all public places.

Women are better drivers than men.

vocabulary
phrasal verbs

1 Read the text and discuss the difference in meaning between the pairs of phrasal verbs in 1–8 below. Remember that the particle may help you to work out the meaning.

Last Saturday I'd decided to **stay in** because I'd **been up** late the night before at a friend's house. Unfortunately she didn't have room to **put me up** for the night, and I **wasn't back** until after two. Anyway, I didn't **stay up** very long on Saturday night as I was really tired. I'd been planning to **sleep in** late on Sunday morning as well, but got woken up quite early by a friend who wanted to **pop in** for a chat. As I was **letting** her **in** at the front door, we heard a really loud banging sound from the back of the house. My first thought was that the dog had been **shut out** all night and was trying to **get in**, but then we realised the sound was coming from the cupboard under the stairs. Well, it turned out that somebody had **broken into** the house while I was asleep and had got **shut in** by accident! I must have **slept through** the sound of him trying to **get out**. We called the police, who came and **let** him **out**, and I heard later that he'd been **locked up** for a number of break-ins in the neighbourhood. If my friend hadn't dropped round, who knows how long he might have been in there for!

1 To *stay in* and to *stay up*.
2 To *let … in* and to *let … out*.
3 To *break into* and *get out*.
4 To *be up* and to *be back*.
5 To *put … up* and to *lock … up*.
6 To *sleep in* and to *sleep through*.
7 To *shut … in* and to *shut … out*.
8 To *pop in* and to *get in*.

2 Use these phrasal verbs to say what needs doing to the room in the picture below.

clean up   clear out   tidy up   clear away   throw out

3 The meaning of *round* is the same in all four of these sentences. Explain what it is.
1 I'll be round soon.
2 We had friends round for dinner.
3 Drop round any time you like.
4 He called round earlier.

In which of 1–4 could other particles be used with a similar meaning?

4 Complete the replies to these comments with a phrasal verb from **1**, **2** or **3**.
1 'I hear you had burglars last night.'
  'Yes, they .... through an open window.'
2 'Look at this place! There are things everywhere!'
  'Don't worry, I'll .... it .... at the weekend.'
3 'I haven't got anywhere to stay.'
  'Don't worry, we'll .... you .... for the night.'
4 'Isn't your brother up yet?'
  'No, he likes to .... on Sunday mornings.'
5 'So what time will you pick up the children?'
  'I'll .... at about 8, if you'll be in then.'
6 'Why didn't you come to the club last night?'
  'I did but it was too busy and the doorman wouldn't .... me ....'

suffixes

1 For each word in the box:
1 underline the suffix
2 explain the meaning of the word
3 define the meaning or use (e.g. *verb from noun*) of the suffix
4 give at least two more examples with that suffix.

Notice that some suffixes have more than one meaning.

EXAMPLE 1 *mouthful* 2 *how much food or drink you can put in your mouth* 3 *the amount contained* 4 *spoonful, handful*

> ~~mouthful~~ plumber legalise ripen tallish washable
> simplify delightful homeless hyphenate wealthy
> guitarist diversity refusal trainee bravery wastage
> technophobe exploration pesticide judgement
> adulthood heroic capitalism engineer upwards

2 **a** What adjectives ending in *-al* correspond to these nouns?
nose mouth eye mind ear

b What adverbial forms correspond to these adjectives?
fast hard difficult silly friendly cowardly

c How do these changes affect vowel pronunciation?
able → ability   drama → dramatic
hostile → hostility   confer → conference

d What happens to word stress in these changes?
elastic → elasticity   photograph → photographer

word formation

1 What do you think the picture shows? Quickly read the text, without filling in any of the gaps, to find out if you were right.

2 **a** Complete spaces 1–10 with words formed from the words in capitals at the end of those lines. For each one, decide:
- what part of speech it is
- which words can be formed from that stem
- whether it is positive/negative (adjective), singular/plural (noun or verb), or what tense it is (verb).

All the correct answers have suffixes, and **9** has two suffixes.

b Check that your completed text makes sense.

3 What do you think of Chalayan and Topen's ideas?

chair wear

Top fashion ....designers.............. Hussein Chalayan and Paul Topen have recently come up with something quite **(1)**............ : furniture that is ready to wear, and ready to take away. Their latest **(2)**............ , consisting of a coffee table and four chairs, was displayed in Avignon during its City of Culture **(3)**............ , following its appearance in London Fashion Week.
The pieces, according to Chalayan, enable **(4)**............ to take their environment with them, and this is very much a feature of the **(5)**............ approach for which he is internationally famous. The chair covers are removed and quickly transformed, with the **(6)**............ of a little Velcro, into four quite different dresses. Equally **(7)**............ is the way the chair legs are used. These fold up, creating a set of suitcases with wooden handles. The table, also made of wood, just needs a quick pull to bring about its instant **(8)**............ into a skirt made of 20 rings, with the four legs forming the hem. Part of the **(9)**............ of this collection, undoubtedly, is the fact that the furniture does actually work. To prove it, the models sat on the chairs – without a single **(10)**............ .

DESIGN

REMARK

COLLECT

CELEBRATE

WEAR

FUNCTION

ASSIST
INVENT

CONVERT

ORIGIN

BREAK

writing formal and informal letters

1 Who do you, or members of your family, receive letters from? What kind of letters are they? How do they differ in layout, content and style? What are the advantages of writing to someone instead of speaking to them?

2 Quickly read the two letters and fill in each gap in the instructions with a suitable word.

A You work as a (**1**) .... in a big hotel. When a well-known rock band spent the night there recently, they held a noisy party that left a trail of destruction. Write a letter to a (**2**) .... of yours, (**3**) .... what took place and how it affected (**4**) .... personally.

B You are the (**1**) .... of a large hotel. Recently, a famous rock band stayed there overnight, and held an impromptu party. Considerable noise and damage was caused. Write a letter to the (**2**) .... , (**3**) .... what happened and stating what you want them to (**4**) .... about it.

A

Dear Tom,

I just thought I'd drop you a line since I'm halfway through my summer job as a porter here at the hotel and it's a while since I was last in touch. The job
5 here is certainly an eye-opener in many ways! How are you getting on at the youth camp? I hope the kids aren't driving you mad ...

I must tell you about a visit we had from Sanders and his backing group last night. You've heard of him,
10 of course? He only stayed one night, which was fortunate since he managed to get himself into trouble with the management pretty quickly! You should have heard the noise coming from his suite later on in the evening!

15 Being on duty at the time, I was hanging around the reception desk as usual when the manager came storming out of the bar and headed straight for the phone. He was in a right state, I'm telling you! Anyway, he obviously calmed down enough to talk to
20 someone in Sanders' suite – his manager maybe – and eventually they turned the music down.

This morning, they left soon after breakfast and I think the boss heaved a sigh of relief to see the back of them. From what I hear, they had also been
25 throwing things around a bit in the suite, which didn't make them any more popular! I didn't come off too badly though – I helped take down their luggage to the limo they had waiting outside, and Sanders himself gave me a hefty tip. Perhaps he hoped that I would
30 put in a good word for them!

I think I'd better put the light off now and get some sleep since I'm on duty at 7 a.m. tomorrow. Don't work too hard!

All the best,

35 Miles

Dear Mr Sanders,

I am writing to express my extreme displeasure over the behaviour exhibited by you and your guests while you were staying at my hotel on the night of
5 28th August. Not only did your actions cause considerable inconvenience, but they also incurred significant expense, which I hope you will take immediate steps to remedy.

To recap the circumstances briefly, it was at
10 around midnight that the disturbance started. Having supervised the cleaning of the dining-room, I was sitting in the bar with some colleagues of mine when our conversation was interrupted by loud rock music blasting out of your suite. This was soon
15 followed by the sound of glasses being smashed and outbursts of raucous laughter. It was apparent that a celebratory party was under way. After some time I phoned your suite and spoke to your manager, who promised that the music would be turned off
20 immediately. In the event it was at least another half an hour before peace was re-established in the hotel.

Unfortunately, that was not the end of the matter. The next morning after your departure, it was brought to my attention by the cleaning staff that
25 the suite was in a state of devastation. Various vases and items of crockery had been smashed and plants had been thrown off the balcony. In short, it was obvious that you and your guests had shown a lamentable lack of respect for the hotel and its
30 property.

In view of the above, I would be very grateful if you could immediately reimburse the cost of the breakages incurred, as outlined on the attached sheet, plus additional costs of cleaning and repairing
35 the suite.

Yours sincerely,

Malcolm Betteridge

Malcolm Betteridge
Hotel Manager

3 1 What events are mentioned in both letters? How do the writers differ in their feelings about what occurred?

2 How would you describe the style of text A, and of text B?

3 How would you describe the tone of each letter?

4 What differences are there in the beginnings and endings of texts A and B? Which similar expressions (e.g. *Dear Sir*) do you know, and when are they used?

4 a In which part of text A is each of these?
  • giving advice to the reader
  • asking about the reader
  • the reason for writing
  • the reason for closing the letter
  • giving news about the writer
  • a description of the main events
  • their consequences for the writer

Which expressions show that the reader and writer already know each other? In what other ways do letter writers often indicate this?

b In which part of text B is each of these?
  • a description of the main events
  • the writer's request for specific action
  • something that made things even worse
  • the writer's response to the situation
  • the background to the situation
  • the reason for writing

Which expressions do you think are common in letters of complaint? What others do you know?

5 a Which verb forms do the writers use to describe what happened? What examples of participle clauses are there in both letters?

b What do you notice about the order of subject, auxiliary verb and main verb after *Not only* (text B line 4)? Make a list of adverbial expressions that are followed by this word order, for example:
Rarely have I seen …
Not until summer will there be …
Is this structure formal or informal?

6 Compare the style of language used in texts A and B. Underline examples of 1–10.
  1 contracted forms (e.g. *I'd*)
  2 use of passives
  3 abbreviations
  4 exclamation marks
  5 impersonal forms (e.g. *It …*)
  6 subject / auxiliary inversion
  7 short, simple sentences
  8 colloquialisms, idioms and phrasal verbs
  9 conversational comments and questions
 10 direct tone (e.g. use of imperatives)

7 Read the instructions for letters 1–4 and underline the words that tell you what you have to write, to whom and why. What style and tone would be appropriate for each letter? Choose one of them and write about 300 words.

1 Your family own a holiday flat by the sea. Recently, a group of tourists stayed there, but they made a terrible mess of the place, and upset the neighbours. Write a letter to one of the tourists, stating what happened and what action you expect.

2 You recently rented a small flat. Before you moved in, the owner assured you it was quiet and warm, and that all the appliances were in good working order. However, you soon discovered that none of this was true. Write a letter to the owner, explaining what has gone wrong and what you expect him / her to do about it.

3 Several tourists recently stayed at a seaside holiday flat owned by your family. They left the place in a terrible state and also upset the neighbours. Write a letter to a friend, describing what happened and what the consequences were for you.

4 A week ago you moved into a small flat. The owner had described it as warm and quiet, with everything working perfectly, but this was not what you found. Write a letter to a friend, describing your experiences and mentioning the funny side of it.

exam factfile

American spelling is acceptable if used consistently.

THERE IS ANOTHER MODEL FORMAL LETTER ON PAGE 163 IN THE WRITING BANK

review

1 Add a suffix to the word in capitals and put the new word in the correct place in the sentence.

EXAMPLE All political parties were after the fall of the dictatorship. LEGAL
All political parties were legalised after the fall of the dictatorship.

1 John's wife left him because of his approach to life. PESSIMIST
2 That electrician tried to fix two of the lights, and now none of them work. TRAIN
3 Many people living on the streets in the capital are in fact refugees. HOME
4 The witness couldn't see clearly, but she says the attacker was a man. TALL
5 When we looked, we noticed that the ceiling was cracked. UP
6 He was rewarded for his behaviour with a special dinner in his honour. HERO

2 Match verbs 1–6 with meanings a–f.

1 stay up   a put someone in prison
2 clear away   b visit
3 call round   c tidy things that have been used
4 check in   d return
5 lock up   e go to bed late
6 be back   f register on arriving at a hotel

3 There is a mistake in most of these sentences. In each case, say what it is and correct it, without changing the participle clause.

1 Waking up early in the morning, my room was bright and cheerful.
2 Not wanting to make any mistakes, I checked all the figures again.
3 Regarded as one of the most poisonous reptiles in the world, our boss was nearly bitten by an escaped cobra.
4 Having run all the way to the station, the train was just leaving as I arrived.
5 Wearing some old clothes, the cooker was fixed by my uncle.
6 Criticised for not trying anything new, the band changed their musical style completely.
7 Not having studied enough, yesterday's exam was just too difficult for me.
8 Sitting in the sunshine on the river bank, the fish were clearly visible below us.

4 Form complete sentences with participle clauses, adding commas where necessary.

1 after / close / the front door / I realise / I leave / the key in the house
2 in spite / live / so close to college / Carolina / always late
3 adore / by a small group of fans for many years / he / not become / famous until recently
4 see / the film twice already / I not want / see it again
5 Christina's latest single / a big hit / sell / over 100,000 copies a week
6 not expect / a maths lesson yesterday / I not bring / my calculator to school
7 look after / properly / this exquisite clock / last / a lifetime

5 Complete the puzzle with words from this unit using 1–13 as clues. The word down means 'somewhere to stay or live in'.

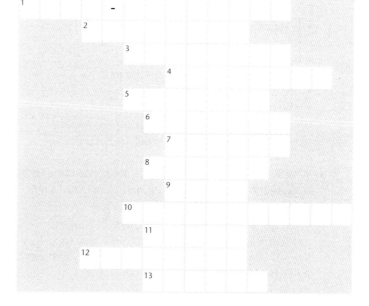

1 house joined to another on one side
2 house joined to others on both sides
3 cups, plates and dishes
4 without anywhere to live
5 person who repairs water pipes, taps, etc.
6 movement of furniture to another house
7 person who pays to live in the same house as their landlord
8 room where someone both lives and sleeps
9 room in a hospital
10 where you try on clothes in a shop
11 set of rooms in a hotel
12 where a photographer develops film
13 someone who rents a property

unit 8   *in the past*

vocabulary and speaking

talking points

1 Think back to when you were a child. What do you remember about your favourite:
toys   clothes   food and drink
TV programmes   friends and relatives?

2 a Which historic event would you most like to have witnessed? Why?
  b What is the most important event you can remember happening?

3 Which films or books do you know in which characters travel back in time?

4 Do you agree that people are fascinated with the past? Why might this be so?

5 Would you like to trace your family tree? Why / Why not? How would you go about doing this?

1 Choose two of the pictures and discuss what the following would have been like at that time.

education   health and life expectancy   women's roles   family life   crime   entertainment

2 **a** Match the adjectives in the box with what they usually describe. Some may fit into more than one category and some may not fit into any.

EXAMPLE *elderly – people*

• people   • inventions   • food   • particular time periods   • buildings

antique   ~~elderly~~   old-fashioned   extinct   obsolete   medieval   primitive
historic   historical   quaint   archaic   classical   fossilised   antiquated
aged   traditional   dated   stale   superseded   prehistoric   past it
out-of-date   behind the times   past its sell-by date   expired

b What could you describe using the words that don't fit into any of the categories?

3 In 1–10, explain the difference between the two expressions in bold.

1 As well as the **souvenirs** we bought at the airport, we also have fond **memories** of our month by the sea.

2 At school we had to **memorise** whole pages of stories in Latin, but I can't **remember** now what they were all about.

3 Prisoner 1173 felt no **remorse** for his dreadful past; instead he looked back with **nostalgia** on the days when he was young and free.

4 On the day my uncle retired, he received a company pen as a **memento**, and a **memo** from the head of the company.

5 It was certainly an **historic** moment when Columbus first set foot on American soil, although there is still disagreement over the **historical** details of his life.

6 The **commemoration** of the 60th anniversary of the end of the war will take place next to the **memorial** to those who died.

7 I know we said we would **review** all staff members' pay at the next meeting, but I don't **recall** when the meeting is!

8 My grandparents are forever **reminiscing** about what life was like when they were young, although sometimes they don't **recollect** things that happened quite recently.

9 Jeff's wife **reminded him to** change his socks, which **reminded him of** his mother.

10 If she thinks young people are only interested in their future careers, she's **living in the past**; nowadays a lot of teenagers find **living for the present** much more fun.

reading gapped text: text organisation

1 Why are some people interested in dinosaurs? Try to think of at least three reasons.

2 **a** The text covers these different aspects of dinosaurs. Quickly read the text following gap 1 and paragraphs A–H and label the paragraphs **1**, **2** or **3**.

 1 Why dinosaurs became extinct.

 2 The history of dinosaur discovery.

 3 Why dinosaurs fascinate so many people.

 What is the purpose of the very first paragraph?

 b Choose from the paragraphs **A–H** the one which fits each gap (**1–7**). There is one extra paragraph which you do not need to use.

 The first paragraph has been done as an example. Use the words and phrases in bold to help you.

3 1 Find all the expressions used in the text to mean 'dinosaurs'.

 2 Rewrite the sentence *Not until the 19th century … become clear* (line 20) so that it begins 'The truth …'.

 3 Which phrase in the same paragraph explains the meaning of *obsolescence* (line 30)?

 4 What is grammatically unusual about the sentence beginning *Climatic upheaval …* (line 56)? Where is the question answered?

 5 Use the context to work out the meaning of *do in* (line 59).

 6 Find two phrasal verbs in paragraph B that mean 'kill' in this context.

 7 Find a synonym for *unearthed* (line 21) in paragraph D.

 8 Find three expressions in paragraph E that mean the same as *extinct* (line 86).

 9 What do you think *the food chain* (line 108) is?

4 What do you think is the most likely explanation for why dinosaurs became extinct?

exam factfile

In Reading Part 3 the first and last paragraphs are never missing so there will always be clues before and after a gap.

WHY DINOSAURS WON'T GO AWAY

From Spielberg's *Jurassic Park* to the BBC's *Walking With Dinosaurs* and Disney's *Dinosaur*, T-rex and his friends have brought in the audiences in their millions, all around the world. The 1954 film
5 *Godzilla – King of the Monsters* was a huge hit in both Japan and the US – and led to no fewer than 14 sequels. We Europeans are particularly thrilled by the beasts. But then we were also the first to learn the awful truth: that despite what we might think, we
10 humans are not The Greatest Creatures That Have Ever Lived.

1 | D

The first indications of **this humiliating little fact** appeared about 300 years ago. Someone in Oxfordshire dug up a huge bony object which ended up in the possession of a Professor Robert Plot of Oxford University.

The specimen had some similarities to the leg-bone of a cow – but judging by its size, an impossibly tall cow. Unable to find any other explanation, Professor Plot decided that the bone had come from a long-dead human giant.

2

Not until the 19th century, when entire skeletons had been unearthed from many sites across Europe, did **the truth** become clear. Some time in the distant past, colossal reptiles had ruled the continent. By 1842 these monsters had been given the name dinosaur, from the Greek for 'terrible lizard'.

3

Others believe we still know little about their place in our consciousness. According to American expert WJT Mitchell, we do not yet understand what the dinosaur really means to us. Sometimes we see it as a scientific wonder; at other times as a children's toy, a company logo, a terrifying monster, or as a synonym for obsolescence – something hopelessly out of date.

4

If the appeal of dinosaurs is the association with enormous power that suddenly ends, then the makers of the *Walking With Dinosaurs* television series got it exactly right, showing us both the triumph and tragedy of the terrible lizards. They realised that, like descriptions of the horrors of war, it doesn't matter how many times you hear about dinosaurs, there is still **something even more awful** about them you still haven't heard.

5

Twice as long as a bus and weighing over 100 tonnes, liopleurodon really is the largest carnivore the world has ever seen – and makes poor T-rex look tiny by comparison. Its astonishing size and power made it an immediate favourite with young (and many not-so-young) viewers everywhere, and plastic liopleurodons started appearing in shop windows within weeks.

6

Since then we have had death by genetic changes, death by continental break-up, and most famously, death by meteor impact. An impact between a very big rock and the Earth's surface at something like 100,000 kph, with the violence of 10 million nuclear bombs.

7

Academics would naturally prefer that the explanation of the extinction of the dinosaurs were simple. Indeed, there are still those who insist there is only one explanation (namely, their own). But there is one last, powerful argument against the single-disaster theories. Dinosaurs were the dominant life-form on this planet for 160 million years. During that time – over 40 times longer than humans have been around – dinosaurs had seen it all. Climatic upheaval, moving continents, volcanic eruptions, meteor impacts? They survived them all. Only the incredibly rare event of several global catastrophes striking all at the same time could finally do the dinosaurs in.

A It's the last of **these roles** that seems strange – why should dinosaurs remain so popular when they are frequently used as a symbol of failure to adapt? 'To be called a dinosaur in a rapidly changing, competitive economy is not very attractive commercially,' says Professor Mitchell.

B **That** ought to have sorted them out, you would think. But no. Most palaeontologists today do not believe that even this monumental impact was enough, by itself, to get rid of T-rex. Instead, they go for the theory of death by all of the above: a combination of volcanic eruptions, genetic and geological changes – with meteor impact as an added extra.

C The producer answered **these criticisms** by admitting that some of the pictures were based on guesswork, but also pointing out scientists do not – and perhaps never will – know everything about dinosaurs. So why should we all sit quietly until the academics eventually decide when we should be permitted to be thrilled?

D ~~The first indications of **this humiliating little fact** appeared about 300 years ago. Someone in Oxfordshire dug up a huge bony object which ended up in the possession of a Professor Robert Plot of Oxford University.~~

E **Nowadays**, of course, everyone knows something else about them: they don't exist anymore. Dinosaurs were once the all-powerful and unchallenged rulers of the world – and now they are gone. Some argue that the fact that they are no longer around may be an important part of their appeal. Attempting to explain our fascination, one psychologist has described them as 'big, fierce, extinct – in other words, scary but safe'.

F Take the episode about marine dinosaurs. When it started, no doubt most of the millions who eagerly sat down to watch felt sure that T-rex was the biggest carnivore ever seen on earth. Within the first 60 seconds, they had been spectacularly proved wrong. They saw some unfortunate little dinosaur seized by the three-metre jaws of liopleurodon, the crocodile from hell. **The beast** swallowed its victim like a bit of hamburger before vanishing back beneath the waves.

G **Which** is two-thirds correct – and the bit he got wrong is significant. For the assumption that the bone must be human is based on the assumption that humans have been, and always have been, the greatest.

H Inevitably, some scientists complain about **all this**, saying that their subject is not being taken seriously. But discovering the fate of dinosaurs is the hot topic in palaeontology right now, and almost every week there is a new theory for their disappearance. A few years ago, a favourite theory was death by volcanic eruption. By throwing huge amounts of dust into the atmosphere, these could have blocked the sun's light, killing vegetation and thus destroying the food chain.

grammar
narrative verb forms and linking words

1 Correct the underlined verbs in 1–6 and then match them with uses a–f below.

1 I <u>read</u> a book when my best friend Lisa rang me for a chat.
2 Ross <u>is going to sell</u> his motorbike, but then he changed his mind and kept it.
3 Years ago I <u>had been drinking</u> very sweet lemonade, but I don't any more.
4 When we woke up in the morning, we noticed that someone <u>broke</u> a window during the night.
5 As soon as she saw his photo, Valerie <u>was recognising</u> Lomax as the attacker.
6 I <u>used to be standing</u> in the queue for hours when at last the ticket office opened.

a A past action at a specific past time, or a past situation.
b An activity in progress when something else happened.
c Something that happened before a past event, or a specific past time.
d An action over a period of time before a past event, or a specific past time.
e Past plans that have not (yet) been carried out.
f Something that happened repeatedly in the past, but does not happen now.

2 Fill each gap using a past form of the verb in brackets.

On a winter's day in 1974, a policeman .... (drive) slowly along a country road when he .... (receive) an urgent message to go to a house where a burglar alarm .... (go off) a short time earlier. Arriving on the scene, he .... (find) the house was securely locked and it .... (take) him some time to get in, as nobody .... (live) there. Once inside, he .... (see) a trail of footprints that .... (lead) across the floor of a completely empty room. All of them .... (make) by the same left foot, and they .... (appear) to stop at the opposite wall. A neighbour .... (begin) to tell him the tale of a one-legged priest who .... (live) there, and started talking about ghosts, but the policeman .... (reply), 'So if he could walk through walls, why .... he .... (make) the alarm go off?'

3 a These linking words and phrases are used in time clauses. Check the meanings of any that you are unsure of. Which two are rather formal?

as   at the same time as   as soon as   now that
prior to   since   subsequently   then   until/till
when   once   by the time   while   whenever
the moment   immediately

b Underline the linking expressions in these sentences.
1 Our train had no sooner left the station than it stopped again.
2 The Minister of Transport had hardly/scarcely begun to speak when protestors interrupted her.

What other word order is possible in each case?

c Join these pairs of sentences by using the correct form of the verbs in brackets and adding the linking expression in bold. Give two answers in each case.

EXAMPLE
Karen (buy) a DVD player. She (begin) to watch films on disc. **as soon as**
As soon as Karen had bought a DVD player, she began to watch films on disc.
Karen began to watch films on disc as soon as she had bought a DVD player.

1 I (watch) my favourite TV programme. There (be) a knock at the door. **while**
2 We (practise) that new dance a few times. We (find) it easy. **once**
3 I (sit down) to have a break. The phone (ring). **no sooner**
4 I realised that I (dream) all the time. I (wake up). **the moment**
5 I (stand) there for 15 minutes. The shop assistant (serve) me. **by the time**
6 The ship's crew (recover) from one tropical illness. They (fall ill) with something else. **scarcely**
7 Street Sounds' new single (come out). It (go) to number one in the charts. **immediately**

d Look at the pictures on page 93 and tell your partner the story, using a variety of past forms and time links from above.

4 The stories in **2** and **3d** are 'Urban Legends' or 'Urban Myths', unusual stories which spread very quickly and which may or may not be true. There are more of these on page 152. Taking turns with your partner, tell one story each using a variety of verb forms and linking expressions.

common errors

I used to live near the border when the war started.
What is wrong with this sentence? Why?

open cloze

1 **a** Read the text quickly to get the main ideas without filling in any of the gaps. Then complete gaps 1–7 only. Use these clues to help you.

1 What noun collocates with *take* to mean 'participate in'?
2 What preposition collocates with *day* to mean 'day without work'?
3 What result conjunction would fit here?
4 What time conjunction would fit here?
5 What expression with *in* means 'quickly enough'?
6 What is the comparative of *badly*?
7 Does the context indicate a positive or a negative word?

b Work in pairs. Student **A** study 8–11, fill in the gaps, and write similar clues for each on a piece of paper. Student **B** do the same with 12–15. Exchange clues and complete the text.

The Gucci Kangaroo

Some years ...ago.... , the yacht *Italia* called into the Australian port of Fremantle while taking **(1)**............ in a round-the-world race. As they had the day **(2)**............ , two crew members decided they would like to see a bit of the outback, **(3)**............ they hired a four-wheel-drive vehicle and set off into the bush. There were trees right up to the roadside, and **(4)**............ a large kangaroo suddenly jumped out in front of their vehicle, the driver couldn't brake in **(5)**............ to avoid hitting it. The two men were badly shaken up by the accident, but the 'roo had come off far **(6)**............ : it was, apparently, dead. They propped it up against the side of the vehicle and tried to revive it, but **(7)**............ any success. After a while they decided to move **(8)**............, but they thought it would be fun before they left to **(9)**............ a photo of Australia's national symbol dressed in a Gucci jacket. **(10)**............ put the expensive garment on the unfortunate animal, one of the men posed for a photo for his family back **(11)**............ . No sooner had he done so, however, **(12)**............ the 'roo, which had only been stunned, came round and leapt to its feet. Completely recovered **(13)**............ its recent experience, it hopped back into the bush and quickly disappeared, **(14)**............ wearing the Gucci jacket. In the pockets the kangaroo also took with it a passport and several hundred Australian dollars, as **(15)**............ as a membership card for a smart Italian nightclub.

c Do you think this is a true story? Why / Why not?

listening multiple choice: question types

EXAM FOCUS

paper 4 part 1 multiple choice

In the first part of Listening you hear four short extracts from monologues or dialogues, played twice. For each extract you read two questions or unfinished statements followed by options A, B and C. Questions will deal with general or specific information, and may focus on the speakers' opinions and feelings, the points they make or the reasons for making the points.

- You will hear different text types, contexts and speakers, so it is useful to know what the questions are about before you start listening.
- Knowing the focus of each question is useful for identifying language clues that may help answer the questions, e.g. *language indicating opinions*.
- Once you have heard each extract twice, don't spend time worrying about any unanswered questions as you may miss the beginning of the next extract.
- Don't leave any questions unanswered – it's better to make a guess.

1 Read 1–6. Is the focus of each question specific, general, feeling or purpose?

2 🔊 You will hear three different extracts. For questions **1–6** choose the answer (**A**, **B** or **C**) which fits best according to what you hear. There are two questions for each extract.

Extract one
You hear a man talking about someone he remembers from his schooldays.
1 The teacher often used to
  A set difficult questions for homework.
  B ask the same question again and again.
  C refuse to answer the pupils' questions. [1]

2 This extract tells the story of how
  A a geography teacher decided to change the way he taught.
  B the pupils made a geography teacher feel embarrassed.
  C geography lessons became much more interesting. [2]

Extract two
You hear a young woman talking about a place she remembers from her childhood.
3 She usually went swimming in
  A spring.
  B early summer.
  C late summer. [3]

4 What was her reaction to the film?
  A She was amused.
  B She was angry.
  C She was bored. [4]

Extract three
You hear part of a talk about the Classical Period of Greek history.
5 The speaker believes there has been too much emphasis on the role of
  A Sparta.
  B Athens.
  C Persia. [5]

6 What is the speaker's main aim in his talk?
  A to claim that the rise of Athens quickly led to the fall of Sparta
  B to stress the role Sparta played in making Greece powerful
  C to link the military successes of Athens with its democratic system [6]

speaking narrating; being a good listener

1 **a** When someone is describing past events, both speaker and listener may use informal expressions to keep the story moving. Look at these expressions used by speakers and put them into the categories below. Can you add more to each category?

> You'll never guess what … Well in the end …
> That reminds me of the time … To cut a long story short …
> Have I ever told you about …? So there I was …

Introducing the story

....

....

Holding the listener's attention

....

....

Finishing the story

....

....

b Add more expressions to these boxes.

> **Encouraging the speaker**
> Go on! So what did you do? What happened in the end, then?

> **Sharing the speaker's feelings**
> How incredible! That must've been awful for you. What a shock!

2 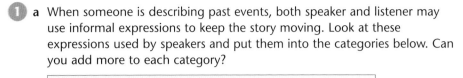 Listen to this anecdote (amusing short story) and add two more expressions to each of the categories in **1b**.

3 Take it in turns to tell one of the stories shown here.

2 YEARS LATER…

vocabulary idioms

1 The idioms in 1–3 are associated with memory – or lack of it. Use the context to explain the meaning of each one.

1 I'd met that girl at the party somewhere before, but right at that moment her name **escaped me**. I was frantically **racking my brains** trying to recall where I'd seen her, when she happened to mention the coffee bar on the high street. That **jogged my memory** and after a moment's thought I had it: she was called Clara.

2 *Before the day of the exam, I'd spent hours studying that poem until at last I'd* **learned it by heart**. *But the moment I sat down in the exam room, disaster struck:* **my mind went blank**. *I felt sure that if only I could remember the first few words, they'd be enough to* **refresh my memory**.

3 It must be five years since I last went to Ireland, but I can remember my stay on the coast as if it was yesterday. The one thing I can't quite recollect is the name of the first place we went to, though **it's on the tip of my tongue**. It's right next to Croagh Patrick, the Holy Mountain. And it's a fishing port. 'Port' – **that rings a bell**, and it's on the west coast, so … 'Westport', that's it!

2 Match the pictures to seven of the idioms in **1**, then use them to give an appropriate response to 1–7 below.

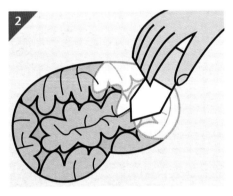

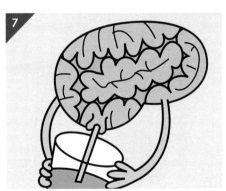

1 Isn't there an easier way of remembering people's phone numbers?
2 Did you see that quiz show on TV last night? They asked someone the simplest of questions but she couldn't say a thing.
3 Have you ever met Conchita, my cousin from Uruguay?
4 Whereabouts are the remains of the medieval castle?
5 I thought you'd completely forgotten my birthday this year.
6 I liked that song they brought out last Christmas. What was it called?
7 I'm sorry officer, but I don't remember anything about a gold necklace.

collocations: adverb + adjective

1 Which two of the adverbs collocate with the adjective to complete 1–12?

1 The two historical events were *loosely / densely / closely* connected.
2 Drinking alcohol is *strictly / harshly / expressly* forbidden there.
3 By the end of the 20th century, rock bands like that seemed *ridiculously / greatly / ludicrously* out-of-date.
4 It was *painfully / anxiously / perfectly* obvious that our athlete was going to lose.
5 The slave trade made certain individuals *totally / enormously / fabulously* wealthy.
6 Everything was *greatly / poorly / superbly* organised at last year's Expo.
7 The public were *deeply / fully / profoundly* shocked by the awful tragedy.
8 I was not *purely / entirely / wholly* convinced by his explanation.
9 The flat we rented was *mercifully / surprisingly / considerably* free of street noise.
10 When Lola became famous, she bought a(n) *lavishly / extremely / tastefully* decorated flat in New York.
11 We were *thoroughly / extraordinarily / unbelievably* lucky to win.
12 Your help during the crisis has been *greatly / widely / completely* appreciated.

2 Use adverb + adjective collocations from **1** to complete 1–6.

1 The emperor was a(n) .... man.

2 The mountain village is still .... of motor vehicles.

3 It is .... to take photos in the gallery.

4 Dave's clothes are .... , most people think.

5 Archaeologists found a(n) .... temple buried in the sand.

6 You have to be .... to win the lottery.

The Old England Restaurant in the heart of London is the place where you can step back in time to the 15th century to dine with the royal court at a truly Medieval Banquet.

Eat, Drink and Be Merry

The magnificent banquet is held in the atmospheric cellars of the Merry England restaurant, close to the Tower of London and Tower Bridge.

Your Medieval Banquet includes:

Four delicious courses

Unlimited beer and wine throughout the meal

Over two hours of top live entertainment, including medieval music and dancing, and star comedians every night

We look forward to welcoming you to the London experience you will never forget!

writing reviews

1 Read these instructions and answer the questions.

An international guide for travellers has asked readers to review a restaurant that they have been to. You saw this advertisement and decided to eat there. Describe your experience there and say how the restaurant compares to the claims in the advertisement. Write your review in about 300 words.

- Who are your readers? What style should you write in?
- What do you have to read? Why?
- What two things do you have to write about?
- What kind of vocabulary is needed?

2 Read the advertisement. What are the main claims it makes? What do you think you would like or dislike about an evening there?

3 **a** Read the review opposite and discuss these questions with your partner.
  1 On a scale of 1–10, how much does the reviewer like the restaurant?
  2 Which paragraphs reflect which parts of the instructions?
  3 How would you describe the style of the text – informal, neutral or formal?

b Read the text in more detail and answer these questions.
  1 Were her first impressions generally positive?
  2 Which of the four courses did she like best?
  3 In what ways was she disappointed?
  4 In what circumstances would she recommend the restaurant?

4 The advertisement says *you can step back in time to the 15th century*, and the reviewer agrees that there is *quite an authentic medieval atmosphere*, but does she think claims 1–5 are justified? What are her exact words in each case?
  1 *Unlimited beer and wine …*
  2 *Four delicious courses*
  3 *Over two hours of top live entertainment …*
  4 *… star comedians every night*
  5 *… experience you will never forget*

5 Which of these does the writer use to
  a be positive?
  b be negative?

  1 *not particularly to either of our tastes*
  2 *They certainly looked … but*
  3 *though rather noisy*
  4 *a reasonable success*
  5 *could be improved*

exam factfile

A review should inform and interest the reader and give the writer's opinion of the film, book, restaurant, etc. being reviewed. It may include narrative and description, with appropriate topic vocabulary, and should be written in a style suitable for the reader.

Old England in the centre of London promises an interesting evening out and reflects a growing trend for themed restaurants. This one's set in medieval England.

Our first impression when we went in, was of a large, 5 dimly-lit room with huge, long wooden tables and walls hung with tapestries depicting medieval scenes. After we had been seated at a table, waitresses in period costume came and brought us drinks in metal goblets. A small group of musicians appeared up in the gallery, burning torches 10 were lit, more diners arrived and the banquet was under way!

The first course, which was roast pigeon, was not particularly to either of our tastes as it was served in an extremely rich sauce. The wild boar that followed was quite 15 tasty although my friend complained that hers was rather tough. The third course, baked fish with a variety of vegetables, was rather bland. Finally, dessert was a selection of traditional tarts and pies. They certainly looked the part but we could have done with a lighter sweet, like a fruit jelly 20 or mousse. The drinks flowed freely enough and the atmosphere was cheerful, though rather noisy!

All in all, the evening was a reasonable success and we both felt that quite an authentic medieval atmosphere had been created. Nonetheless, I would say that the standard of 25 the food didn't live up to our expectations and they could do with a lot more choice on the menu. The entertainment wasn't quite what had been advertised, since, for some reason, the comedians did not appear on the evening we were there, and the dancing only got going in the last half 30 hour or so. If these things could be improved, then I would definitely recommend it as something a bit different for an evening out; whether I would classify it as an unforgettable experience, however, is questionable.

6 Choose one of these reviews. Use narrative tenses, topic-related vocabulary, and expressions from **5**.

1 Readers of an international magazine have been asked to contribute reviews of unusual restaurants they have visited. When you saw this advertisement you had a meal at one of those it mentions. Describe your evening, and compare the restaurant to what is claimed in the advertisement. Write your review in about 300 words.

2 An entertainment guide for your town has asked for reviews of local restaurants or bars. Write a review of your favourite restaurant or bar in about 300 words.

EAT AT MEAL TIMES!

MEAL TIMES, the world-famous restaurants, take you back to your favourite historical setting for the dining experience of a lifetime.

WE'VE THOUGHT OF EVERYTHING

From the music to the furniture and costumes, we've made sure that every last detail is authentic. The food and service, of course, is superb, and the entertainment includes surprises that will delight you.

A CHOICE OF CENTURIES

Each of our magnificent restaurants is set in an exciting time in history. The choice is yours!

●

Greek myths and legends

●

Ancient Egypt

●

The Wild West

●

50S AMERICA

TABLES ARE MUCH IN DEMAND – SO BOOK EARLY TO AVOID DISAPPOINTMENT!

● THERE IS ANOTHER MODEL REVIEW ON PAGE 164 IN THE WRITING BANK

review

1 Write suitable questions for these answers. Use a different past form of the verb for each one.
1 I was just going to bed then.
2 No, I hadn't – but I had spoken to him on the phone once.
3 Yes, I was going to – but I didn't see her yesterday.
4 I think she'd been swimming, because her hair was still wet.
5 Yes, I did – but nowadays I only have time to play once a week.
6 No, I didn't – it was the most boring one I've seen.

2 Complete each sentence with one of these linking expressions.

> by the time   hardly   the moment   no sooner
> scarcely   while

1 .... I was walking home one night, a man offered me a lift in his car.
2 .... had Dawn finished one novel when she started writing another.
3 .... I got home I sensed that something had gone badly wrong.
4 .... had she paid one bill when the next one arrived.
5 .... my sister was five, she'd learned to read.
6 .... had Charlie's parents gone out than his friends came round.

3 Which idiom describes these situations?
1 You study something and remember it perfectly.
2 You can nearly, but not quite, remember something.
3 Something helps you to remember something else. (2 idioms)
4 Something reminds you of something else, but you don't know exactly what.
5 You can't remember something specific.
6 You can't remember anything at all.

4 Match the adverbs with the adjectives and use the collocations to rewrite 1–6.

> ridiculously   wealthy
> fabulously   obvious
> surprisingly   convinced
> strictly   out-of-date
> ~~poorly~~   ~~organised~~
> painfully   forbidden
> entirely   free

EXAMPLE They didn't run Sports Day very well.
Sports Day was poorly organised.

1 His family have a huge amount of money.
2 You must not smoke on this aeroplane.
3 Unusually, that city has no crime at all.
4 She believed everything he said.
5 Cars like that seem very unfashionable now.
6 Everyone else could see that she didn't love him.

5 Complete the crossword with words from this unit.

across
1 not young
5 not fresh, e.g. bread
8 short note to someone at work
11 associated with religion
12 surviving parts of ancient objects and buildings
13 replaced by something newer
17 no longer alive as a species
18 object built to remind people of the past
19 attractively old-fashioned
20 generic term for large animal

down
2 design used on firm's paper, products, etc.
3 old story that may or may not be true
4 to think about the past with affection
6 old-fashioned – words, laws, etc.
7 feeling of deep guilt
9 learn by heart
10 no longer fashionable
12 something that helps you remember
14 belonging to an earlier society or time
15 valuable old object
16 to dig up

unit 9 | *seasons*

vocabulary and speaking

1 Look at the three pictures. What is the significance of each of the activities shown? What else is celebrated in each of these seasons, and what other traditions (in your country and abroad) are there at that time?

talking points

1 How do the seasons affect **a** what you wear? **b** your studies or work? **c** your free time?

2 What would life be like if one of the seasons became much longer, or a lot more extreme? Do you think this is already starting to happen?

3 What would it be like living in a country where there is constant light in summer, and perpetual darkness in winter? Or somewhere that celebrates Christmas and New Year in summer?

4 Why do we have seasons in sports and hobbies? Could they be changed?

5 Read this quotation – do you think it accurately describes each of the seasons? Why / Why not?
'light, greenery, warmth and joy in midwinter, … the spring with symbols of rebirth … sunlight and open air during the summer, and thoughts of death and the uncanny at the onset of winter.'

2 a In your country, which months of the year are considered to be spring, summer, autumn and winter? Why? What are the differences in daylight and darkness hours, temperature and humidity? How do these affect living things? How do the differences affect you?

b With which season(s) do you associate each of these words? What do they mean?

> frosty   heatwave   misty   changeable   sweltering   blizzard   overcast
> raw   mild   dreary   scorching   arctic   sticky   hazy   bright   bleak

3 Many words connected with the seasons have both literal and figurative meanings. For each of these verbs, give examples of the two meanings, and link the literal one to a particular season.

   EXAMPLE 1 *The apple trees have begun to **blossom** early this year. (spring)*
   2 *After a slow start, their relationship began to **blossom**.*

> melt   sow   flood   bake   chill   sprout   fade   thaw   bloom   shed

4 a Which common health problems do you associate with each of these symptoms?

> coughing   breathlessness   lethargy   sneezing   nausea   itching
> inflammation   runny nose   watering eyes   insomnia   fatigue
> depression   sore throat   vomiting

b Do any of them occur at particular times of the year?

reading multiple choice: question types

EXAM FOCUS

paper 1 part 2 multiple choice

The second part of Reading consists of four texts with two multiple-choice questions each. The texts are linked by topic, but are taken from a range of sources. The questions may be incomplete sentences or direct questions. There are four options for each one.

1 Read the stems of the questions only without looking at options A–D.
2 Read quickly through the text without worrying too much about unfamiliar words or expressions. Identify the parts of the text that relate to each question.
3 Decide on your own answer and then compare it to A, B, C and D. Choose the one that is nearest in meaning to your own understanding of what the text says.
4 Confirm your choice by finding evidence that your answer is right and the other three are wrong.
5 If you can't decide, guess and move on to the next question, and then the next text.

exam factfile

The texts in Reading become progressively longer from Parts 1 to 4.

1 Quickly read texts A, B and C, and answer these questions.
1 What is the theme of all three?
 a the mountains in winter
 b winter dangers
 c the risks of skiing
 d common winter illnesses
2 What text type is each one?
3 What kind of technical language is used in all three?

2 a Read the stems of questions 1–6 and decide which of these each one focuses on:
 • the writer's purpose
 • making a comparison
 • reference to something else in the text
 • giving an example.

b For questions **1–6**, choose the answer (**A**, **B**, **C** or **D**) which you think fits best according to the text.

'WE'VE BEEN CERTIFIED!'
Seasonal Affective Disorder Lightbox are proud to announce that we have gained the prestigious Certification for Medical Devices and comply with all the latest European legislation.
OUR CE MARKING IS CE 0120

The effective remedy for winter blues and depression

S.A.D. is now officially recognised by doctors and psychiatrists as a medical condition thought to affect millions of people.

S.A.D. has a lot in common with the hibernation
5 cycle of animals. As the days grow shorter and the light becomes less intense, it increases the desire to 'hibernate'.

Although S.A.D. symptoms are rare among people living within 30 degrees of the equator, where the
10 length of the days varies little with the seasons and the sun's rays remain bright throughout the year, they may start to develop them if they move further away from the equator.

Typical problems include:
15 ● depression, feelings of gloom and despondency
 ● lethargy, lack of energy
 ● anxiety, feeling unable to cope
 ● social problems: irritability, being withdrawn
 ● sleep: finding it hard to stay awake during the day,
20 but having disturbed nights
 ● temporary difficulties in relationship with partner
 ● craving for carbohydrates and sweet foods

Historically, treatment for depression involved the use of drugs. However, in recent years research
25 showed that S.A.D. sufferers responded, often quite dramatically, to Bright Light Treatment. Our fully proven lightboxes have been specifically designed and are a recognised method of alleviating S.A.D. You should start to feel the benefit within 4–10 days of
30 using one for just half an hour each morning.

1 The text likens Seasonal Affective Disorder to
 A the need of some creatures to sleep all winter.
 B living near the equator.
 C the emotions of those whose relationships have broken up.
 D the psychological consequences of drug abuse.

2 What does *them* in line 12 refer to?
 A symptoms
 B days
 C seasons
 D rays

B

WINTER ILLNESSES

Getting a cold from the cold weather is a myth. Viruses cause chills, though you'd never think so reading Victorian romances in which a good soaking leaves the heroine at death's door. Why do
5 we get more sniffles in winter? Because we spend more time indoors, often in stuffy, poorly ventilated homes and offices.

Then there is the myth that alcohol protects against the winter cold. This appealing idea comes
10 from the image of the Alpine St Bernard dog with a keg of brandy hanging from its collar. Alas, although St Bernards comforted thousands of climbers and skiers, it is questionable how many they actually saved. Alcohol actually has a chilling
15 effect. The myth lives on because alcohol does have a temporary warming effect. It makes blood rise to the surface of the skin, resulting in flushing. But as skin temperature rises, body temperature falls.
20 A winter myth skiers frequently claim is 'mountain sickness'. Don't believe it. Few go above 1,800 m. Go to 3,000 m and stay there for long periods and you may develop some symptoms: your physical coordination may be affected, for
25 example, while at 3,500 m you may start experiencing headaches, irritability, insomnia, nausea, vomiting and shortness of breath. These symptoms are well known to mountaineers in the Andes and Himalayas. Regulars on the slopes of
30 Switzerland, France and Italy may indeed experience similar effects but the causes are very different. The typical skier goes straight from the office to the resort, up the nearest lift and into vigorous exercise. Breathlessness and fatigue then
35 become nausea and 'mountain sickness'.

C

WOMAN UNDER ICE

A woman in Norway has been brought back from the dead after surviving the lowest temperature recorded in a human being. 29-year-old Anna Bagenholm was declared clinically dead after a skiing accident in
5 which she became stuck under thick ice and submerged in freezing water for 40 minutes. Her body temperature had fallen to 13.7°C – almost 24 degrees below the normal 37°C. On her arrival at Tromso hospital, it took doctors nine hours' work to
10 bring her round. She then spent 60 days in intensive care, 35 of them on a ventilator to assist her respiration.

Ms Bagenholm had been descending a frozen stream with two friends when she slipped and fell
15 head first down the 30-degree slope and under a section of cracked ice. Professor Mads Gilbert, at the University Hospital of Tromso, described what happened: 'She was wedged between rocks and she was banging on the ice and scratching at the
20 underside. There must have been air-pockets under the ice because she kept struggling for 40 minutes. Then she stopped.'

Eventually a rescue team arrived, dug a hole in the ice downstream and pulled her out. She was not
25 breathing and had no pulse, but resuscitation was begun immediately and continued while she was flown by air ambulance to hospital in Tromso. Once there she was put on a heart bypass machine for three hours to bring her blood back to normal
30 temperature.

3 What is the overall aim of the text?
   A to encourage people to take more exercise
   B to discourage people from drinking alcohol
   C to correct people's mistaken beliefs
   D to advise people to be careful on high mountains

4 Among those who often suffer serious mountain sickness are people who
   A ski at 1,800 metres in the Andes or Himalayas.
   B ski in Switzerland, Italy or France.
   C spend a lot of time at 3,000 metres.
   D climb in the Andes or Himalayas.

5 What did the *nine hours' work* (line 9) include?
   A using a machine to help her breathe
   B starting to resuscitate her
   C warming up her blood
   D cooling her head

6 The text was written in order to
   A warn people against skiing in dangerous places.
   B report a remarkable incident.
   C criticise the rescue services and the woman's friends.
   D describe the medical facilities in Norway.

3 1 In which countries is S.A.D. likely to be a problem?

2 What traditional remedies for common illnesses do you know?

3 What other stories of miraculous escapes from death do you know?

grammar   recognising phrasal verbs

 a Read the explanation then say which of 1–6 contain phrasal verbs.

> A phrasal verb can consist of
> * a verb followed by an adverb, e.g. *step down*
> * a verb followed by a preposition, e.g. *stem from*
> * a verb followed by both an adverb and a preposition, e.g. *miss out on.*
>
> The adverb and preposition are sometimes called 'particles'. Not all multi-word verbs are phrasal verbs. A verb may be followed by an adjective, as in *play fair* or by another verb, for example in *make do.* Also, a preposition after a verb may in fact be part of a phrase, e.g. *she lives in the city.*

1 I'm afraid, Chris, that we'll have to <u>let you go</u>.
2 I don't know who <u>dreamt up</u> this crazy idea.
3 On hearing the alarm, everyone in the theatre <u>walked straight</u> to the exit.
4 I know we can <u>count on</u> your support against them.
5 All his carefully laid plans <u>fell apart</u> at the last minute.
6 Amelia <u>fell in</u> love with the little house straightaway.

b Phrasal verbs may be transitive (they need an object) or intransitive (they don't need one). Which of the phrasal verbs in 1–6 above are transitive, and which intransitive?

phrasal verbs and objects

 Read the rules in the box, then say which sentences in 1–3 are correct.

> An object can sometimes be placed between a verb and a particle, but there are rules.
> * Intransitive verbs do not take an object and therefore cannot be separated:
>   *The weather was good as our plane* **touched down**.
> * Some transitive verbs are not separable:
>   *One of the technicians* **dealt with** *the problem very quickly.*
> * Other transitive verbs are separable, and the particle can go before or after the noun object: *We* **noted** *all the details* **down**. *We* **noted down** *all the details.*
> * If, however, the object is very long, it usually goes after the particle:
>   *The two riders managed to* **shake off** *the men who had been following them through the desert all day.*
> * If the object is a pronoun, it must go before the particle:
>   *When you have finished writing the document,* **print** *it* **out**.

1 a The police are looking into the murder.
  b The police are looking the murder into.
  c The police are looking it into.
  d The police are looking into it.

2 a I didn't want my old school books so I gave them away.
  b I didn't want my old school books so I gave away them.

3 a It took ages to hammer an agreement with the other sides in the conflict out.
  b It took ages to hammer out an agreement with the other sides in the conflict.

2 **a** Read the dictionary entries. How do you know if the verb can be separated? How do you know if it is transitive or intransitive?

‚set 'off to begin a journey

be 'heading for sth (also be 'headed for sth especially in *AmE*) to be going in a particular direction or to a particular place

‚slow 'down/'up| ‚slow sth/sb↔'down/'up to go or to make sth/sb go at a slower speed or be less active

‚run 'out if a supply of sth runs out, it is used up or finished

‚carry 'on (with sth)| ‚carry sth↔'on to continue doing sth

‚tire sb/yourself 'out to make sb/yourself feel very tired

'come across sb/sth to meet or find sb/sth by chance

‚cheer 'up| ‚cheer sb/sth↔'up to become more cheerful; to make sb/sth more cheerful

---

Extracts from the *Oxford Advanced Learner's Dictionary*, sixth edition

b Tell the story shown in the pictures. Use the phrasal verbs in **a** and your own ideas. What happens in the end?

EXAMPLE break down *Roy and Lucy's vehicle broke down in heavy snow.*

Nouns can be formed from transitive or intransitive phrasal verbs by:
1 joining both parts of the verb, e.g. knock out – *knockout*
2 hyphenating the two parts, e.g. slip up – *slip-up*
3 putting the adverb or preposition first, e.g. put in – *input*
4 using the *-ing* form of the verb, e.g. set up – *setting-up*

compound nouns formed from phrasal verbs

1 Read the notes, then form nouns from the phrasal verbs in 1–8.
1 I'd like two meals to take away, please.
2 You can check your luggage in over there.
3 My cousins were brought up very strictly.
4 The money coming in is far less than our outgoings.
5 Violence broke out following the controversial court ruling.
6 Please print it out and give one to all the staff.
7 In tonight's programme listeners can phone in to give their opinions.
8 Get the mechanic to go over the engine very thoroughly.

listening

sentence completion:
focusing on clues (2)

EXAM FOCUS

paper 4 part 2 sentence completion

In this part of Listening you complete a gap in each of nine sentences by writing a word or short phrase. The text is usually a monologue, although a second speaker may give prompts. The questions are in the order of the text.
1 Identify the key words in each question and think of other forms of the key words or phrases.
2 When the tape is played, listen out for the key words and synonyms. Remember that the clues on the recording may come before and/or after the answer.
3 You do not have to rephrase what you hear, although if you do and your answer is correct you will get the mark.
4 When you have finished, check your answers make sense and that the complete sentence is grammatically correct.

exam factfile

In Listening Part 2 your spelling must be correct, although you will not be asked to spell unusually difficult words, e.g. *yacht*, *rhythm*.

1 What effects do you think very high temperatures have on people's behaviour?

2 **a** Look at the underlined words in 1–5 in **3a** and think of other forms and synonyms.

> **EXAMPLE** 1 *investigation, enquiry, study; hot, heatwave, high temperatures; increase, rise.*

b For 6–9, underline the key words and think of other forms and synonyms.

3 **a** 🔊 You will hear part of a talk about the influence of the weather on people's moods. For questions **1–9**, complete the sentences with a word or short phrase.

Recent <u>research</u> says that <u>heat</u> makes people <u>more</u> [**1**   ].
It <u>seems</u> that [**2**   ] is <u>increasing</u> as a <u>result</u> of <u>climate change</u>.
There is more <u>street crime</u> <u>during</u> [**3**   ].
People are often <u>aware of</u> [**4**   ] violence involving their <u>neighbours</u>.
In New York, [**5**   ] <u>increased</u> by <u>three-quarters</u>.
Drivers become involved in more cases of [**6**   ] in summer.
Some kinds of criminal violence are less common in [**7**   ] countries.
Some suggest that the real reason is too much [**8**   ] .
In winter, people prefer to stay in [**9**   ] .

b Check your answers. Look at the transcript on page 153 and find the synonyms of the key words.

speaking discussing pictures

EXAM FOCUS

paper 5 part 2

In Speaking Part 2 you might be asked to speculate, (for example on what will happen or might have happened), evaluate what you can see, compare, give your opinions, or make decisions.

Here are some expressions you can use when comparing aspects of different pictures.

Summers in northern countries aren't that hot, especially *when compared to* those in Mediterranean countries.
Temperatures there are *a great deal* higher *than* here.
The weather is *nothing like as* good *as* in some countries.
Compared with that one, *this* one is *more* interesting.
This one is *by far the more* striking *of the two* pictures.

① Look at the examples in the boxes and add more to each one.

> **Opening the discussion**
> I think we should look at features like …
> We should consider aspects such as …
> The factors we need to take into account include …

> **Discussing preferences**
> Which would you rather …?
> Which appeals more: … or …?
> Which do you find more attractive: … or …?

> **Expressing preferences**
> Given the choice, I'd …   My choice would be …
> If I had to choose, I'd …
> … appeals to me rather more than …
> On balance, I'd …   Rather than …, I'd …

> **Persuading your partner**
> Don't you think, though, that …?
> But wouldn't you go along with me that …?

> **Commenting on a decision**
> Good, that's agreed then.   So we're agreed then.
> That's settled, then.

② 🔊 **a** Look at the pictures. Compare the different aspects of summer shown. How do they make you feel?

b You've been asked to judge a competition called 'Summer'. Discuss which of the pictures best illustrates this and should win the competition.

c Imagine you are entering the competition. Discuss with your partner what other aspect(s) of summer your picture would show.

vocabulary
idioms

1 Complete 1–10 with one of these words, and explain the meanings of the idioms.

> bright   clouds   cold   dry   frosty   heat
> rain   rainy   season (x2)

1 Why don't you put that money in the bank and save it for a .... day?
2 I know we've lost every match so far, but rather than get depressed, let's look on the .... side.
3 My uncle has serious money problems but he's sure he's going to win the lottery; my aunt thinks he's got his head in the ....
4 I like to buy vegetables when they're fresh and in .... , rather than get frozen ones.
5 Ben was going to do a parachute jump, but at the last minute he got .... feet and decided to stay on the plane.
6 Easter, the summer months and Christmas are the high .... , when tickets cost a lot more.
7 Everyone got very angry, and in the .... of the moment Mark threatened to hit Colin.
8 The Socialist Party now have 49.9% of the votes, so they're nearly home and ....
9 When Mr Simms went to the bank to borrow yet more money, the manager gave him a .... reception.
10 Everybody else in the class had 'flu, but I felt as right as .... , and carried on going to lessons.

2 Complete the acrostic using these clues. The word they form vertically is something that is supposed to bring good luck.

1 How do you feel if you are right as rain?
2 Being very keen to do something is the .... of getting cold feet.
3 When you are home and dry, you have successfully .... the end.
4 When melons are in season.
5 People who save money for a rainy day don't .... it all at once.
6 It is more .... to go on holiday in high season.
7 If you do something in the heat of the moment, you do not .... about the consequences.
8 What you call somebody who looks on the bright side of life.
9 If you've got your head in the clouds you are not ....

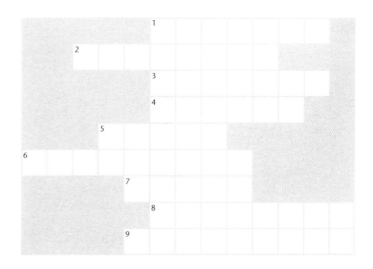

phrasal verbs

1 **a** Answer these 'weather' questions.
1 What happens when the sun *goes down*, and when it *goes in*?
2 When happens when it *comes up*, when it *comes out* and when it *beats down*?
3 Which of the above do you associate with *brighten up*, and which with *cloud over*?
4 What happens when rain *pours down*, and when it *eases off*?
5 Why might a river *dry up*, and when might it *fill up* again?
6 At what time of day does it *warm up*, and when does it *cool down*?
7 How do people feel when the heat *builds up*, and if it doesn't *let up*?
8 What is the difference between a lake that *freezes over*, and a pipe that *freezes up*?
9 What has happened if people have been *flooded out*, or if a sporting event has been *rained off*?
10 What do people on holiday do to *cool off*, and how do they *chill out*?

b Which of the verbs in **a** are intransitive, and which can take an object?

c In what circumstances do people *brighten up*, *ease off*, *dry up*, *warm up* and *cool down*?

key word transformations

1 Look at the three possible answers for each of 1–3. Which is correct?

1 The thugs only have themselves to blame for being sent to prison.
serves

It .... serves the thugs right that they have been / serves right the thugs that they have been / right serves the thugs that they have been .... sent to prison.

2 Your term work is good, but your exam marks could be better.
room

Although your term work is good, ... there is room for improvement by / there is room for improvement in / in the exam room you need improvement .... your exam marks.

3 Union leaders suddenly stopped negotiating with the bosses, and left angrily.
stormed

Unions leaders .... stormed out of the negotiations / stormed the negotiations out / stormed out negotiating .... with the bosses.

2 For questions **1–6** complete the second sentence so that it has a similar meaning to the first sentence, using the word given. **Do not change the word given**. You must use between **three** and **eight** words, including the word given.

1 A rock fell on his head and left him unconscious until several minutes later.
knocking
A rock fell on his head .... several minutes.

2 Some people will do absolutely anything to appear on television.
lengths
Some people .... appear on television.

3 There is a lot more sunshine than we expected.
turned
It .... than we expected.

4 You'd better watch out in case someone steals your purse.
eye
You'd better .... your purse in case someone steals it.

5 Using a mobile phone when you are driving is illegal.
law
It .... mobile phone when you are driving.

6 Nobody else had any money left so I had to pay for everyone's drinks.
foot
I had to .... because nobody else had any money left.

writing summary

1. What is hay fever? Do you know anyone who suffers from it? In which season do people in your country suffer from it most?

2. Read quickly through the text. Which parts of it deal with
   a the symptoms of hay fever?
   b ways of reducing its effects?
   c what causes it?

HAY FEVER

Hay fever is an allergy which makes part of each year a misery for millions of people in countries all over the world. It is brought on by breathing in pollen, which irritates the nose; and by pollen coming into contact
5 with the eyes, creating inflammation. You can get hay fever in any month from early spring to late autumn, as it depends on which of the many types of pollen you are allergic to. Those most likely to lead to problems are from grasses and trees – especially birch trees in
10 northern climates, and also olive trees in warmer countries. The condition tends to run in families.

Most sufferers sneeze frequently, and have a blocked-up sensation in the nose, which may also be runny. The eyes itch and water, and the throat or mouth may also
15 be irritated. Headaches are common, as is an inability to concentrate for any length of time, and there is a general feeling of being unwell (and often, not surprisingly, very unhappy).

There are many tablets, sprays and drops available to
20 treat hay fever, but it also helps if you can avoid too much potential contact with pollen. Begin by keeping an eye on the pollen count, and where possible don't go outside if it is high. Remember that in the pollen season, you can often follow the count in radio,
25 television and newspaper weather reports. Avoid opening doors and windows unnecessarily, above all first thing in the morning when pollen counts are usually at their highest.

If you really do have to go out, wear sunglasses to
30 stop pollen getting in your eyes, and keep out of areas like parks or fields, particularly in the early evening when there is a lot of pollen at ground level. The best time to be out of doors is following heavy rainfall. When driving, keep the windows closed and if you are
35 buying a car, ask your garage which ones are fitted with pollen filters. Finally, wear a hay-fever mask (available in pharmacies) if you need to do jobs in the garden like mowing the lawn. Better still, get someone else to do them!

3 Work out the meanings of these words and phrases by finding clues in the text.

misery (line 2) *brought on* (line 3) *condition* (line 11) *itch* (line 14)
keeping an eye on (line 21) *keep out of* (line 30) *mowing the lawn* (line 38)

4 Identify the key words in these instructions. Which parts of the text are relevant?

In a paragraph of between **50–70** words, summarise **in your own words as far as possible** the causes of hay fever and how it affects people's health, as described in the text.

5 Look at these two summaries. Summary A includes all the main points, but is too long. Summary B contains the same points but is within the word limit. Identify where each technique 1–7 below has been used.

A

Hay fever, which is often passed on from parent to child, occurs in the warmer months when pollen from plants and trees gets into the nose and into the eyes of people who are allergic to it. There is a wide variety of pollens, which means that people can be affected by it at any time except in the winter. Symptoms include sneezing, a blocked and runny nose, eyes that itch and are watery, an irritated throat or mouth, headaches, difficulty concentrating, and generally feeling rather ill.

B

Hay fever, which is often hereditary, occurs in the warmer months, when pollen gets into the nose and eyes of people allergic to it. There is a wide variety of pollens, meaning that hay fever can strike at any time except in winter. Symptoms include sneezing, a blocked and runny nose, itchy and watery eyes, an irritated throat or mouth, headaches, difficulty concentrating, and generally feeling ill.

1 Avoid repetition or unnecessary information wherever possible.
2 Use participle clauses instead of full clauses.
3 Leave out unnecessary articles.
4 Leave out unnecessary adverbs and adjectives.
5 Use the active not the passive where possible.
6 Use adjectives instead of relative clauses.
7 Don't use long explanations where one word can say the same thing.

6 **a** Read these instructions, identify the key words and decide which parts of the text are relevant.

In a paragraph of between **50–70** words, summarise **in your own words as far as possible** the ways that people who suffer from hay fever can reduce their exposure to pollen.

b Make notes on the relevant points, in your own words where you can.

c Write your summary, using techniques from **5** to make it as concise as possible.

review

1 Some of these sentences contain a mistake. Correct those that are wrong.

1 While we were walking in the forest, we came a small cottage across.
2 He set off, confident in his ability to find the way.
3 Why don't both of you try to cheer up?
4 After three days together, his patience ran finally out.
5 They carried for hours on the conversation.
6 You're going to have to deal the problem with sooner or later.

2 Complete 1–6 with a suitable pronoun and one of these particles.

off   up   for   out   down   on

1 She read the e-mail then printed ....
2 You might get a second chance, but don't count ....
3 That's a fantastic invention! I wonder who dreamt .... ?
4 If you read out the names and addresses, I'll note ....
5 We were hungry and thirsty, so when we saw the café we immediately headed ....
6 No matter how fast we ran from the dogs, we couldn't shake ....

3 Match words in column A to those in column B to form phrasal verbs with the meanings in column C.

A	B	C
1 cool		rain heavily
2 brighten	away	become solid ice
3 freeze	up	become less hot
4 ease	down	disappear slowly
5 thaw	off	become sunnier
6 melt	over	become unfrozen
7 pour	out	become less heavy

4 Correct the errors in these idioms.

1 Matt often says things in the rain of the moment and then regrets it later.
2 Gail had been planning to run in the city marathon, but I think she got frosty feet.
3 I know we're in a bit of trouble, but let's look on the dry side.
4 Since Paolo played so badly last month, he's been given a cold reception by his team mates.
5 Kat should be thinking about her interview tomorrow, but she's got her head in the sun.
6 Don't worry about your temperature. Take your medicine and you'll soon be as right as heat.

5 Find 22 words from this unit in the wordsquare and match them with the meanings below. The words can read in any direction, including backwards.

S	O	F	B	A	R	C	T	I	C	P	E	L	I
H	N	R	S	Y	G	R	E	L	L	A	M	E	N
U	V	O	T	R	G	N	I	H	C	R	O	C	S
Y	A	S	I	A	W	K	O	L	D	E	S	T	O
M	O	T	C	T	Z	E	K	E	L	J	S	P	M
A	E	Y	K	I	A	L	H	R	I	A	O	R	N
L	E	R	Y	D	E	S	A	B	E	L	L	P	I
A	K	T	O	E	D	A	N	U	L	V	B	E	A
T	S	E	V	R	A	H	G	E	O	M	I	L	D
I	N	J	I	E	F	I	N	R	P	U	S	H	A
T	H	A	W	H	T	G	Y	I	E	M	A	W	S
U	P	G	R	A	D	E	A	T	A	E	O	I	E
D	E	I	F	M	C	X	I	C	O	S	Y	C	S
E	T	A	N	R	E	B	I	H	C	H	I	L	L

1 extremely cold, with a thin layer of ice
2 when snow and ice melt
3 to change to a higher status
4 to sleep deeply through the winter
5 hot, damp uncomfortable weather
6 extreme tiredness
7 extremely cold
8 something that runs in the family
9 to irritate, so that you want to scratch
10 to make cooler
11 medical condition caused by a reaction to something
12 when trees produce flowers
13 small, warm and comfortable
14 money paid for harm caused
15 inability to sleep at night
16 to plant seeds in the ground
17 fine powder from flowers
18 extremely hot
19 to lose leaves, or get rid of
20 to lose colour
21 cutting or picking of crops
22 not very cold

vocabulary and speaking

1 Complete each sentence with the correct form of one of these phrasal verbs, and then discuss the answers to the questions with your partner.

> take part in   give up   take up   join in   bring out   catch on   take in

1 Do you like hobbies you can do on your own, or do you prefer to .... activities with other people?
2 a Which new hobbies and pastimes have .... recently, and why did they become so popular?
  b Are there any that you'd like to .... ? Is there anything that you regret not .... as a child?
3 Why might someone have to .... their favourite leisure activity? Have you ever had to .... any?
4 Which pastimes involve .... a lot of rules?
5 Do you agree that it's more important to .... something than to win?
6 Which sports do you think .... the worst in people? In what way? Why does this happen?

2 a The verbs in the box all describe gestures and actions. Which part of the body do you associate which each verb?

  b Take turns choosing verbs from the box. For each one, explain it to your partner. They must guess which word it is, asking you questions if they need to.

> nod   point   frown   sniff   stretch   clap   wink
> scratch   shrug   hug   chew   pinch   stare   whistle

  c Which of the verbs in the box can also be used as nouns?

  d Which adverbs are often used with the verbs in the box (e.g. *chew noisily*)?

  e In your country, are any of these actions and gestures not acceptable in public?

3 a Explain the differences between these pairs of words.
  1 *characteristics* and *quirks*
  2 *eccentricities* and *superstitions*
  3 *habits* and *obsessions*
  4 *temptations* and *compulsions*

  b Match sentences 1–8 with one of the eight words in **a**.
  1 Carmen always goes to bed before 11 p.m.
  2 James Martin is a multi-millionaire, but he lives in an old caravan.
  3 My aunt believes breaking a mirror brings seven years' bad luck.
  4 Raymond can't stop thinking about football.
  5 I nearly bought a bottle of champagne even though I knew I couldn't afford it.
  6 Some people talk more softly than others.
  7 When he's nervous, my father always straightens his tie.
  8 Felicity feels she has to brush her hair every few minutes.

talking points

1 What temptations do you find hard to resist?
2 Give some examples of 'bad habits'. Which are the most difficult habits to stop? Why? What suggestions do you have for people who want to stop?
3 Which bad habits most annoy you in other people? What good habits would you like to have?

reading gapped text:
lexical and grammatical links (2)

1 **a** What type of things do people collect? Do you collect anything? Have you heard of any strange collections? Why do you think people collect those things? Have you ever collected anything like that?

b Read quickly through the gapped text and missing paragraphs and note down all the kinds of collections mentioned. Are any the same as you thought of in **a**?

2 **a** A well-written text has good linking between clauses, sentences and paragraphs, and it avoids unnecessary repetition. Parts of a sentence can be replaced or left out without changing the meaning. Study the text and decide what these words replace:
do (line 2); *do so* (line 27); *not* (line 50); *one* (lines 51 and 52); *so is she* (line 56); *doing so* (line 73); *so* (line 80).

What has the writer left out before or after these expressions?
mean to (line 2); *16th* (line 21); *put on* (line 34)

b Choose from the paragraphs **A–G** the one that fits each gap (**1–6**). There is one extra paragraph which you do not need to use.

Use these questions as clues:
What has been omitted after *Pete Kelly's* (line 13) and *Karen Salt's* (line 53)?
What do *ones* (line 23), *does* (line 53) and *do so* (line 59) substitute?

c Which paragraphs did you fit into the text by recognising that words had been replaced or left out? How did you do the others?

YOU ARE WHAT YOU KEEP

You are the collector in the gallery of your life. You collect. You might not mean to but you do. It might be owls or pussycats, photos or fluff or funny facts. It might be monsters, mice or men. One person in three, it is estimated, collects tangible things. Cliff
5 Pearcy collects 'noisy toys'. Roy Reed collects comics. Jane Reynolds collects snails. Dave Swift has amassed a collection of monsters worth £25,000.

> **1**

Some of the collections that have been put together are fairly common – records, model houses. Others are strangely beautiful
10 – branches that have fallen from trees, for instance. But they all reveal an enormous amount: ask someone what they collect and their answer will tell you who they are.

> **2**

Pete Kelly's consists of 'anything'. Sometimes he makes a collection of objects, arranges them and then leaves them in parks
15 for other people to find – a gesture of gentle generosity. He has a collection of classified ads (like 'Pigs For Sale') which he leaves between packets of cheese in supermarkets.

> **3**

Tim Miller has been collecting objects found from London's river banks since he was nine, and he can tell you how many
20 centimetres you need to dig to reach certain periods of the past. 25 cm is early 19th century. 90 cm is 16th. The past is always underground.

> **4**

These new ones, it is hoped, will build on the success of 'The Museum Of', which is dedicated to exploring what museums are
25 for, and the relationship between people and museums. The thinkers behind the project want to explore why people collect, and what it means to do so. They hope that visitors who may not have considered themselves collectors will begin to see that they, too, collect.

> **5**

30 Most of them, however, agree that women tend to collect in a partially functional way. For example, Jane Reynolds, president of the Conchological Society, combines a strong academic interest in snails with a collection of snail postcards, jewellery, toys, or clothes with snails on – but she will also wear the clothes, put on
35 the jewellery.

> **6**

Some collectors say they started or stopped making collections at crux points: the beginning or end of adolescence – 'it's a growing-up thing; you stop when you grow up' says one. Other traumatic times are mentioned, such as the end of a relationship. For time –
40 and life – can seem so uncontrollable that a steady serial arrangement is comforting. Crucially, by embodying the past in a collection you can refuse to accept that the past is gone, so childhood need never be over, loss need not be loss.

A Male collectors, meanwhile, tend to segregate the
45 collection and its function. Daragh Reeves, the 'can man',
has collected 1,500 drinks cans, but they are unopened.

B Depressed by this, he revisited his childhood home and
found the remnants of his collection. There is no
alternative, he feels, to restocking it with every single item
50 it once contained. If not, there will always be two
collections for him: the present, tangible one and the past,
intangible one – the memory of his childhood collection.

C Karen Salt's certainly does. She collects teddy bears and is
round-faced and cuddly. Sophie Jones collects miniature
55 coloured glasses. Why? 'I like them because they're small.'
Being only seven, so is she. She also wears round, well-
polished spectacles which reflect the glasses in her
collection.

D For the urge to do so is almost universal, though there are
60 many types of collecting. Some experts say that there is a
strand of 'consumer collecting', which happens in direct
response to advertising and marketing strategies. Others
say it is a residue of the hunter-gatherer mindset, an
appetite.

65 **E** Some of his discoveries will no doubt find their way into
the planned 'Museum of the River Thames'. Others on the
way include 'The Museum of Collectors', 'The Museum of
the Unknown', 'The Museum of Emotions', and 'The
Museum of Me'.

70 **F** These are among some 40 collections that are being shown
at 'The Museum Of' – the first of a series of temporary
museums which, over the next two years, will celebrate the
collections of ordinary people. In doing so, they will
legitimise a popular culture of museums, not the high-
75 culture, expert-led authoritas that museums normally
represent.

G 'It's to do with the absurdity of life. It would give me
pleasure to find something like that and I hope it gives
others that pleasure. Maybe it will cause someone to
80 remember or recollect something. If so, it has succeeded.'
For 'collections' are intimate with 're-collections';
museums and memory are close. The word 'museum' is
from 'seat of the Muses' and the nine Muses were originally
goddesses of memory.

3 What do these words refer to?
it (lines 2 and 3); *they* (line 12); *they* (line 27); *them*
(line 30); *his* (line 65); *these* (line 70); *that* (line 78)

4 1 Explain these expressions from the text:
gesture (line 15); *it's a growing-up thing* (line 37);
be over (line 43); *mindset* (line 63); *on the way* (line
66); *it's to do with* (line 77).
2 Think of synonyms for these words: *amass* (line 6),
reveal (line 11), *segregate* (line 44).
3 Find two words in the last paragraph of the main text
that indicate 'importance'.
4 Find two words in paragraphs B and D that mean
'what is left'.

5 1 What is your opinion of the collections mentioned in
the text, and the people who collect them?
2 Do you agree with what the text says about the
following? Why/Why not?
  • What collections tell us about the collectors.
  • Why people collect.
  • The difference between female and male
    collectors.
  • The nature of traditional museums.
3 What would you put in each of these museums?
  • *The Museum of the Unknown*
  • *The Museum of Emotions*
  • *The Museum of Me*
4 What other kinds of museum would you like to see?

grammar
introductory *It*

 a Look at these four examples. Which form in each pair is less formal?

> **EXAMPLES** *To live in Rio de Janeiro must be very exciting.*
> *It must be very exciting to live in Rio de Janeiro.*
>
> *That anyone can believe his story is astonishing.*
> *It is astonishing that anyone can believe his story.*

We often begin complex sentences with *It* instead of using the infinitive or *That, Why, Where, What,* etc.

In written English we do not normally replace a noun in this way.

> *The extra room will be very useful.*
> ~~It will be very useful the extra room.~~

b Rewrite sentences 1–6 so that they begin with *It*.
1 To work all weekend isn't much fun.
2 That everyone survived is a great relief.
3 To meet your sister at the airport was quite a surprise.
4 When the election will actually take place is uncertain.
5 Why her husband disappeared has never been satisfactorily explained.
6 To cross the Himalayas in a balloon would be an incredible experience.

c Complete these sentences with your own ideas. Continue with one of these words – try to use each one once.

> | that | to | where | why | what | when |

> **EXAMPLE** It was very exciting *to meet my cousin from Australia for the first time.*

1 It wasn't clear …
2 It's sometimes not easy …
3 It was a huge relief …
4 It's a complete mystery …
5 It's hard to decide …
6 It's really irritating …

emphatic *It*

 a We can use *It* to emphasise part of a sentence. What is being emphasised in 1–4?
1 It was at seven in the morning that we finally went home.
2 It was the fog that caused the accident.
3 It's the money that's most important to me in a job.
4 It's not the building that makes their house so attractive, it's the garden.

b Begin these sentences with *It* to emphasise the underlined words.
1 Compulsory military service in Britain was phased out <u>in the 1960s</u>.
2 <u>Carol</u> crossed the finishing line first.
3 The murder took place <u>outside the nightclub</u>.
4 Jenny decided to buy <u>the light green blouse</u> in the end.
5 <u>A person's appearance</u> isn't the most important thing.
6 My brother loves collecting <u>old vinyl records</u>, not CDs.
7 She's not going out with <u>Simon</u>, she's going out with Robbie.
8 A cure for the disease was discovered <u>only after years of research</u>.

emphatic *What* and *All*

 a We can also use *What …* or *All …* for emphasis. In the examples which word means 'The thing that', and which means 'The only thing that'?

> *What I like most is lying on the beach in summer.*
> *All we have left is a few drops of water.*

b Rewrite these sentences so they begin *What* or *All*.
1 I strongly believe the death penalty is wrong in any circumstances.
2 I'm only asking for a few pounds until Friday.
3 I really want to visit lots of interesting countries.
4 I don't understand why some people are so cruel.
5 The only thing I could say was 'I'm sorry'.
6 Staying in bed late on Saturday morning is something I really enjoy.

c Choose one of the categories below and write six sentences using emphatic *It, What* and *All*. Include some negatives and *want, need, most enjoy, really like, hate, can't stand,* etc.

> hobbies and sports   film and TV   food and drink
> clothes and fashion   everyday routine   the arts

---

common errors

The thing what I like most is staying in bed all morning.
What is wrong with this sentence? Why?

sentence adverbs

1 Read the explanation then do **a** and **b** below.

> We can begin a sentence with an adverb (or adverbial phrase) to give emphasis, often when giving our own opinion about something.
>
> *Wisely*, my parents have always saved some money for the future.
> *Surprisingly*, many people name the Prime Minister as their favourite politician.

a Rewrite each of 1–7 with one of these adverbs. There's one you don't need to use.

> admittedly   theoretically   apparently   typically
> unfortunately   generally   ~~oddly~~   astonishingly
> coincidentally

EXAMPLE There was nobody there when I opened the door, which was strange.
Oddly there was nobody there when I opened the door.

1 In most cases, people in our country retire at age 65.
2 I've left all my homework at home, which is a pity.
3 Her last record sold a million copies in a month, which was amazing.
4 He invited us out for a drink but then said he had no money, which is the kind of thing he often does.
5 They obtained all the cash quite legally, it would seem.
6 I must confess that I had already seen the questions, but the answers still weren't easy.
7 The new law is supposed to mean there will be fewer cars on the city's roads.

b Look at the pictures below. Use a variety of sentence adverbs to tell the two stories.

open cloze

1 Read the text through quickly and explain the two meanings of the title.

2 Choose the correct alternative for 1–15 by studying the context of the missing words. Is the other option wrong because **a** it does not fit grammatically? **b** it fits the gap but not the overall meaning?

> **EXAMPLE** *as (like does not collocate with 'describe')*: **a**

> **exam factfile**
>
> In the open cloze you are not given a choice of words; you have to think of the missing word yourself.

ANTI-STRESS ROOM IS A SMASH HIT

When Mr Watanabe, who describes himself *as/like* an ordinary Japanese businessman, and three of his female colleagues entered the stress-relief room it (**1**) *resembled/looked* like a tidy antiques shop with gilt-framed paintings, an elaborately decorated screen, (**2**) *and/or* statuettes and an ornate vase.

Two hours later, (**3**) *although/however*, Mr Watanabe and friends left the place looking as (**4**) *if/when* it had been hit by a typhoon. The pictures were torn, the screen, statuettes and table broken, and pieces of the vase scattered all (**5**) *above/over* the floor.

(**6**) *There/It* was in July last year that the stress-relief room was (**7**) *set/smashed* up by Yoshie Ogasawara. (**8**) *All/Everything* you have to pay is 10,000 yen (about £50) and you get the use of the room for two hours. (**9**) *This/These* will include as much beer as you can drink, as many karaoke songs as you can sing and as (**10**) *little/much* damage as you can do.

'Everyone gets stressed out occasionally,' Ms Ogasawara explained, 'but perhaps especially (**11**) *so/because* in Japan. (**12**) *What/That* happens here is that people are expected to keep up appearances. This room is a way for them to let off steam.' It is not (**13**) *common/uncommon* to hear middle-ranking managers screaming abuse at their seniors (**14**) *during/while* smashing the room. One customer wrote to Ms Ogasawara after what (**15**) *should/must* have been a particularly satisfying smashing session: 'I can't thank you enough. You have made me look at things in a new light.'

listening multiple choice: inference

EXAM FOCUS

paper 4 part 3 multiple choice

In Listening Part 3, you hear a single dialogue and have to answer five multiple-choice questions about it. Each question has four options, which may either complete a sentence stem or answer a direct question. Questions may test your comprehension of gist, detail and opinion.

- Before you listen, look at the instructions and the five questions or sentence stems. Think about the topic and what you are likely to hear.
- Don't worry if there are some words you don't recognise. They may not be necessary for overall understanding, or they could be in a part of the text that is not actually tested.
- Don't stop listening as you write your answers. Write them in pencil as you might want to change them the second time you listen.
- If you're not sure of an answer, put a line through any impossible or unlikely ones. Choose one of those that remain by guessing.

exam factfile

In Listening, some answers may come from implied information: information that is not stated directly.

1 a 🔊 Listen to the first part of the recording. What is Obsessive–Compulsive Disorder?

What happened as a result of his obsession with cleaning?
A His wife left him.
B He lost his home.
C He lost his job.
D He asked for help.

b 🔊 You will hear an interview with Christopher Blair, a clinical psychologist who specialises in Obsessive–Compulsive Disorder (OCD). For questions 1–5, choose the answer (A, B, C or D) which fits best according to what you hear.

1 What kind of action is 'touching wood'?
A a superstition
B a compulsion
C a habit
D a sign of nervousness `1`

2 What would some people do next if they failed to comb their hair twice?
A get out of bed again
B brush their teeth again
C have another shower
D re-check their appearance `2`

3 What does Dr Blair imply about OCD sufferers?
A They should not be ashamed of having the condition.
B They are often unaware that they have the condition.
C They should recognise they are likely to fail in their careers.
D The causes of their condition are entirely genetic. `3`

4 What is the interviewer's position?
A She doesn't understand OCD.
B She finds OCD alarming.
C She doesn't take OCD seriously.
D She has suffered from OCD herself. `4`

5 What is Dr Blair's attitude towards 'self-help' as a treatment for OCD?
A open-minded
B sceptical
C enthusiastic
D dismissive `5`

2 Are you superstitious? What about? What superstitions are common in your country? Is there anything wrong with being superstitious?

speaking   finding the right word

1 When we are talking, as native speakers or learners, we are sometimes unable to think of exactly the expression we need. Look at these three common ways of getting round the problem.

1 We use an explanatory phrase: *It's a place where …/*
It's a thing for (+ ing) …/It's someone who … .

2 We paraphrase by using a more general term: *You need the right equipment.*

3 We ask the listener for help: *What's the word for … ?*

2 a 🔊 With a partner, look at all three pictures. Imagine that an international magazine is going to publish a special edition on what today's young people do in their spare time. You have to decide which photo best illustrates this topic. Before you begin, study the example on page 153 and underline the parts of the dialogue where the speakers get round the problem of not knowing the right word or expression.

b What would you say if you didn't know the word for 'volume'?

3 🔊 Suggest three other scenes that would depict typical free-time activities of many young people. Then choose one for the same magazine in **2**, using the techniques in **1** where necessary.

vocabulary
phrasal verbs

1 Read the explanation then identify the phrasal verbs in 1–10 below and explain their meaning.

> Three-part phrasal verbs, e.g. *grow out of* are normally found in informal language. They consist of a base verb (*grow*), an adverb particle (*out*) and a preposition (*of*).
>
> In most cases the preposition is followed by its own object, e.g. *she soon grew out of* **the habit**. A few, however, have a direct object right after the verb, e.g. *I talked* **my friend Susana** *out of leaving school*. Any pronoun must be in the same position: *she soon grew out of* **it**; *I talked* **her** *out of leaving school*.

1 I know I eat too much, but I am trying to cut down on chocolate, at least.

2 Young children often go in for the same hobbies as their parents.

3 Experts put Janet's emotional difficulties down to a trauma she suffered as a child.

4 Do you get on well with your parents, or do you have a lot of arguments?

5 Some of the oldest items in Tim's collection date back to the fifteenth century.

6 If you give in to the temptation to buy everything you fancy, you'll soon have no money left.

7 If you think someone is suffering from stress, look out for signs such as severely bitten fingernails.

8 I'm afraid you've just got to face up to the fact that you're addicted to alcohol, Mr Stevens.

9 Nobody has come up with an infallible solution to the problem of compulsive behaviour.

10 You don't know what you're letting yourself in for by accepting that job offer.

2 Complete sentences 1–10 with the correct forms of the phrasal verbs from **1**.

1 After months of denying he was ill, Paul finally .... reality and sought medical help.

2 Angela .... the brilliant idea of going on holiday in a place which caters for all our different hobbies.

3 My sister managed to avoid biting her nails for a whole month, but just before her exams she finally .... temptation and started again.

4 I'm trying to .... the amount of time I waste watching rubbish on TV.

5 At first I .... her unwillingness to talk .... boredom, but then I realised she was extremely nervous.

6 Eccentrics who live alone often find it hard to .... other people.

7 I have never .... sport; I don't even like watching it on TV.

8 Dorothy's psychological problems .... when she used to live with Gary.

9 I soon found out what I'd .... myself .... when the course actually began.

10 Whenever I go to the street market, I always .... any really old records to add to my collection.

3 Form ten verbs with these meanings by choosing one word from each column in the box.

EXAMPLE to escape – *get away from*

1 to abolish
2 to respect
3 to have no respect for
4 to support someone
5 to escape punishment for
6 to be involved in something
7 to reach the same level as
8 to work on something you are behind with
9 to find time to do something
10 to start doing something that needs concentration

catch	down	to
do	up	for
get	forward	on
look	round	with
stick	away	from

collocations: adverb + adjective

1 In each of 1–12, form an adverb + adjective collocation by choosing from this list, and then complete the sentences below to illustrate the meanings.

> little   deeply   violently   hilariously   casually
> densely   currently   excruciatingly   wildly   theoretically
> ~~fully~~   prohibitively   universally

EXAMPLE I think young people are .fully. justified in *wanting to lead more independent lives.*

1 The most .... populated region of my country is …
2 It is .... expensive to shop in …
3 I find it .... irritating when …
4 I prefer to be .... dressed when I …
5 It is .... painful when you …
6 Some people in my country are .... opposed to …
7 It's .... inaccurate to say that …
8 To be .... popular, a book or film must …
9 It's a(n) .... -known fact that …
10 The most .... funny thing I've ever seen is when …
11 In my country, it is .... fashionable to …
12 Although it's difficult in practice, it is .... possible to …

2 **a** Match the adverbs on the left with the adjectives on the right to form collocations.

acutely	ashamed
bitterly	astonished
enormously	disappointed
insanely	embarrassed
thoroughly	jealous
utterly	impressed

b For each picture, write a sentence using one of the collocations from **a**.

gapped sentences

1 In 1–4 think of another meaning for the word. In 5–8, think of two meanings. Remember not to change the form or part of speech of the word.
1 capital – noun (*city, letter*)
2 add – verb (*increase amount, say something else*)
3 pass – verb (*give to somebody, go past*)
4 poor – adjective (*having little money, less than expected*)
5 free – adjective (*not occupied*)
6 set – noun (*furniture and scenery in a play*)
7 beat – verb (*mix quickly*)
8 position – noun (*how well you do in a race*)

2 Think of one word that fits both sentences. Then write a sentence of your own with a different meaning of exactly the same word.

EXAMPLE Everyone at the hospital ...looked. terribly anxious as they waited for news of their relatives.
When we were children I admired my elder brother, while Anna ...looked. up to Janet, our elder sister.
As soon as I got up in the morning I looked everywhere for my purse, but I still couldn't find it.

1 When Jack realised he had won the lottery, he was so excited that he went .... at the knees.
Channel 3's new comedy programme is notable only for its extremely poor acting and very .... jokes.

2 Those tourists don't look adequately .... for the long hard walk to the top of the mountain.
Your mother and I are simply not .... to put up with this kind of behaviour any longer, Kevin.

3 The maximum speed of the car is .... to 250 kph.
His ambitions in life seem to be .... to working as little as possible and socialising as much as possible.

writing 'for & against' essays

1 Read this advice for writing a 'for and against' essay, and give a reason for each piece of advice.

EXAMPLE Open with a general statement about the subject.
This will introduce both the topic and the text type.

1 Develop each argument you have presented.
2 Avoid using contracted forms (like *isn't*) and conversational expressions.
3 Don't repeat words and phrases from the instructions too often.
4 Try to avoid using 'I think …' or 'In my opinion …', at least until the last paragraph.
5 Good linking of sentences and paragraphs is particularly important in this kind of text.
6 Close by summing up, and possibly also giving your own opinion.

2 **a** Read these instructions and the text extract. What is the main argument of the text? Which other points from it do you need to discuss?

You have read this extract from a text in an English coursebook. Write an essay (300–350 words) for your tutor, giving arguments for and against the opinion it expresses.

Today's global society is making all of us more and more alike. Increasingly, the way we look and act is almost indistinguishable from that of our fellow citizens. 'Individuals' as we used to know them are fast becoming an endangered species as governments and big businesses do their best to replace them with standardised human beings who think, do and buy whatever they are told to.

b Read quickly through the model essay and note down which main points are made and where, as in the example.

FOR	AGAINST
similar clothes everywhere	
(2nd paragraph)	

3 **a** Underline the main linking expressions in the model essay, and think of an alternative for each one.

EXAMPLE Firstly – *To begin with*

b Find examples in the essay of these punctuation marks and explain their use in each case. What other uses can they have?

EXAMPLE apostrophe: *use in paragraph 1 – possessive; other use – to indicate missing letter(s).*

brackets (paragraph 6)
hyphen (twice in paragraph 4)
colon (paragraphs 3 and 6)
semi-colon (paragraphs 1, 2 and 4)
quotation marks (paragraphs 2 and 3)

In many ways, the world is getting smaller. Vastly improved global communications quickly spread new ideas, with immediate impact on people's lifestyles everywhere. Some would claim that this is destroying true individualism; others that it is creating a much more diverse population.

Firstly, people are starting to look almost identical. Everyone wears the same 'uniform' of baseball cap, T-shirt, jeans and designer trainers; or else slavishly follows the latest fashion as advertised on global TV stations, and reinforced by the selling power of multinational clothes manufacturers and retailers. In the same way, they play the same video games, listen to the same bland music and go in for the same leisure activities as countless millions of others around the world.

What is even more alarming, however, is the way that government and large organisations are attacking individuality. Politicians and employers are united in their suspicion of those who are 'different': the nonconformists, the free spirits, the eccentrics. Consequently, there are new laws limiting people's freedom of action, CCTV surveillance cameras and intrusive company rules that apply even outside working hours.

Conversely, many would argue it is exactly these kinds of pressure that are encouraging growing numbers of people to get away from the over-regulation and enforced conformity of mainstream society. Millions are taking charge of their own lives by becoming self-employed; others are adopting alternative lifestyles, for instance as travellers, or radical greens.

Furthermore, young people nowadays feel much freer to live as they wish, and far less constrained by traditional attitudes to gender, age, class and so forth. They are also a lot more mobile, able if necessary to leave small villages or towns and seek independence in big cities, or even abroad. There they find a huge range of fashions, music and things to do that enable them to express their individuality in an infinite variety of ways.

To sum up, there are two opposing trends: the increasing power of the state, the corporations and the media to control individuals' lives, and the rapid growth of new ways of living that allow people to be themselves. Fortunately, the stronger the big organisations become, the more the young (especially) will assert their independence and individuality.

4 **a** Choose either the task in **2a**, or this one:

Read this text and write an essay for your tutor giving arguments for and against the point of view it contains.

> Life is becoming more and more stressful. Whether we are at school, university or work, there is growing pressure on us to increase our efforts, to succeed, to outdo others. We are also feeling the strain in the little spare time we are allowed, as leisure activities become ever more intense and often more competitive.

Think about the following when planning your ideas:
- What general comment could you make about stress in the 21st century to introduce the topic?
- How can school or work be stressful?
- Why do you think there is growing pressure on us to increase our efforts?
- In what other ways can leisure activities be stressful? What are the positive effects of leisure activities?
- What other examples can you give of how life is (or isn't) stressful?

b 1 Note down as many arguments as you can think of, so that you have roughly the same number of points on both sides. Try to understand all these points of view: this will make your writing more convincing.
  2 Group all the points on one side or the other, and put them in a logical order. Note down the reasons and/or examples you will use.
  3 Decide how you will organise your essay into paragraphs, and what your conclusion will be.
  4 Write your essay, bearing in mind points 1–6 in **1**.

● THERE IS ANOTHER MODEL 'FOR AND AGAINST' ESSAY ON PAGE 165 IN THE WRITING BANK

review

1 Emphasise the underlined words by rewriting these sentences twice: once beginning with emphatic *It*, and once with emphatic *What*.

> **EXAMPLE** <u>The cost</u> of the treatment puts me off.
> *It's the cost of the treatment that puts me off.*
> *What puts me off is the cost of the treatment.*

1 The amount of time you waste <u>is terrible</u>.
2 She needs <u>a good holiday</u> more than anything else.
3 To find buried treasure <u>must be a wonderful feeling</u>.
4 Giving up smoking <u>can be very difficult</u>.
5 That Sylvia soon felt better <u>came as no surprise</u>.
6 His angry response to the question <u>wasn't expected</u>.
7 Why she left so suddenly <u>wasn't clear</u>.
8 Moving house would be <u>an excellent idea</u>.

2 Complete 1–6 with one of these adverbs.

> Apparently   Typically   Wisely   Oddly
> Unfortunately   Coincidentally

1 .... just as I was about to sell my bike, it was stolen.
2 .... shop work is not very well paid.
3 I decided to phone my best friend. .... , just at that moment she rang me.
4 He was absent on the day of the test. .... , he was ill, although I had my doubts.
5 I heard voices in the room. .... , when I opened the door there was no one there.
6 The workmen found an unexploded bomb while they were digging. .... , they didn't touch it.

3 Complete the collocations from this unit by putting an adjective into each gap.

> **EXAMPLE** The Manchester United players were confident they would beat Real Madrid, and were bitterly ...disappointed... when they lost.

1 A lot of men no longer wear suits and now go to work much more casually ....
2 Phil was acutely .... when his mother showed his girlfriend photos of him taken when he was a baby.
3 I trapped my fingernail in the door and it was excruciatingly .... for hours.
4 Look what a terrible mess you children have made! You should be thoroughly .... of yourselves!
5 A lot of people thought it was hilariously .... when a Hollywood star fell flat on his face, but he wasn't laughing.
6 Judy suddenly felt insanely .... when she saw her ex-boyfriend out with someone else.

4 Use clues 1–20 to complete the puzzle with two-part and three-part phrasal verbs.
Which adverb + adjective collocation do the letters down spell?

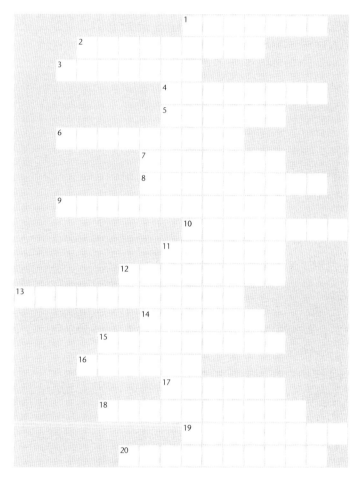

1 to become popular
2 to become too old or big for
3 to have as a hobby
4 to make something appear
5 to maintain
6 to attribute to
7 to be involved in something
8 to persuade not to do
9 to escape from
10 to accept facts or responsibilities
11 to understand or remember information
12 to stop doing/using over a period of time
13 to assemble
14 to take part in
15 to reduce consumption of
16 to allow to be defeated
17 to start doing a hobby
18 to exist since
19 to admire
20 to have an idea or find a solution

unit 11 | hazards

vocabulary and speaking

1 Look at this 'stress scale'. Is there anything you find surprising? Where on the scale would you place these events?

starting a new job
trouble with boss or headteacher
complete change of image (dress / hairstyle, etc.)
moving house
breaking up with a girlfriend / boyfriend

2 **a** Use some of these expressions to talk about the pictures.

> stressful alarming perilous fraught with danger
> hazardous catastrophic nerve-racking intimidating

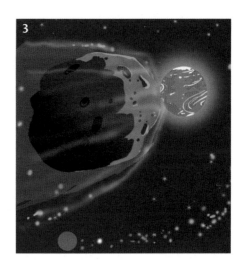

b Say how you would feel in each situation, using as many different adjectives as you can.

3 Imagine these situations.
- You have been wrongly accused of something.
- You have lost your purse or wallet with a large sum of money in it.
- You are going for a job interview.
- You are alone on the streets of a foreign city at night.
- You have suddenly received some very bad news.
- You have agreed to go on a blind date.

In which might you feel *uneasy, apprehensive, dismayed, vulnerable* or *petrified*?
When might you have *misgivings* or *butterflies*?
Which could make you *panic*?
In which would you feel *unconcerned, indignant* or *resentful*?

4 **a** Which of these adjectives do we use for people who take risks, and which for people who don't?

> cautious wary bold cowardly daring impetuous prudent
> rash adventurous faint-hearted reckless

b Which of them have positive connotations, and which have negative ones?

reading multiple choice: focusing on stems

EXAM FOCUS

paper 1 part 4 multiple choice

The last part of Reading is a single text followed by seven multiple-choice questions. The text types, question types and focus of the questions are the same as in Reading Part 2 but the text itself is longer.

- If a question focuses on an individual word, ensure you look at its meaning in context.
- Don't choose an option just because it makes a statement that you agree with, or believe to be true.
- Be careful with options that use the same language (especially unusual expressions) as that in the text.

exam factfile

The questions in Reading Part 4 always follow the order of the information in the text, with the exception of global questions, which are normally at the end.

1 Read quickly through the text and decide what its purpose is. What common theme do the five sections share? Which of these adjectives would you use to describe the tone of the text?

alarmist   light-hearted   down-to-earth   hysterical   defeatist   naive

2 **a** Read the text carefully, and answer these questions in your own words. You may want to give more than one answer in some cases.

1 Which word in the title or introduction is used ironically?
2 What will happen if you land using a companion's parachute?
3 What should you do if your car breaks down in the desert and you have little water?
4 What should you do if you are attacked by killer bees?
5 What should you do to escape from a black bear?

b Study the five multiple-choice questions on page 154. Decide which of A, B, C or D is closest to your answer(s) in each case.

HOW TO *wrestle* AN ALLIGATOR

(and practical ways to deal with those other everyday disasters)

Suppose you are trapped in the jaws of a hungry crocodile. You struggle frantically but the pain is excruciating and the enormous reptile doesn't want to let you go.

5 Don't despair, a new guide tells us what to do in this and other 'worst-case scenarios'.

HOW TO WRESTLE FREE FROM AN ALLIGATOR

You are most likely to encounter an alligator in Florida. In Africa and Australia, it will be a crocodile – but the way to escape is
10 the same in either case. Nile crocodiles kill hundreds of people a year, but death by alligator is rarer.

If you are on land, try to get on the creature's back and put downward pressure on its neck. This will force its head and jaws down. Then cover its eyes; that should calm it down. In
15 fact, always go for the eyes and nose, using any weapon you have, or your fist. If the jaws close on your leg or arm, tap or punch the creature on the snout. Alligators often open their mouths when tapped lightly – sometimes dropping what they've taken hold of – and back away.

20 But if the alligator has you firmly in its jaws, you must prevent it from shaking you or from rolling over – these instinctive actions will cause severe tissue damage. Try to keep its mouth clamped shut so it does not begin shaking.

And when – or rather if – you get free, seek medical help
25 immediately: alligators have a lot of unhygienic bacteria in their mouths.

HOW TO SURVIVE IF YOUR PARACHUTE FAILS

The good news is that modern parachutes are built to open, even if there have been mistakes in packing them. However, if
30 even your reserve chute fails, signal to a companion whose chute has not yet opened. Wave your arms and point to your chute. When your companion (and new best friend) gets to you, hook arms. The two of you will be falling at terminal velocity, about 200 kph, and when your friend opens his or her chute
35 neither of you will be able to hold on because the G-forces will triple or quadruple body weight. To prepare, hook your arms into the other person's chest strap all the way up to your elbows, and grab hold of your own strap to link you securely. When the chute opens, the shock will probably dislocate or
40 break your arms. Your friend must try to hold you with one arm while steering with the other. If his or her canopy is big, you may hit the ground slowly enough to break only a leg and your chances of survival are high.

HOW TO SURVIVE IF LOST IN THE DESERT

45 Walk slowly to conserve energy. No matter how hot it is, wear long-sleeved clothing – it reduces sweating and water loss. Don't panic, especially if people know where you are and when you were due back. If you have a vehicle, remain with it – do not wander. If you are on foot, try retracing your steps. Always
50 move down-country. Travel along ridges instead of in valleys; you'll be seen more easily. (If you are not *absolutely* sure you can retrace your route, stay put.) When walking, rest for ten minutes every hour. Drink water; don't ration it. Avoid talking and smoking. Breathe through your nose, not your mouth.
55 Avoid eating if there is not a lot of water – digestion consumes water. Newspaper or tinfoil laid out in a triangle is an international signal of distress. So are three shots from a gun or blasts from a whistle.

HOW TO ESCAPE FROM KILLER BEES

60 A killer bee is a hybrid strain between African bees and honeybees. Accidentally introduced to America ten years ago, they have been
65 spreading ever since. They are much more aggressive bees. They attack en masse, and are a danger even to those who are not allergic to bee stings –
70 horses and people have been stung to death. Normal honeybees will chase you for about 50 metres, but killer bees will chase you three
75 times that distance. Speed is of the essence. If bees begin
flying around and / or attacking you, put as much distance as you can between you and them; swatting only makes them more angry. Get inside as fast as possible; if no shelter is
80 available, keep running – through bushes or high weeds if there are any. A bee will leave its sting in your skin. Remove it by raking your finger-nail across it in a sideways motion. Do not pinch or pull it out – this may squeeze more poison into your body. If you try to take refuge by diving into a swimming pool,
85 river or lake, the bees are likely to be waiting for you when you surface.

HOW TO ESCAPE FROM A BEAR

If you are walking in bear country and see a bear in the distance, make your presence known by talking loudly,
90 clapping, singing or occasionally calling out. Or wear bells that chime as you walk. Whatever you do, be heard – it does not pay to surprise a bear. Avoid hiking with dogs; they often antagonise bears and trigger an attack. An unleashed dog may even lead a bear back to you. If you are attacked, lie still and
95 be quiet. An attack by a mother black bear often ends when she thinks she has killed the victim. If that doesn't work, fight back with anything you can. Go for the eyes or the snout. Do not attempt to climb a tree to escape. Bears climb faster and better than you. If you are in a car, stay in it – though bears are
100 extremely strong and can tear a car apart looking for food.

3 Answer these questions.
1 Why is it sometimes safer to be held tightly in an alligator's jaws?
2 Why would it be important that your companion's parachute had not yet opened?
3 Why would your companion be your 'new best friend'?
4 Why would you damage your arms when the parachute opened?
5 Why do you think you shouldn't breathe through your mouth in the desert?
6 Why do you think you should run through bushes if killer bees are chasing you?
7 How safe are you from a bear attack in your car?

4 Which of the five situations in the reading text would you find most alarming? Is there anything else you would try to do?

grammar
modals: present and past forms

1 Which of these modals can be used, in which forms, to express functions 1–9?

EXAMPLE deduction *can't be/have been, could/couldn't be, could/couldn't have been, must be/have been.*

> can   could   may   might   must   ought to
> shall   should   will   would

1 ability
2 giving permission
3 making an offer
4 prohibition
5 prediction
6 making a request
7 possibility
8 obligation
9 giving advice

2 **a** Correct the mistake in each of a–h, and match the sentences with rules 1–9.

EXAMPLE They may waiting for us.
They may be waiting for us – rule 5.

a We must write in ink, must not we?
b You don't ought to stand so near the fire.
c I'll could make breakfast if you like.
d 'Will she pass?' 'Yes, I think she'll.'
e You would help me carry this?
f Their train might been delayed.
g 'Where's George?' 'He must went home.'
h You must ever not do this again.

1 A modal is never followed by another modal.
2 We never use forms of 'do' to make modals negative or interrogative.
3 We form the negative by putting 'not' after the modal (or after *ought*).
4 We form questions by putting the subject after the modal (or after *ought*).
5 To talk about the present or future, we can use a modal + *be* + present participle.
6 To talk about the past, we can use a modal + *have* + past participle.
7 In the passive, we use a modal + *be* (or *have been*) + past participle.
8 In negative question tags, we do not normally use the full form of modals.
9 We cannot use the shortened forms of *will* and *would* on their own.

b Which function from **1** does each correct modal in a–h express?

3 Rewrite 1–8 using the modal in brackets.

1 I suppose it's possible he forgot to tell you. (might)
2 It was wrong of you to say that to her. (ought to)
3 There's a chance the prisoner wasn't caught, but I doubt it. (may)
4 It's September, so I imagine they've finished their holidays by now. (will)
5 Don't you regret not applying for the job? (should)
6 Is there any likelihood the others took a different path? (could)

7 He wants to leave school now, but I think it's a bad idea. (should)

8 I bet your mother was furious when she found out. (must)

4 **a** 📼 Sometimes the meaning of modals depends on intonation. You will hear 1–8 spoken twice: once with meaning **A** and once with meaning **B**. As you listen, decide which is which and number them in the order you hear them.

1 They should have arrived by now.
   A They probably have arrived.
   B Why haven't they arrived?

2 I could have passed the exam.
   A If only I had studied harder.
   B I don't know the result yet.

3 You shouldn't have spent so much money.
   A That was stupid of you.
   B That's very kind of you.

4 He might have sent me a birthday card.
   A I don't know if he has, but I hope so.
   B He didn't, but he should have done.

5 You should have seen her last night.
   A You were supposed to see her but you didn't.
   B She looked amazing.

6 I could have played 'Quake' all night.
   A I enjoy it so much, but they didn't let me.
   B I decided I didn't want to.

7 They might have been badly hurt in the accident.
   A They weren't hurt, but they were lucky not to be.
   B It's possible they were hurt but we're still not certain.

8 He couldn't have seen you there.
   A Don't worry – he wasn't ignoring you.
   B Don't worry – your secret is safe!

b When you have checked your answers, practise saying 1–8 with both meanings.

> **common errors**
>
> *Their plane can have landed by now.*
> What is wrong with this sentence? Why?

key word transformations

1 Read the instructions and the example. The answer is correct apart from one missing word. What is the word, where does it go, and how does it change from the first sentence?

Complete the second sentence so that it has a similar meaning to the first one using the word given. **Do not change the word given.** You must use between **three** and **eight** words, including the word given.

Losing the map was very nearly an utter disaster for the expedition.
disastrous

Losing the map could ....*have been disastrous*.... for the expedition.

2 Rewrite sentences 1–6, using the clue below each one. All the answers require modals, plus other changes.

1 It would've been a good idea if you'd done some thorough revision this week.
   revised
   You .... this week.
   (adjective to adverb)

2 It's possible that I broke it by accident, though I didn't notice doing so.
   might
   I .... it, though I didn't notice doing so.
   (noun to adverb)

3 I'll phone them now in case our arrival is delayed.
   not
   We .... time so I'll phone them now.
   (noun to verb)

4 I'm sure you were awfully shocked when you heard the news.
   come
   It .... when you heard the news.
   (adverb to adjective, adjective to noun)

5 An immediate decision to accept the plan is likely.
   well
   They .... to accept the plan.
   (noun to verb, adjective to adverb)

6 It's obvious that the company made a mistake in spending so much money.
   ought
   The company .... spent so much money.
   (adjective to adverb)

listening multiple choice: focusing on stems (2)

1 a 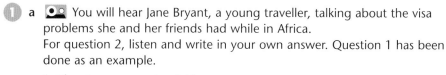 You will hear Jane Bryant, a young traveller, talking about the visa problems she and her friends had while in Africa.
For question 2, listen and write in your own answer. Question 1 has been done as an example.

1 The visas were not valid because
someone had tricked them into buying them.
....

2 What were they worried about while they were in the compound?
....

b Look at the options on page 155 and match the answers with options A, B, C or D.

2 a 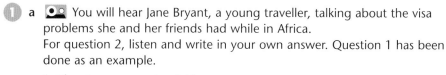 You will hear an interview with Dr Eva Chapman, who ran into difficulties on the East–West borders during the Cold War.
Listen and write in your own answers for questions 1–5.

1 When she was a small child, Eva and her mother
....

2 The bus was held up at the Polish border because
....

3 Why did she feel so guilty when she admitted the passport was hers?
....

4 What did she do in the office?
....

5 What happened when she got back on the bus?
....

b 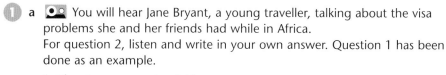 Match your answers with the options on page 155, then listen again to confirm your choices.

3 If you are entering a country in another continent, what sort of questions might you be asked? What must / mustn't you take with you? Why?

speaking speculating and hypothesising

1 The diagram shows ways of speculating, depending on how sure you are of something. Match these expressions to the correct degree of certainty, as in the examples.

> It's a foregone conclusion that …   It must have …   It may well …
> The odds are that …   I shouldn't think that …
> We can't rule out the possibility that …   I very much doubt whether …
> There's no chance it'll …

impossible	unlikely	possible	probable	certain
—	**–**	**?**	**+**	**+**
It couldn't have …	*I'd be surprised if …*	*I suppose it might be … if …*	*I wouldn't be at all surprised …*	*It's bound to …*

2 **a** 🔊 In pairs, look at picture A. Use expressions from **1** to answer 1–5.
   1 Focus first on the people. Speculate about their age, nationality, etc.
   2 Consider what kind of place it probably is, what they could be doing there and what else might be happening.
   3 Talk about what might have just happened, where and why.
   4 Suggest how they might be feeling and what they may be thinking. What can you infer from their expressions and body language?
   5 Say what you think they might do next. What else could happen?

   b Do the same with picture B.

3 🔊 Look at C and D. Ask your partner hypothetical questions about the people in the pictures. Think about the past, present and future as in **2**.

vocabulary
collocations: adjective + noun

1 Three of the four adjectives in each group (1–8) collocate with one of these nouns. Decide which noun goes with which group, and cross out the incorrect adjective.

attempt chance danger escape fear risk situation warning

1 final
stern
advance ....
critical

2 potential
futile
desperate ....
heroic

3 slim
hard
remote ....
fair

4 cruel
imminent
constant ....
grave

5 high
utmost
calculated ....
negligible

6 tense
volatile
considerable ....
precarious

7 narrow
lucky
miraculous ....
tough

8 sheer
unfounded
morbid ....
irrational

2 Rewrite 1–7 using one collocation from each of the groups above. More than one answer is possible.

EXAMPLE Betty could so easily have been killed when the house caught fire.
Betty had a lucky/miraculous escape when the house caught fire.

1 A helicopter crew tried bravely to rescue the survivors, but it was impossible.
2 The explorers knew exactly what might happen when they decided to take a short cut.
3 Although he couldn't explain it, Guy was petrified of entering the room.
4 I'm afraid that people without shelter are unlikely to survive in these conditions.
5 After the revolution, we knew things could change suddenly and unexpectedly.
6 We will let you know in good time if there's going to be a storm in the area.
7 During their voyage down the river they could have been attacked by crocodiles at any time.

idioms

1 Which of the following idioms are about

a running away?
b facing / dealing with a situation?
c taking a risk?
d being vigilant?

1 to make a run for it
2 to make a quick exit
3 to keep your wits about you
4 to take the bull by the horns
5 to make yourself scarce
6 to need eyes in the back of your head
7 to stick your neck out
8 to throw caution to the wind
9 to dice with death
10 to give someone the slip

2 **a** Use an idiom from **1** to say what you did in each of these situations.

EXAMPLE You decided to bet all your money on one horse in one race.
I threw caution to the wind.

1 You took a chance that could have led to you being killed.
2 You only stayed for ten minutes at a boring party.
3 Someone was after you, but you got away by going down a side street.
4 You were tempted to relax, but realised that dangers still lay ahead.
5 You told everyone that you would definitely pass a very difficult exam.
6 You were nervous about asking your parents for a lot of money, but in the end you plucked up the courage to do so.

b For the three idioms not used in **2a**, write your own example.

word formation

1 To fill in gaps in word formation exercises, you sometimes need to add both a prefix and a suffix to the base word. Look at the example and make similar words from a–e.

EXAMPLE simplify – *oversimplify, oversimplification*

a doubt
b lead
c agree
d patience
e organise

Which of the words you have formed have a negative meaning?

2 For each of 1–5, decide what kind of word is needed. Note down the part of speech required, and – where you can – whether the word should be positive or negative, singular or plural. Then choose one of the words from **1**.

1 As the traffic jam worsened, some drivers began .... honking their horns.
2 The advertisement .... implied that batteries were included in the price.
3 The band split up because of a .... over the 'musical direction' they should take.
4 Mobile phones are .... useful, but they may be dangerous if used too much.
5 His essay was completely .... , with no identifiable beginning, middle or end.

3 Occasionally, a gap requires a compound noun (e.g. *teacup*), a compound adjective (e.g. *widespread*) or noun formed from a phrasal verb (e.g. *upkeep*). Match the words on the left with those on the right, and say what the compounds mean.

night	take
out	speaker
sight	fall
loud	payer
road	cry
tax	seeing
in	works

4 **a** Look at the title of the text. What is an *auction*? What kind of things are auctioned? Read the text quickly. What, according to the writer, is only an imagined danger at auctions, and what is a real danger there?

b For questions 1–10 use the word given in **capitals** at the end of some of the lines to form a word that fits in the space in the same line. There is an example at the beginning (**0**).

Some of the answers need both a prefix and a suffix, and two require compounds.

c If you wanted to buy something at an auction, which of the idioms on page 132 might be appropriate?

At the auction

There are a lot of (**0**) *(noun, negative, plural)* misconceptions about bidding at auctions. People have told me that they are afraid to scratch their nose for fear of (**1**)........... becoming the owner of a vintage Porsche. This is very (**2**)........... . You will have more trouble making sure that the auctioneer sees your raised hand. I confess I still find bidding an extremely (**3**)........... process. I look on in amazement as a man beside me tilts his head a fraction and his bid receives immediate (**4**)........... . Of course, the auctioneer has known these people for years and is familiar with their every (**5**)........... expression. Don't try it. First, it's a good idea to watch an auction from the sidelines. Go to a (**6**)........... one rather than an evening one if you want to see the big bidders: it can get quite exciting as the price rockets upwards, with the final (**7**)........... anyone's guess until the very last moment. Before you bid, decide on the top amount you are prepared to pay. The estimate in the catalogue is (**8**)........... just a guide and the bidding can always go much higher or drop well below. Resist the (**9**)........... to compete. It's only too easy to start increasing your bid just because someone else keeps raising it. If you're not careful, you'll find yourself trying to 'win' at a price that would have been (**10**)........... in a calmer moment.

CONCEIVE

INTENTION
LIKE

MYSTERY

ACKNOWLEDGE

FACE

TIME

OUT

VARY

TEMPT

THINK

writing summary and comprehension questions

EXAM FOCUS

paper 3 part 5 summary

Check you know what to do in the summary task by filling in gaps 1–6.

Read both texts carefully, then underline the (1) ...... in the instructions. Underline the (2) ...... parts of both texts, making sure you have about the same number of points from each text. Make (3) ...... in your own words. (4) ...... include any ideas not in the texts. Choose the best (5) ...... for the points then write your summary in a neutral style. Link the sentences together appropriately then (6) ...... your summary for errors and repetition.

1 Read quickly through these texts and answer these questions.

1 What text types are they?

2 Which of a–d best describes the main topic of both?

a The popularity of dangerous sports and hobbies.

b The rapid increase in risk-taking in modern-day society.

c The kinds of risks we inevitably face during our lives.

d The kinds of risk we face and why we take risks.

2 Read the texts more carefully and answer questions 1–4 with a word or short phrase (you needn't use complete sentences). There is a clue for each one.

Risk-taking for fun – from white-water rafting to jumping out of aeroplanes – is on the increase. Sometimes the risks are huge; mostly they are unpredictable, like sailing accidents in violent storms. Dozens of climbers and sailors die every year, but most of the time nothing goes wrong: tourists needn't do much more than hang on to the inflatable and believe they're risking life and limb when in fact it's hardly more risky than a theme-park or fairground ride.

But why the fashion for taking risks, real or not? There are lots of theories around. The point that most make is that western city life is now tame and over-controlled. Physical exercise is usually no more than aerobics in the gym on a Thursday, or a game of football or tennis in the park at the weekend. So holidays are the one time when people can get away from their everyday lives.

Risk-taking, soft or extreme, may also be a backlash to ultra-protective western society. Kids aren't often left alone to fall out of trees, dodge the traffic, or make mistakes. Laws and insurance companies try to stop people swimming in rivers, jumping off bridges, or doing anything else that might be dangerous. Some say that people are starting to get fed up with this, and that the risk-taking we're seeing is a reaction against society trying to make everything safe.

Others think we're fooling ourselves that our technology can protect us from nature; that unsinkable boats, insulated jackets or anti-frostbite boots make us invulnerable. But it's only when something drastic or unforeseeable happens, like a little river suddenly becoming a raging torrent, that we realise just how powerful nature is.

1 What impression of tourists does the writer give in the first paragraph?
(*What do the references to theme-parks and fairgrounds tell you?*)
....

2 Why does the writer use the word *invulnerable* (line 34)?
(*What does our technology provide us with?*)
....

From the moment we are born into the world we are at risk.

In our journey through life we will be exposed to a variety of risks, each of which might shorten that journey. Some of these we can do nothing about; our very existence on planet Earth is fraught with danger. Others are imposed upon us, whether we like it or not. Others we accept by our own choosing with full knowledge of the possible consequences. And others we accept in ignorance as part of the normal processes of everyday life, yet future generations living in more enlightened times will no doubt issue the appropriate health warnings.

If we are lucky we may avoid all the hazards, and we shall die of nothing other than 'old age'. More likely we shall fall victim to one of these hazards and our death certificates will record some identifiable cause.

Maybe it is *because* we are mortal that we take risks. We drive on our overcrowded roads well aware of the accident statistics. We lie in the sun, we walk in the mountains and we work with machinery. And we do *not* wear bullet proof vests when we go into town. If we were *ever* to cure disease and find a way of halting the body's ageing process, we might be a little more cautious, but even then we should still know that one day we may fall prey to some natural disaster or malicious act over which we will have no control.

Deciding to expose ourselves to danger involves evaluating the benefits and our perception of the risks. Yet when we examine people's actual decisions we often find them to be totally irrational. They refuse to engage in activities which have known, but quite negligible, risks yet fearlessly participate in those whose dangers are far greater.

line 24

3 What does 'If we were *ever* to ...' (line 24) say about the writer's thoughts on curing disease?
(*Is the writer optimistic or pessimistic?*)

....

4 Explain in your own words why people's decisions about risk-taking are often irrational.
(*Look at the last sentence.*)

....

3 Read these instructions. Then look at the summary below and answer questions 1–6 about it.

In a paragraph of between **50–70** words, summarise **in your own words as far as possible** the categories of risk described in the texts.

Certain risks are involuntary and unavoidable. These include dangers in the natural world plus those deliberately created by other people, for example armed violence. Others, such as sunbathing, are voluntary but avoidable, although we may not be aware of the danger. People also voluntarily take risks for enjoyment, for instance by going climbing or sailing. These activities may entail serious risk, or just seem more dangerous than they really are.

1 Which points are from which text?
2 Why are the points in that order?
3 In what style is the summary written?
4 Is it sufficiently well organised and linked?
5 Is it the correct length?
6 Does it avoid repetition, lifting and language errors?

4 Underline the key words in these instructions and select the relevant points from both texts. When you have written your summary, ask yourself questions 1–6 in **3**.

In a paragraph of between **50–70** words, summarise **in your own words as far as possible** the reasons given in the texts why people deliberately take risks.

review

1 Choose the correct alternative and explain what it means.
1 I *shall be/couldn't have been* there on time tomorrow.
2 Phil and Lisa love each other's company and they *couldn't/wouldn't* be happier together.
3 I suppose there could be a sequel to this film but I *shan't/shouldn't* think so.
4 My coat's missing; it *may be taken/may have been taken* by that girl who just left.
5 They *ought not to have left/have not ought to leave* the school premises without permission.
6 I *must/wouldn't* be doing this if my mother hadn't forced me to.

2 Respond to 1–5 using the modal in brackets.
1 'I got badly sunburnt on the beach yesterday.' (should)
2 'It's midnight and your sister still isn't home.' (must)
3 'That lunatic driver didn't stop, even though the traffic lights were red.' (might)
4 'I hope your quiz show will have finished by the time my film starts.' (might)
5 'Did your parents object to your plans?' (would)

3 Correct the mistakes in each of these idioms.
1 There are so many dangers here that you need wind in the back of your head.
2 There are too many of them; the only thing we can do is make a head for it.
3 Rather than let things get even worse, she decided to take the neck by the horns.
4 When the situation in the bar turned nasty, we made a quick slip.
5 I think we'd better dice ourselves scarce before anyone sees the damage!
6 He gave the police the wits by hiding under a car.

4 Complete each sentence so that the meaning of the collocation is clear.
1 Flying may seem risky, but compared to travelling by car there is a negligible risk …
2 As we walked through the dark forest, I had an irrational fear …
3 The organisers of the race across the Sahara gave competitors advance warning …
4 Agent 005 and her accomplice had a lucky escape …
5 When the two rival gangs met, the tense situation …
6 This is a hostile part of the country, but I don't think we're in imminent danger …
7 Rescue teams in the Himalayas made futile attempts …
8 It's a month since they disappeared in the jungle, but I suppose there's still a remote chance …

5 Complete the crossword with words from this unit.

across
1 having a serious or violent effect
5 to hit something gently
7 another word for 'cautious'
8 filled with danger
10 a danger or risk
13 too afraid to move
16 not able to live for ever
18 confident and brave
19 doubts about doing something
22 unable to be wounded, hurt or damaged
23 useless or pointless (attempt)

down
2 place giving protection
3 to hit (an insect) hard
4 acting without thinking carefully first
6 sensible and careful
9 deliberately harmful
11 to become or seem older
12 of little importance
13 dangerous
14 not dangerous or exciting
15 having no logical reason
17 likely to happen very soon
20 very serious and worrying

unit 12 | futures

vocabulary and speaking

talking points

1 Read the two statements below. Which one do you agree with?

a 'The rate of technological, economic and social change is now so fast that it makes predictions of future trends so inexact as to be practically a waste of time. The future is, literally, unimaginable.'

b 'In many countries the rate of change has slowed considerably, and will continue to do so. Today's young people have colour televisions and video games, whereas their parents' generation had black and white TVs and pinball machines. Compare that, though, with what *their* parents had: poverty, hunger and, often, the awful effects of war.'

2 What do you think it is possible, and impossible, to predict for the year 2020? Give reasons.

3 What aspects of life do you believe will get better, and which may get worse, in the coming years? Why?

1 These predictions were made in the 1970s about life in the early 21st century. Which have come true, or partly true? Why do you think some of them were correctly predicted, and some weren't? Which might still be proved correct?
1 'All dental treatment will be pain-free.'
2 'Deserts will no longer exist, as we will have learnt how to increase rainfall.'
3 'We will no longer have to get up and walk over to the TV to change channel.'
4 'Electric cars will have become the most common form of private transport.'
5 'Average life expectancy in some countries will be over 100 years.'
6 'We will be able to re-grow entire arms and legs that we have lost in accidents.'

2 What are the differences between these?
1 an *astrologer* and a *fortune-teller*
2 to *envisage*, to *forecast* and to *foretell*
3 the *outlook* and the *outcome*
4 to *foresee*, to *anticipate* and to *contemplate*
5 *in future*, *in the future* and *to have a future*
6 *futuristic*, *trendy* and *cutting-edge*
7 *state-of-the-art* and *ahead of its time*

3 Which of these two visions of the future do you find more likely? Why? How does your own vision differ?

4 Read the two texts below. From the ten words in bold, make five pairs of words with similar meanings.

It was an **unpromising** start to the day when we set off on our **ill-fated** journey. **Inauspicious** black clouds gathered overhead and there was an **impending** sense of gloom among us. We could not know what the forthcoming days would bring or that only six of us were **destined** to return, but our future disasters were **looming** ever closer even then …

Did I ever tell you about the time I went on a blind date? The friend who arranged it for me has very different taste in men, so it was **on the cards** that I wouldn't get on with him. The evening was obviously **doomed** to failure from the beginning when I lost my purse on the way to the restaurant, so it was **odds on** that I was going to be late. However, we must have been **fated** to be together, as the evening turned out to be a complete success.

reading gapped text: predicting text content

EXAM FOCUS

paper 1 part 3 gapped text

In Part 3 of Reading, you are given eight paragraphs of a text and have to put seven missing paragraphs into numbered gaps. There is also an extra paragraph which you do not need to use.

This task type tests your ability to appreciate the following:
- **Global meaning**: the gist, or what the text is mainly about.
- **Text structure**: how the information in the text is organised.
- **Coherence**: the logical sequence of ideas within the text.
- **Cohesion**: linking using reference words, conjunctions, vocabulary, substitution and ellipsis.

1 Read only the title and the first sentence of each paragraph in the main text. What is the text about?

2 Read the whole text. As you reach gaps 1–7 use the answers to these questions as clues to its structure.

1 Do you think the next paragraph will discuss other crimes, or say what happens in this case?
2 Will the next paragraph describe another incident, or talk about violent crime in general?
3 Will this paragraph deal with other crimes, or statistics about murder victims?
4 Will this paragraph discuss criminal activities related to this trade, or introduce the topic of digital stimulants?
5 Will this paragraph give more background information, or change the subject?
6 Will this paragraph give a specific example of chip implantation, or consider computer crime in general?
7 Will this paragraph refer to research into electronic addiction, or studies of particular criminal organisations?

3 Choose from the paragraphs **A–H** the one which fits each gap (1–7). There is one extra paragraph which you do not need to use.

Use these clues to help you: *This* (line 7) *growth* (line 14) *Instead* (line 31) *one put into … elbow* (line 57) *this kind of* (line 65) *addicted* (line 70) *unconscious manager* (line 74) *bank's* (line 75) *So, too* (line 89).

HIGH-TECH
CRIME OF THE FUTURE

It begins with a beam of high-intensity radiation. Silent and invisible. It disables the electronics of the alarm and telephone system of the bank manager's house, and then the gang bursts in. Wearing identical clothes and caps to confuse the CCTV and
5 communicating by untraceable mobile phones, the gang of four criminals incapacitate everyone in the house with stun guns.

1

This, law enforcement experts believe, is the future of organised crime where villains will use a combination of cutting-edge technology and old-fashioned brute force to defeat increasingly
10 sophisticated security systems. Rather than coshes and sawn-off shotguns, the criminals of tomorrow will be skilled in crimes that produce massive profits but with a fraction of the risk of armed robbery or smuggling. It is not far away.

2

Kidnapping is thought to be a particular growth area. This is
15 because new security technologies such as retina scans and fingerprint recognition require a living subject. Long thought to be the stuff of science fiction, such devices are becoming increasingly common. However, one negative result is that crimes in which staff are abducted and forced to help criminals are also
20 set to rise.

3

Commodities traded by the organised criminals of tomorrow will also change. Increasing profits will lead to a search for effective money-laundering solutions. Small, high-value items such as computer memory chips, rare metals and even meteorite
25 fragments will be traded between gangs in an effort to avoid leaving electronic trails.

4

Senior National Criminal Intelligence Service analysts are also warning of the threat of digital stimulants, illegally transmitted across the Internet. These could create new forms of addiction far
30 worse than that sometimes caused by interactive PC games.

5

Instead, users will hook up to machines which will directly stimulate the pleasure centres of the brain. Some may go further and have silicon chips implanted in their bodies.

6

A silicon chip implanted into the body will be able to pick up a
35 signal transmitted across the Internet, or using radio waves. It will give extremes of pleasure more addictive than the most intense virtual-reality experiences – and be controlled by criminals.

7

'Cyberspace offers criminals opportunities to create unprecedented and terrible new forms of addiction,' said
40 Professor Warwick. 'The question is not whether electronic stimulants can be created, but how soon they can be put on the market.'

A With the price of these chips having risen 400 per cent recently, police believe a new spate of robberies and factory
45 break-ins is just around the corner.

B 'The purpose of organised crime is to generate profits,' says one expert. 'To identify the key areas of criminality in the future, you simply have to identify the areas that will be generating the most money. Biotechnology and information
50 technology are the two biggest revolutions of this century, and we have to look at each of them and see where the potential for money is from the criminal point of view. Organised crime will become more sophisticated and more networked, and it is the challenge of law enforcement to look
55 where those networks may expand in the future.'

C Last year Kevin Warwick, Professor of Cybernetics at Reading University, had one put into his left elbow, which allowed computers to communicate directly with his body. He could switch machines on and off simply by scratching his head.

60 **D** Murders of this sort, fortunately, are likely to become less common. Increased penalties for carrying firearms, along with a greatly increased likelihood of being shot dead by the police, will lead to more criminals using non-lethal weapons to incapacitate victims, such as stun guns and CS gas sprays.

65 **E** Although the technology to deliver this kind of cyber-stimulant does not yet exist, experts in the field admit that it is only a matter of time. Experiments on chimps and other animals have already shown that when they are wired externally, via an electrode implanted into the pleasure
70 centres of the brain, they become so addicted to the sensations it produces that they forget to eat and can die for lack of food.

F A lap-top computer and portable palm reader is then produced and the hand of the unconscious manager is placed
75 on top. Within seconds, the gang have dialled into the bank's computer and gained top-level access to thousands of accounts. After transferring money the gang leaves, sealing the doors of the home with a foam which turns rock solid in seconds, and makes its getaway in two identical vehicles
80 equipped with anti-reflective number plates to frustrate speed cameras.

G At an FBI-sponsored gathering of international law enforcement agencies in Germany last month, one NCIS officer claimed that criminals had begun to exploit areas such
85 as virtual banking and on-line gambling, and were now developing a new generation of stimulants, the effects of which could be experienced without actually possessing them.

H So, too, are cases of blackmail and extortion. Although banks
90 refuse to discuss the subject, it is believed that there have already been at least four instances of extortion in which criminals have threatened to disrupt the systems of city institutions with high-intensity radiation devices.

4 **a** What do these words refer to?
It (line 13) *Some* (line 32) *It* (line 35) *each* (line 51)
which (line 87) *the subject* (line 90)

b What has been omitted before these words?
Silent (line 1) *coshes* (line 10) *using* (line 35)
more (line 36) *be* (line 37) *implanted* (line 69)
can (line 71) *were* (line 85)

c How is *Kevin Warwick* (line 56) referred to in line 40, and *NCIS* (line 83) in line 27?

5 What changes do you think there will be in the way the police operate in the future?

grammar
future forms

 a This text contains six future forms used incorrectly. Find them, correct them, and in each case say why that form should be used there. The first one has been done as an example.

I still can't quite believe it, but this time tomorrow <u>we have</u> dinner in New York City.

(1 ~~we have~~ – we will be having – future action in progress at a certain time)

It's a place I've always wanted to visit, and at last I'm actually just about to go. Our plane is taking off at 10 tomorrow morning, with our arrival scheduled for 11.30 local time, though by then we will be flying for nearly eight hours, of course.

Last night, Jilly phoned some friends of hers who live in Brooklyn and they meet us at JFK airport. Then the plan is for us to go straight to our hotel in midtown Manhattan. We'll have been staying at the Paramount on West 46th Street, which is really handy for Broadway and Times Square.

I'm on the point of starting to pack my case, though I don't intend to take much with me as I want to leave plenty of room for new clothes, CDs and all the other things that are so much cheaper over there. The problem is, by the middle of the week I am spending every last one of my precious dollars!

b Imagine you are in these situations. Write a response for each one, choosing from the verb tenses in **a**.
1 A friend asks you about the departure time of your flight to Rio de Janeiro.
2 Your teacher says you must finish your essay by 10 o'clock. You are confident you can do so.
3 Someone asks you for a date for next Friday night. Refuse, without hurting their feelings.
4 You are with friends late in the evening and they ask you how you will get home. You have arranged for someone to collect you at 11 p.m.
5 A classmate asks you to think ahead to when you pass Proficiency, and count the total number of years you spent studying English.
6 A friend asks if it is all right to phone you at 6.30 a.m. on a Sunday morning. It isn't!

c Look at these expressions used to talk about the immediate future and find two others in the text in **a**.
set to   on the verge of   on the brink of

Which of them are followed by the infinitive, and which by *-ing*?

All these expressions can be used with past forms of the verb 'to be' to talk about the future in the past, e.g. *Scientists were on the point of making a major breakthrough. I was / had been on the point of phoning her when she sent me an email.*

Use each of the above expressions to talk about events that are or were in the news.

 a Match the uses of *will* and *going to* in 1–6 with functions a–f.
1 Your hairdryer's broken? Don't worry, I'll fix it for you now.
2 The phone number isn't here. I know – I'll look in the Yellow Pages.
3 These suitcases are awfully heavy. Will you give me a hand with them?
4 Ray and I are going to get engaged on New Year's Eve.
5 Watch out! Your purse is going to fall out of your bag!
6 There will / is going to be an extra day in February this year.

a to make spontaneous decisions
b to make predictions based on current evidence
c to make an offer
d to make requests
e to state decisions already made
f to state facts

b Look at these five situations. In each case decide whether both verb forms are correct, or only one.
1 The bill will be enormous!
The bill is going to be enormous!

2 You stay here and I'm going to go round to the back door.
You stay here and I'll go round to the back door.

3 I'll be 30 next year.
I'm going to be 30 next year.

4 Empty! Will you lend me some cash?
Empty! Are you going to lend me some cash?

5 I've got to go to school now. I'll post that letter for you.
I've got to go to school now. I'm going to post that letter for you.

3 **a** We sometimes use a form of *be to* with future reference. In 1–4, underline the expression used and explain what it means.

---

1 **150-storey tower block to be built**

2
Passengers are to remain seated until the vehicle has stopped moving.

3 SCHOOL MEMO

Pupils are not to bring mobile telephones to class.

4
We must take action soon if we are to prevent sea levels rising alarmingly.

---

b Think of five new rules for where you study or work. Write them in sentences using *are to* and *are not to*.
Swap rules with your partner. Do you think their rules are reasonable or not?

c What kind of future do the underlined words refer to? What continuous verb forms could replace them?
Jane Austen <u>was to</u> become one of the most popular authors of all time.
The band <u>were to have</u> brought out a new single last month.

d Think of some events (in the news or personal) that were planned but did not happen. Tell your partner about them and explain why they didn't happen.

EXAMPLE *The new cultural centre was to have opened last May, but it didn't because the funding ran out.*

---

common errors

He was on the point to walk when the bus appeared.
What is wrong with this sentence? Why?

---

open cloze

1 1 In pairs, you are going to design your own cloze. Student A look at 'Sailing to the stars 1' on page 150; Student B look at 'Sailing to the stars 2' on page 157. Both are about a plan to use solar energy to power spacecraft at tremendous speeds. Study your text and delete eight suitable words choosing from these:

> prepositions   conjunctions   relative pronouns
> modals   parts of phrasal verbs
> dependent prepositions   parts of collocations
> reference words (e.g. *this*)
> linking words (e.g. *however*)

2 Exchange books and complete each other's text.

3 Check your answers with your partner.

4 Were there any gaps which were particularly hard to fill? What part of speech are they?
Which of the following are unlikely to be tested in an open cloze? Why?

adjectives
contracted forms (e.g. *isn't*)
pronouns
main verbs
articles
nouns
hyphenated words
adverbs of manner (e.g. *slowly*)

listening   three-way matching: ways of agreeing and disagreeing (2)

1 **a** You are going to read about the issue of animal species that have been introduced from other countries. What do you know about this? Can you give any specific examples from your country?

b Read the dialogue on page 156 and match missing sentences A–E with gaps 1–5.

c 🎧 Listen to the recording and check your answers.

d 🎧 Listen again, without reading the tapescript, and answer 1–5.

You will hear part of a radio programme in which David and Chloe discuss the issue of non-native animals in the countryside. For questions **1–5** decide whether the opinions are expressed by only one of the speakers, or whether the speakers agree. Write **D** for David, **C** for Chloe or **B** for Both, where they agree.

1 Non-native animals are creating a problem. ⬚ **1**

2 The red squirrel will probably be replaced by the grey squirrel. ⬚ **2**

3 Most imported animals are brought in on boats. ⬚ **3**

4 Something must be done about the problem. ⬚ **4**

5 All imported animals will have to be destroyed. ⬚ **5**

2 🎧 You will hear part of a radio programme in which two people, Lucy and Joe, discuss likely future trends in terms of size. For questions **1–6**, decide whether the opinions are expressed by only one of the speakers, or whether the speakers agree. Write **L** for Lucy, **J** for Joe or **B** for Both, where they agree.

1 In the future, most things we produce will be much smaller. ⬚ **1**

2 Mobile telephones cannot become any smaller than they are now. ⬚ **2**

3 Computers as we know them now will disappear quite soon. ⬚ **3**

4 Cars will inevitably be smaller in the future. ⬚ **4**

5 Government policy will result in some items becoming smaller. ⬚ **5**

6 Modern technology is reducing the need for wood. ⬚ **6**

3 Check your answers, then study the tapescript on page 159 and identify the expressions used for agreement and disagreement.

4 Do you think things will generally become larger or smaller in the future?

speaking   turn-taking and interrupting

1 **a** Read the expressions in the boxes and add more to each one.

> **Encouraging your partner to speak**
> What are your thoughts on this?
> Isn't that right, (your partner's name)?
> How would you have reacted to a situation like that?

> **Interrupting**
> If I could just make a point here …
> Hang on a moment …   I'm sorry but I …

> **Stopping your partner interrupting**
> Just a moment, please …
> If you'll let me continue …
> I'm sorry, but could I just finish what I'm saying …

b Which of the expressions are polite, and which aren't?

2 🔊 You are going to role-play part of a Paper 5 interview but with two examiners instead of one. Make groups of four and decide who will be the two examiners and who will be the two candidates.

1 **Examiners** ask the candidates three questions each about their homes, work or studies, childhood, plans for the future, etc.
Candidates answer as fully as possible.

2 **Candidates** look at the picture and think about the sort of questions you may be asked.
Examiners ask the candidates to say what idea of the future it shows. What changes to family life do they think there will be in their country in the future?

3 Change roles so that the candidates become the examiners.

4 **Candidates** look at cards 1 and 2 and think about the topics.
Examiners ask the first candidate about one of the cards then ask the second candidate about the other card.

5 **Candidates** try to predict what topic related to the cards you might be asked about.
Examiners choose a topic related to the cards and ask the candidates to discuss it.

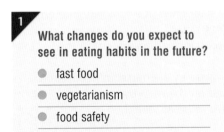

1
What changes do you expect to see in eating habits in the future?
- fast food
- vegetarianism
- food safety

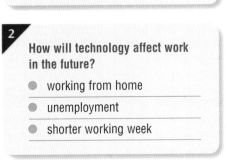

2
How will technology affect work in the future?
- working from home
- unemployment
- shorter working week

vocabulary frequently confused words

1 Some words have the same pronunciation as others, but are spelt differently. Correct the mistake in each of 1–8, and then write a new sentence to illustrate the meaning of the word you have replaced.

EXAMPLE Factories will soon have to stop dumping industrial ~~waist~~ *waste* into the river.

My waist measurement is 60 cm.

1 You've put on wait since you started working in that cake shop.
2 I didn't even have enough money for my bus fair home.
3 Our dog loves to berry bones in the back garden.
4 The kids want lots of tomato source on their burgers.
5 You can sew those seeds in plant pots in the spring.
6 For breakfast I usually have serial and a cup of coffee.
7 The two youths hid until the police car was out of site.
8 I couldn't bare the suspense at the end of that film.

2 **a** The words below have more than one common meaning. Which meaning do pictures 1–6 show?

> lie   play   ~~branch~~   charge   figure   hold   match

EXAMPLE branch – *part of a tree*

b What is the other common meaning of each word?

3 **a** In 1–10, both words in bold are possible. Explain the different meanings of the sentence in each case.

EXAMPLE They're unfriendly in that village: they don't like **strangers/foreigners**.

strangers – They don't like people they don't know.

foreigners – They don't like people from other countries.

1 Julie's always been a very **sensitive/sensible** child.
2 The coach will stop **briefly/shortly** at Stratford-upon-Avon.
3 Our neighbours have decorated their house in a **classic/classical** style.
4 It's a lovely restaurant: everything is very **tasty/tasteful**.
5 Although I was surprised by what happened, it was a very interesting **experience/experiment**.
6 I heard two teachers having **a discussion/an argument** in the staffroom.
7 There's a **single/unique** Egyptian vase in the museum's collection.
8 The **boundary/border** is indicated on the map by a red line.
9 Investigations showed the painting to be absolutely **priceless/worthless**.
10 Some people get very **irritable/nervous** when they are kept waiting.

b Write a sentence of your own which can be completed with only one of the words in each of 1–10, leaving a gap for this word. Then give your sentences to your partner to complete with the correct words.

multiple-choice cloze

1
a Read quickly through the two texts, without filling in any gaps, and decide what text types they are.

b For questions **1–12**, read the two texts below and decide which answer (**A**, **B**, **C** or **D**) best fits each gap.

- For 1 and 3, you need to choose from four frequently confused words.
- For 2, complete a collocation.
- For 4 and 5, complete idioms.
- For 6, complete a phrasal verb.

Do the missing words for 7–12 complete collocations, idioms or phrasal verbs?

TOMORROW'S MEALS

Our relationship with food is changing dramatically, and many scientists **(1)**........ that one day we will select what we eat according to our own particular health needs. Within 20 years, if their predictions **(2)**........ true, we will know so much more about how different types of food affect us that every item we buy will be based on our own individual needs. Already, multinational food companies have begun to manufacture 'functional foods' that provide extra medical **(3)**........, in addition to the usual nutrients they contain. Also in the **(4)**........ are products that will bring psychological benefits, for instance drinks that aid concentration, and even fruit that has been genetically modified to contain medicine. Time will **(5)**........ whether such foods can actually ever become popular, but some doctors wonder whether we really know what we are **(6)**........ ourselves in for if we allow them onto our supermarket shelves.

	A	**B**	**C**	**D**
1	foresee	preview	prospect	forebode
2	are	result	turn	come
3	profits	benefits	promotions	premiums
4	pipeline	tunnel	way	corridor
5	tell	prove	say	confirm
6	deceiving	letting	introducing	making

SCALING THE ATLAS

It was only mid-afternoon but we were tired when we pitched our tents on the slopes of the mighty Atlas mountains. We had planned to cross the highest part of the African range later that evening, but our hopes were **(7)**........ when the spring weather suddenly worsened. Karim, our guide, advised us to bring **(8)**........ our stop for the night: 'The pass', he said, pointing up at the white peaks towering above us, 'may be blocked by snow.' Most of us, I think, felt slightly relieved to be given an excuse to **(9)**........ off the ascent. It had been a hard day's walk under a scorching Moroccan sun, and as the track became steeper and the air thinner we knew what still **(10)**........ ahead of us. Lauren and James, though, were keen to keep going, presumably on the **(11)**........ that the weather might suddenly clear. The rest of us could appreciate their impatience to reach our destination, but in the end everyone seemed to go along with Karim when he said 'All in good **(12)**........ . Don't worry, the Sahara will still be there on Friday.'

	A	**B**	**C**	**D**
7	spoiled	finished	dashed	smashed
8	ahead	up	in	forward
9	keep	drop	put	bring
10	stood	lay	looked	waited
11	potential	likelihood	feasibility	offchance
12	time	interval	moment	pause

writing proposals

 a A proposal is a written plan put forward for readers to think about and decide upon. Quickly read through the instructions and the model text below. As you do so, write a heading for each paragraph.

b Read the text more carefully, and answer these questions.
- In what style is it written?
- Does it mainly focus on the past or the future?
- What is the purpose of each paragraph?
- What follows each recommendation?

You are attending an international conference on 21st century issues, and have been asked to write a proposal on how to deal with the problems which mankind will face concerning transport. Write your proposal in 300–350 words.

As we embark upon a new century, it must be fairly evident to all of us that transport is very soon going to be a problem of major proportions, to which solutions will need to be found.

During the second half of the twentieth century, the number of vehicles on the roads and planes in the sky increased beyond all expectations; to the point where, today, roads in many countries cannot handle the amount of daily traffic they are subjected to and congested air space presents us with grave cause for concern. In addition to these problems, there is also the situation regarding fuel: oil products are becoming progressively more expensive, and the reliability of future supply is not something we can take for granted.

Looking firstly, then, at the problem of congestion on our roads, and the accompanying atmospheric pollution from exhaust fumes, it will obviously be necessary, at some point, either to construct flyovers over built-up areas or ring roads around all towns and cities. The problem with the latter solution is that there is a danger of carving further and further into the surrounding countryside and transforming what is left of our greenery into concrete and asphalt. Another possible measure – however unwelcome it may be – would be to restrict by law the number of cars allowed in each family, or impose obligatory car-sharing. This would also serve to reduce overall fuel consumption, as would the alternative of electric cars.

Regarding international air travel, here again it may be necessary to impose restrictions: in this case on the number of aeroplanes that are given permission to be in the air at any one time. Surely too, the amount of business travelling required could be drastically reduced if we learn to take advantage of new technological developments such as tele- and video-conferencing.

The idea of curtailing the personal freedom of people in this way may not seem to be a very welcome one. However, for the sake of our future health and safety, the recommendations outlined above must be given urgent consideration, and those accepted should be acted upon in the shortest time possible.

2 a Which words does the writer use to introduce the topics of the third and fourth paragraphs? We could also write *To turn to ...* or *With reference to ...*; what other expressions like these do you know?

b What expressions does the writer use to make recommendations?

c Which verb forms does she mainly use to describe the problems, and which to discuss the solutions?

3 What would you consider to be the strong points and the weak points of the proposal? What would you add to it?

4 a Which are the key words in this question?

You work for the planning department of your local council. Your boss has asked you for a proposal on how to make your town or district more fun for the people of your age group who live there. Include in your proposal ideas for improving existing leisure and entertainment facilities, and suggestions for new ones. Write your proposal in 300–350 words.

b Write your proposal in a similar style to the model text. Ensure each paragraph has a clear aim and use section headings if you wish. Use appropriate language for making recommendations:
It is strongly advised / recommended ...
There appears to be no alternative to ...
The best solution seems to be ...
The evidence (undoubtedly) points towards ...

exam factfile

A proposal has a similar layout to a report, but is a recommendation for the future, while a report is about something that has happened.

⬤ THERE IS ANOTHER MODEL PROPOSAL ON PAGE 166 IN THE WRITING BANK

review

1 Match definitions 1–8 with words formed from these anagrams.

gameturn   nextempire   yourband   sorefinger
lostshrew   liarbiter   eelcrisps   isisevent

1 dividing line between two areas of land
2 easily hurt or damaged
3 scientific test to prove whether a theory is true
4 extremely valuable
5 strong verbal disagreement
6 in a mood in which you are easily annoyed
7 people from another country
8 having no value or use

2 In 1–7, form collocations using one word from each pair. Then write an example sentence for each.

EXAMPLE cereal / serial   TV / breakfast
breakfast cereal, TV serial
My favourite breakfast cereal is corn flakes.
I must watch the last episode of that TV serial.

1 fair / fare   fun / taxi
2 sow / sew   buttons / seeds
3 wait / weight   heavy / long
4 bear / bare   pain / teeth
5 sauce / source   spicy / river
6 site / sight   beautiful / building
7 waste / waist   slim / absolute

3 Look at the possible answers to 1–6. Which of them sound natural, and which don't?

1 Are you coming to the party at my place on Friday?
   A Yes, I'm to be there.
   B Yes, I'll be there.
   C Yes, I'm being there.
   D Yes, I'm going to be there.

2 What do you think she'll do next?
   A She's going to stand up.
   B She's on the brink of standing up.
   C She'll be standing up.
   D She's just about to stand up.

3 Can I borrow your bike at four this afternoon?
   A Sorry, I'll use it then.
   B Sorry, I'll be using it then.
   C Sorry, I'm using it then.
   D Sorry, I was to have used it then.

4 What time's dawn tomorrow?
   A The sun comes up at 6.47.
   B The sun is coming up at 6.47.
   C The sun is to be up at 6.47.
   D The sun will come up at 6.47.

5 My computer screen's suddenly gone blank. What's wrong with it?
   A I help you with that.
   B I'm going to help you with that.
   C I'll help you with that.
   D I'm due to help you with that.

6 How different do you think life will be in ten years' time?
   A I should think I'm earning a lot of money by then.
   B I don't think I'll have got married by then.
   C I suppose I'll be bringing up kids by then.
   D I imagine I'll have been working for several years by then.

4 Complete these sentences about yourself.
1 I'm just about to …
2 I'm on the point of …
3 I've already made the arrangements. I'm …
4 Next term, I'm going to …
5 Last year, I was to have …
6 This time next year, I'll be …
7 By 2015, I'll have …
8 By 2020, I'll have been …

5 Use the clues to complete the puzzle with adjectives from this unit. The word down describes something that has never happened before.

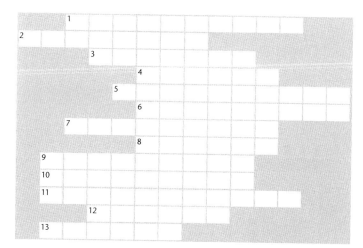

1 extremely modern and unusual in appearance
2 having a future that has already been decided
3 black substance used for making road surfaces
4 the part of the eye that is sensitive to light
5 person who doesn't eat meat
6 full, crowded, e.g. roads
7 the possibility of something happening
8 condemned to future disaster or failure
9 extremely valuable
10 about to happen
11 happening suddenly and without planning
12 an informal word for 'fashionable'
13 extremely fashionable and modern

appendix

Unit 1 Speaking ③

Text A

Counterfeiting money

- copy into computer memory
- change the number on banknote
- print sample note to check printing and colours
- make corrections then print as many as required
- use washing machine to wash and dry notes to look real

Unit 3 Listening

You will hear an interview in which Suzie Molina, a foreign correspondent for a well-known international TV news organisation, talks about her work. For questions **1–4**, choose the answer (**A**, **B**, **C** or **D**) which fits best according to what you hear.

1 What does Suzie like most about doing interviews?
   A She always does them in sunny countries.
   B She can help people do a good interview.
   C She films people with their friends and relatives.
   D She can watch videos of herself afterwards.   1

2 When does reporting make her feel nervous?
   A when a piece of equipment goes wrong
   B when she is getting on badly with her colleagues
   C when she has to act as an interpreter
   D when she doesn't understand the local language   2

3 When does she worry about her own safety?
   A when she does something careless
   B when other journalists predict trouble
   C when things happen faster than expected
   D when she cannot contact the outside world   3

4 How is her job affecting her relationship with her boyfriend?
   A She feels that she doesn't see him enough.
   B He feels that he doesn't see her enough.
   C They don't want to see each other any more.
   D They accept that they can't often see each other.   4

Unit 12 Open cloze

Sailing to the stars 1

A spacecraft could sail on a sunbeam to Mars and beyond. This is not the start of a fairy story but a theory confirmed by NASA scientists. The biggest cost of space is the launch. As it lifts off from the ground, the space shuttle's rockets burn enough energy every second to power 2 million family cars. A shuttle has to carry its experiments as well as its human passengers, with their food, air and water for a fortnight. If it also had to carry fuel for a 100 million mile journey to Mars and back, the launch costs would rise enormously.

Unit 4 Speaking ③ b

Some say NO!

- The effects of introducing GM foods into the human food chain are still unknown, and difficulties in testing means there is no scientific consensus on their long-term impact on health. Following the 'mad cows' scare, the public want to know their food is safe.
- In Europe, much of wildlife is dependent on agriculture for survival. GM crops pose a serious threat to wild plants and the ecosystems they support, and can contaminate non-GM crops.
- American scientists recently reported that the Monarch Butterfly suffered higher death rates when exposed to pollen from Genetically Modified maize.
- Pests can also develop a resistance to GM products through over-exposure and build up an immunity to pesticides.
- Many farmers in Europe are already turning to safer organic methods to reduce the need for chemicals and to meet the huge increase in demand for organic food.
- Once incorporated into the food chain GM genes will be impossible to control, and the process irreversible. Such far-reaching technology cannot be imposed on people, especially when its effects on health and the environment remain unknown.

Unit 1 Speaking ③

Text B

Producing money

- put strips of metal in machine to cut out round coins
- wash and dry coins
- make edge of coins
- stamp with design
- remove any wrong sizes or shapes

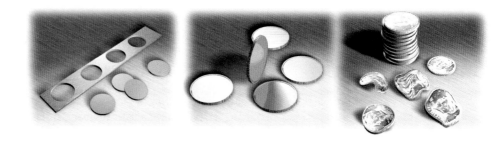

Unit 4 Listening ④

Giles: We lock up more of our citizens than they do in any comparable country, with the sole exception of the United States. What on earth are we doing? This policy is a disaster for all concerned, whether they be prisoners, their dependants or their victims!

Sandy: Well, not entirely. You may think so but …

Giles: Look, the defenders of this unjust and cruel system will tell you that 'prison works', that 'zero tolerance' of even the slightest misbehaviour will somehow magically solve all the problems of crime – despite the fact that study after study proves conclusively that most ex-prisoners are back in court within two years of their release, and that jailing youngsters who have committed minor offences does little more than turn them into hardened criminals …

Sandy: … In what are in effect universities of crime, where they learn new criminal skills, make underworld contacts for the future and so on. But, having said that, for those who *have* committed serious offences, aren't a lot of people starting to feel that sentences should be much longer, that 'life imprisonment' should really mean that murderers stay in jail till they die?

Giles: I don't believe they've thought it through properly. Whenever you ask them where they would keep all these convicts spending maybe 50 or 60 years inside, their answer is simple: 'build more prisons'. But aren't these often exactly the same people who want the state to spend less, so that their taxes can be cut yet again? They know it costs a fortune to keep someone in jail, so what do they do? They call for more private prisons, that's what. Even though all the evidence shows that jails run for profit have an even worse record in terms of reforming prisoners, and that they have too few staff to prevent bullying, and everything else that makes our prisons so atrocious.

Sandy: They're not as bad as they were though, are they? I mean, they haven't been around for all that long and there were bound to be some teething troubles at first. Even their strongest supporters recognise that.

Giles: But conditions inside don't worry them, do they? In fact, they actually appear to believe that our jails are 'too soft', with too much emphasis on education and training, and not enough on punishment. They seem remarkably unconcerned, too, by the loss of the presumption of innocence, if their opposition to bail is anything to go by. Around 60 per cent of accused people held in prison awaiting trial are either later found innocent, or not sent to prison. Like so much of what is now going on in the name of 'law and order', this is totally unacceptable in a society that likes to call itself 'civilised'.

Sandy: So what do you suggest then?

Giles: Well, in the first place we should be *in*creasing the use of cautions for petty offences, especially for teenagers. To many of them it's a shock that they don't want to repeat. It avoids giving them a criminal record that could harm their future career. Among those convicted of more serious offences, there are, inevitably, a few whose crimes are so terrible that they must remain in custody for the rest of their lives, but the vast majority of prisoners would undoubtedly benefit from better preparation for life outside jail. This would include vastly-improved education and training, but also reasonably well-paid work, as they could then afford to compensate the victims of their crimes – and support their own dependants …

Sandy: … I'm sorry but I really don't like the thought of convicted criminals feathering their nests in jail, not while there are so many decent honest people out there in the community who can't find a well-paid job at all …

Giles: ... No no, I'm not talking about letting prisoners line their own pockets. What I am proposing is that they should be allowed to make just enough – and no more – to pay their victims and families. Because links with the outside, I'm utterly convinced, are vital. One of the worst effects of the rush to build new jails is that many prisoners are now held in remote parts of the country, too far away for friends and relatives to visit, with the resulting breakdown of marriages and friendships. This is crazy. We should be doing everything in our power to maintain prisoners' relationships, so that they have a world to go to on their release. And when I say 'release', I mean real freedom, not with Big Brother-style restrictions like electronic tagging or nine to seven curfews, but giving genuine support to help them rebuild their lives. This, of course, is a lot easier if their stay inside has not damaged them too much, so we need to make use of all the resources we have – and some more – to reduce prison overcrowding and combat evils such as institutional racism and violence ...

Sandy: ... <u>No one could disagree with that</u> ...

Giles: ... Above all, though, I believe passionately that the first challenge facing us is this: how to cut the number of people going to prison. There is clear evidence that constructive alternatives like probation and community service are far more effective in reducing re-offending, and we have a duty to get this message across to the public. I'm sick and tired of hearing politicians – and their friends in the media – using the threat to lock up more people as a means of gaining a few more cheap votes. The prison system we've got doesn't work; it destroys. It destroys the lives of everyone it touches and should be a source of shame to every one of us.

Sandy: <u>Well, that's one way of looking at it, I suppose</u>...

Unit 8 Grammar 4

1 1975/college built recently/buildings sinking into ground/engineers study original plans/architect made no allowance for weight of books in library/reduce number of books/still sinking/discover architect made no allowance for weight of water in swimming pool/reduce water level/still sinking/discover architect made no allowance for increasing weight of students

2 1980s Antarctica/Air Force plane flying along coast/penguins on beach/never seen aeroplane/all turn at same time to look left/all turn at same time to look right/pilot flies over penguins/all look up/penguins fall over backwards/can't get up/pilot radios base/Marines arrive/pick up penguins

3 1990s UK/man reading newspaper/sees ad: 'almost new Porsche – £50'/goes to see car, speaks to owner/yes, correct price/test drive/pays £50/asks her why car so cheap/woman explains: happily married for many years/husband runs off with girlfriend/e-mails wife: sell car and send money

Unit 10 Speaking ❷ a

A I'd say it's the second one that shows the most typical scene. I mean, computers play such a big part in your life when you're young – you can listen to music, play games, etc. and just shut out the rest of the world. Particularly if you've got, er, those things you put on your ears to listen through.

B Headphones.

A Right.

B I agree that computers are very important, and of course you can listen to music and at the same time send e-mails, or what do you call it when you look at lots of things on the Internet?

A You mean surfing the Net?

B That's it. Which is another reason why I reckon the second photo is more representative, especially now that such a lot of young people have their own computers in their rooms and all the stuff that goes with them.

Unit 9 Listening ❸ b

One of the effects of extremely hot weather conditions, according to a study carried out recently in the USA, is a significant change in people's mood, leading to a sharp rise in aggressive behaviour. Some, of course, will say that it was hardly necessary to undertake years of costly research to make what might appear to many a fairly obvious point, but with summers apparently heating up, it may mean that a steady increase in violent crime is yet another likely and unwelcome consequence of global warming.

What this study shows is that heatwaves almost invariably coincide with greatly increased rates of violence on the streets, including rioting – hence the term 'long hot summer' that was coined during the Los Angeles riots of the late sixties. The figures for domestic attacks also worsen at such times, which will hardly surprise those living next door to – or, worse still, with – violent individuals. In the same way, the murder statistics frequently show a sudden jump, such as the 75% rise in New York during one particularly steamy August.

On this side of the Atlantic, it has been noticed that the hotter months often bring with them an upsurge in road rage incidents, with motorists more inclined than usual to assault one another for reasons ranging from dangerous overtaking to displaying irritating bumper stickers.

Not everyone however is convinced that heat in itself makes people more violent. Some critics point to the high levels of certain categories of violent crime in northern countries such as the UK, especially when compared to those in some Mediterranean countries where summers are almost invariably much hotter. One explanation put forward for this is that people in more northerly latitudes have a greater tendency to drink excessive amounts of alcohol when the temperature rises, and that much of the violence seen there results from drunkenness, rather than any actual change in mood brought on by the weather.

Some of those who have carried out studies into behaviour on the roads are also sceptical that high temperatures necessarily lead to bad tempers. They believe there is another possible explanation for seasonal variations in levels of violence: people's relative unwillingness to leave the warmth and comfort of their cars to confront other drivers when the weather is cold and wet.

Clearly, more extensive research is needed in a number of areas before the critics can be persuaded of the link between the weather and violence. One area that has yet to be studied is the difference in the effects on people of dry heat and humid heat. Or why, to put it into practical terms, 35 degrees is bearable in Madrid – but not in the much damper atmosphere of, say, London or Paris.

Unit 6 Listening ①c

We hear a lot about European motorway and rail links, and the spider's web of flight paths across the continent, but I bet not many people realise that there's a network of footpaths criss-crossing Europe, too. Known as European Long Distance Paths, or E-Paths, they are the result of at least thirty years' endeavour by the ERA, the European Ramblers Association, whose aim has been to provide walkers with well-mapped, clearly-marked and properly-maintained paths that extend thousands of kilometres, cutting right across international borders.

Often based on existing routes, some parts – inevitably – are better than others and in places it is also possible to travel by horse or bicycle. There are particularly good sections in Scandinavia, Austria and northern Spain, where the old pilgrims' road to Santiago de Compostela is clearly signposted and offers reasonably-priced accommodation for walkers at fairly regular intervals. You'll also find ancient water fountains dotted along the route, and allegedly there's even one that serves the local red wine, free.

Other E-Paths, of course, don't offer quite so much, and there are still a few gaps, particularly in countries that have been involved in armed conflicts in the last ten years or so. Little by little, though, the network is being improved and completed, and it is already possible, for example, to walk non-stop from inside the Arctic Circle to central Italy, or from Portugal to the Ukraine. Though quite how many of us have the time or energy to do so is another matter!

Unit 11 Reading ②b

You are going to read an article about dealing with dangerous situations. For questions 1–5, choose the answer (A, B, C or D) which you think fits best according to the text.

1 Which of these words in the title and introduction is used ironically?
   A practical
   B everyday
   C enormous
   D worst-case

2 What will happen if you land using a companion's parachute?
   A You will damage your arms as you land.
   B You may be uninjured.
   C You will suffer at least a broken leg.
   D You will be killed.

3 What should you do if your car breaks down in the desert and you have little water?
   A stay where you are and wait
   B walk back the way you came
   C eat as much food as possible
   D listen for signals from other people

4 What should you do if you are attacked by killer bees?
   A kill as many as you can
   B run away
   C leave stings in your skin
   D jump into deep water

5 What would you do to escape from a black bear?
   A try to frighten it by making a loud noise
   B climb on top of your car
   C let your dog chase it
   D pretend to be dead

Unit 11 Listening 1 b

1 The visas were not valid because *someone had tricked them into buying them.*
   A the visas had not been obtained before they began their journey.
   B the person who sold them the visas was pretending to be an official.
   C they had not entered the country at the border specified in the visas.
   D they had obtained the visas by offering an illegal gift to an official.

2 What were they worried about while they were in the compound?
   A The soldiers might shoot them by mistake.
   B The conditions there were getting worse every day.
   C They could be kept there for quite a long time.
   D Jane might be accused of taking photos of the refugee camp.

Unit 11 Listening 2 b

You will hear an interview with Dr Eva Chapman, who ran into difficulties on the East–West borders during the Cold War. For questions 1–5, choose the answer (A, B, C or D) which fits best according to what you hear.

1 When she was a small child, Eva and her mother
   A managed to cross from Czechoslovakia into Austria.
   B were caught by the Austrian police after leaving Czechoslovakia.
   C tried unsuccessfully to cross the Czechoslovak–Austrian border.
   D were arrested by the Czechoslovak border police.

2 The bus was held up at the Polish border because
   A a film was being made there.
   B the officials believed that a passenger had shown disrespect.
   C it was so cold that the driver would not go on.
   D the officials accused the driver of insulting the authorities.

3 Why did she feel so guilty when she admitted the passport was hers?
   A At first she had denied it belonged to her.
   B She said that her daughter had wet it.
   C She felt it was her fault that her daughter had wet it.
   D She had been trying to hide under the seat.

4 What did she do in the office?
   A She confessed that she had escaped in 1950.
   B She showed the officials what had happened to the passport.
   C She told them what she thought of the East German government.
   D She spoke very loudly in German.

5 What happened when she got back on the bus?
   A The guards apologised to the driver.
   B The other people on the bus became angry with her.
   C The bus was allowed to continue its journey.
   D The bus had to go back the way it had come.

Unit 12 Listening ❶ b

A Yes, that's true.
B I'm afraid it's quite simple: we'll have to get rid of them.
C Well, it certainly seems to be a matter for concern.
D I really don't go along with that at all.
E Clearly something will have to be done about it.

Interviewer: There's been a lot of talk about the changing nature of the countryside, and one topic that concerns many people is the threat – real or imagined – from imported creatures. In the studio are David Richards and Chloe Gordon. David, what are your views on this?

David: Yes, it seems to me there's a very real danger to our native wildlife from some of the foreign species that have somehow found their way into our countryside. Wouldn't you agree Chloe?

Chloe: 1 (Indicates agreement) ....

David: Yes, take the grey squirrel for instance. It only arrived here a relatively short time ago but it's likely to push out the native red one altogether.

Chloe: 2 (States agreement) ....
The same's happened with the American bullfrog. It's been taking over everywhere since people started bringing it into the country as a pet, and then dumped it in ponds when they got fed up with the incredible amount of noise it makes. But the main reason is that animals are now starting to arrive in food containers on ships, and then escaping.

David: 3 (States disagreement) ....
There's nothing new about importing food from other parts of the world – it's been going on since the nineteenth century and it didn't happen then, so there's really no reason why it should now. Anyway the question is what we do next. We've got to face up to the fact that they're here in very large numbers, and act accordingly.

Chloe: 4 (Indicates agreement) ....
But the problem is what. There just aren't any obvious solutions.

David: 5 (Indicates disagreement) ....
All of them. It's the only way. I know it sounds cruel, but if we don't do something drastic they'll wipe out entire populations of indigenous animals, which is even crueller …

Unit 12 Open cloze

Sailing to the stars 2

The idea of using sunlight to fuel spacecraft was first put forward over 20 years ago, but at that time NASA was in financial trouble and the idea was shelved. Now, however, the future of space exploration looks much brighter, and by 2010 we might actually see a solar sail-driven spacecraft called Interstellar Probe. Its half-kilometre sail would be opened in space, and it would appear for a while to hang there, a kite floating in space. But not for long. Pressure from the sun's rays would accelerate it to speeds five times greater than possible with conventional rockets, and after a certain amount of time it would be zooming towards the stars at 90 kilometres per second.

Unit 4 Speaking ③ b

Some say YES!

- Genetically Modified foods are part of our modern food industry; scientists have been putting barley genes into wheat to make it disease resistant for nearly a century.
- Decades of heavy industry have left us with a planet containing polluted land which needs additional chemicals to make it fertile. GM crops can be altered to reduce the use of pesticides, lessening the impact of chemicals on the surrounding environment.
- Foods can be genetically modified to ensure that they last longer by taking out or adding certain genes.
- They are less likely to lose their colour and keep more of their nutrients. Proteins vital to our diets can be added to foods which don't ordinarily contain them. In time, this will also be true of vitamins, minerals and other nutrients.
- People accept drugs and medicines that have been modified, and frequently swallow pills for the slightest illness. If foods can be adapted to improve quality of life in the first place, why the resistance to biotechnology in agriculture?

Unit 3 Listening ❶a

Interviewer: Today in 'On Camera' we're talking to Suzie Molina, whose face will, I'm sure, be familiar to many of us. I'd like to begin by asking you, Suzie, how you feel about constantly flying off to different parts of the world, often with only a few hours' warning?

Suzie: Well of course I grew up travelling from place to place, so I'm quite used to waking up in a totally different culture from the one I was in yesterday, and finding I've gained or lost several hours, too.

Interviewer: Which countries do you most like working in?

Suzie : Warm ones, as a rule, where the sun shines and people are friendly. Particularly southern Europe and Latin America. That's not to say that people elsewhere are unfriendly, of course: I was in Poland last month and everyone there was great, really easy to interview.

Interviewer: Do you like interviewing people?

Suzie : Yes, I do. Part of my job is to help them relax, and the best thing is when I feel I've achieved something when they come across well on camera. We always let them have a video of their TV appearance, and you know how much it will mean to them, their family and friends if they've done it well.

Interviewer: Are *you* always relaxed, though? What I mean is, how do you handle the pressure when, for instance, you're reporting live to an audience of tens of millions around the world? Do you get very nervous?

Suzie : Oh I usually manage to stay pretty calm, even if now and then you're tempted to start panicking when the inevitable technical hitches occur. A lot depends on the working relationship you have with the rest of the crew, which fortunately in my case has always – touch wood – been good, and sometimes also on your ability to communicate with the local people.

Interviewer: Do you often need to work through an interpreter?

Suzie : No, not often, as I can usually find someone who speaks a language I know, and I've picked up bits and pieces of various local languages and dialects on my travels.

Interviewer: But isn't it sometimes difficult to understand the background to events in some faraway country, particularly if you haven't been there before?

Suzie : Well occasionally perhaps, but I've always been interested in history so in most places I've usually got some idea of the forces that have shaped the current situation there.

Interviewer: Some of the countries you go to are bound to be unstable, perhaps with conflicts going on and a breakdown in law and order. Don't you ever feel frightened in some places?

Suzie : No, not often anyway. I think I can take care of myself in most situations, and we usually know in advance – often from other reporters – where and when things are likely to get nasty, how to get out in a hurry, and so on. Very occasionally, if events move more quickly than anyone thought they would, it can get a bit alarming, but we always have our satellite phone with us and we can call for help if there's nothing else for it.

Interviewer: Some people might say your job is rather insecure in other ways, too, like your employment conditions. How do you feel about having a contract that only lasts two or three years?

Suzie : Oh I'm not bothered about that. I haven't got any commitments and I don't intend to acquire any!

Interviewer: I know you've got a steady boyfriend, though. How do you feel about not seeing him for weeks at a time?

Suzie : Well, we're very fond of each other, but we both value our independence and we're used to being apart for quite long periods of time. My job comes first and I think for him his does too.

Interviewer: Thank you, Suzie.

Suzie : Thanks.

Unit 12 Listening ③

Lucy: Thinking big was fine last century. All our great achievements were conceived on a grand scale, from luxury Transatlantic liners to vast road networks, and from skyscrapers to moon rockets. But the future is different. Technology is advancing so quickly, and attitudes are changing so fast, that before long virtually everything we build and manufacture is going to be a lot tinier.

Joe: I can see the logic of what you're saying, and I'm sure that in some cases you'll be proved right, but I've got my reservations about just how widespread these changes will eventually turn out to be. Electrical equipment, yes – there's no doubt there, though I think some things like mobile phones have now shrunk about as much as they practicably can without …

Lucy: Sorry to butt in, but did you see the monstrosities people were lugging around in that 1980s film the other night? And someone in it actually said 'they're so handy these little phones'. *Little* – it's all a question of what people are used to, and there's always scope for change. It's not that long since computers were massive great things that filled entire rooms, but now even the desk-top PC in its present form has its days numbered …

Joe: No more big grey boxes sitting there: the office will never be the same again, but a lot of other things that are part of everyday life will remain the same, or become even bigger. Planes, for instance: the new jumbos are huge, and apparently giant airships are making a comeback. And you mentioned liners before: what about these monster cruise vessels they're building, the ones that people are going to live on?

Lucy: But we're talking here about very few of each of these things, aren't we? The means of transport that most people use to get about – the car, unfortunately for the environment, it has to be said – is going to become more compact, it's bound to as the cities and roads get ever more crowded.

Joe: Well, they've been saying that was about to happen for the last forty years, haven't they? Ever since the Mini and the little Fiat came out in fact, but there's still no sign of any real change.

Lucy: There will be, before too long. Taxes on particularly wasteful vehicles are going up, in the same way that governments will penalise the manufacture of goods that over-use scarce resources, in other words big products made of wood or oil-based materials. In some cases, of course, technology is actually bringing about some of these changes, without governments having to step in.

Joe: Yes, I'd go along with you there, though my feeling is that it'd *always* be down to technological change rather than politicians deciding what's best for us. For instance, everyone used to have a great long row of encyclopaedias in their living room, which must have accounted for quite a few trees, whereas nowadays the whole thing's held on a single CD ROM.

Lucy: Right.

Joe: But, having said that, I think most people would still rather take a real book with them to the beach, or to bed, or wherever.

Article

An interior design magazine has asked its readers to send in articles entitled *The Ideal Home*. Write an <u>article</u> <u>describing</u> your idea of the <u>perfect flat</u> or <u>house</u>, giving <u>reasons</u> for your <u>choice</u> of <u>building</u>, <u>furniture</u> and <u>decoration</u>.

There's a saying *There's no place like home* and when choosing an ideal home the variety of options available is vast, ranging from sprawling mansion to elegant town house; from luxury penthouse to quaint country cottage. Size, style and position: these are just some of the aspects that need to be considered.

One of the essential elements of my own ideal home would be its location. My home would be in an isolated spot, with breathtaking views of hills and valleys stretching out as far as the eye can see.

As well as its stunning position, a huge, private garden would be vital, divided into different sections: one for flowers, one for homegrown vegetables and somewhere I can relax. There would be a small lake which would attract wildlife, and a willow tree beneath which I'd idle away my time reading or thinking and being lulled by the sound of the birds.

Regarding the house itself, it would be large and it would be several centuries old, because I think old houses have so much more character. To preserve its style all the original features, such as fireplaces, wooden beams and polished floors, would still be in place. The rooms would be full of elegant but comfortable furniture, which again would complement the style of the house, and, as an art fanatic, I would have exquisite paintings on every wall.

Despite my desire for seclusion, at times of course I enjoy company, so there would be a room in the house solely devoted to entertaining. Its furnishings would be more modern; with plush sofas in one corner, a long dining table in another and plenty of floor space for dancing. The walls would be covered in tasteful murals and there might also be a small stage for live music.

My ideal home would be a place of beauty with a sense of history; it would represent the way I want to live, ensuring I could enjoy each aspect of my life freely and in privacy.

- general introduction about the topic to engage reader
- specific vocabulary related to topic included
- written in an appropriate style for an article
- appropriate conditional structures used
- both parts of question (i.e. description and reason) answered
- conclusion recaps generally on content

Set Books: article

The 'Books' section of a Sunday newspaper has asked readers to contribute articles entitled 'Things were different then' on books they have read. Write an <u>article</u> on how *The Great Gatsby* demonstrates the <u>attitudes</u> of <u>early 20th century society</u> in America, and the <u>effects</u> those <u>attitudes</u> have on the <u>life</u> of <u>Gatsby</u>.

THINGS WERE **DIFFERENT** THEN

Rich Society in 1920s America was characterised by a pursuit of pleasure and an absence of ideals where people with an excess of time and money on their hands had a disregard for the lives of other people. F. Scott Fitzgerald called this period 'The Jazz Age'. In *The Great Gatsby*, Fitzgerald exposes the attitudes of 'The Jazz Age' as worthless and dangerous and capable of having disastrous effects on people. It is Daisy and Tom who represent this emptiness and Jay Gatsby who is eventually destroyed.

Daisy and Tom are described as 'gleaming like silver, safe and proud above the hot struggles of the poor.' Their lives are centred on money and status, Tom is brutish and disloyal and Daisy is insincere and devoid of ideas. Neither of them show remorse as tragedy occurs. They are both 'careless people' who 'smashed up things and creatures and then retreated back into their money'.

In contrast, Gatsby is a romantic in search of an ideal that will make his life meaningful. He is an outsider, in love with the undeserving Daisy. He is an object of gossip and speculation amongst the hollow characters that populate his extravagant and artificial parties where 'casual innuendo and introductions' are 'forgotten on the spot', and his vulnerability and isolation make him an inevitable victim.

Through Gatsby, Fitzgerald, like many of his contemporaries, makes a further indictment on American society as he reveals the falsity of the American dream. Gatsby with his accumulated wealth is not guaranteed happiness.

Fitzgerald's characters reveal the inadequacies of 'The Jazz Age' of 1920s America. The destruction and violence that runs through *The Great Gatsby* foreshadows the end of the age itself which was to eventually burn itself out and be replaced by The Great Depression of the 1930s.

- clear introduction links the two themes: the attitudes of society to the book
- relevant quotes from book support points made
- references to specific characters included
- both parts of the question answered
- appropriate use of the present tense to describe events
- written in a suitable style for an article
- conclusion summarises themes

Report

You are spending the summer working as a tourist guide at a safari park. While you were escorting a group of tourists, a serious incident occurred which resulted in two people being injured. Write a <u>report</u> of the <u>incident</u> for your boss, <u>stating who</u> or <u>what</u> was to <u>blame</u> for what <u>happened</u>.

Introduction

The purpose of this report is to explain what happened and state who is to blame for the serious incident that took place on Wednesday 5th August, when two people in the tour group were injured. It is based on information taken from members of the group who witnessed what happened, as well as on private observation.

Events leading up to the incident

The incident occurred at approximately 2 p.m. The group had re-boarded the coach after a meal at the Safari Restaurant and the coach was approaching the Monkey Sanctuary. Many of the tourists on the bus have since reported they felt the driver was going too quickly at this point. Some of them remember commenting on this fact to their fellow passengers and stating they intended to make complaints at the end of the tour. One tourist felt the driver picked up speed as he passed the sign for the sanctuary. Another felt the driver was spending too much time looking out of the window. She remembers feeling nervous about this.

The incident and its effects

A few minutes after the coach passed the sign for the sanctuary, the driver had to brake suddenly in order to avoid crashing into a car which had stopped after a monkey had jumped onto its windscreen. The coach stopped with such force that people were thrown forward in their seats. Most people were shocked by the incident but uninjured. However, one man broke his nose on the seat in front of him and a woman sprained her wrist as she put out her arm to protect herself. The coach then drove back to the First Aid room at the entrance to the safari park, where the two injured members of the group were treated. The driver admits he may have been driving too fast, but denies a lack of concentration.

Conclusion

In conclusion, it is obvious from the testimonies of the tour group that the driver is to blame for the incident. He was clearly driving too quickly and without due care and attention.

- clear introduction: aims stated using the passive
- appropriate use of grammar: reported opinions, facts in past tense, use of passive
- conclusion sums up the contents of the report
- question is answered in full
- written in neutral style, not unnecessarily formal
- suitable layout with clearly labelled paragraphs

Formal letter

You have decided to resign from your job. Write a <u>letter</u> to your <u>boss</u>, <u>describing</u> <u>why</u> you are <u>leaving</u> and explaining <u>why</u> it has been such a <u>difficult</u> <u>decision</u> for you to make. Do not write any postal addresses.

Dear Mr Jones

I am writing to inform you that I wish to resign from my post as Marketing Manager for Marston's Textiles PLC. I would like to leave the company at the beginning of July this year. As you know I have been with Marston's Textiles for over ten years, and have gained considerable experience in the textiles field. However, I now feel it is time to diversify that experience and move elsewhere.

I have been offered and have accepted a post as Marketing Director for an innovative cosmetic company which is setting up in Singapore later this year. Bartlett's Cosmetics already has branches all over Europe and is now hoping to make further breakthroughs in the Far East. Initially the post is for two years, however, with the company's plans for continued expansion it is likely to be extended indefinitely with eventual possibilities of living and working in other countries.

Naturally my family and I will be re-locating to Singapore. Although this may initially involve considerable difficulty, it will ultimately, I feel, be an excellent opportunity for all of us. Bartlett's Cosmetics has offered me an excellent package, which includes paying the children's fees at one of the country's top independent schools, as well as housing us in one of the most prestigious apartment blocks in the city centre. The chance to live outside the UK in such excellent circumstances has also been a major factor in enticing me to accept the job.

I would like to emphasise that my decision to leave Marston's Textiles has not been taken lightly and that it is with considerable regret that I leave a company where not only have I enjoyed exciting challenges and job satisfaction, but I have had the privilege to work with a team of extremely dedicated and professional people.

Yours sincerely

David Cunningham

David Cunningham

- written in formal style
- appropriate opening and closing expressions used
- both parts of the question answered
- suitable layout; no postal addresses included
- appropriate range of tenses used

Review

You have recently been to the cinema to see the re-release of a <u>classic</u> <u>film</u>. Write a <u>review</u> of the film for a <u>city leisure guide</u>, and <u>explain</u> <u>why</u> you think <u>young</u> <u>people</u> today will <u>still</u> <u>enjoy</u> it.

Hitchcock's *Rear Window* is a nail-biting thriller which is as entertaining for young people today as it was when it was first released. The film combines an exciting plot, with an original and gripping way of relating it, and also raises more serious questions about the nature of voyeurism.

The whole film is seen through the eyes of one man, played by James Stewart, who sits in his cramped apartment, temporarily confined to a wheelchair. He entertains himself by looking out of the rear window of his own apartment and watching the activities of the residents in the apartment block opposite. What starts as an amusing pastime, however, gradually becomes a dangerous activity as he becomes convinced that the salesman played by Raymond Burr has murdered his invalid wife. James Stewart enlists the help of his girlfriend, Grace Kelly, and his nurse in order to spy more effectively, and the tension mounts.

In classic suspense style, we remain unsure whether the murder has taken place right up until the climax. By showing the events through one man's eyes, Hitchcock uses a more unusual method as we are drawn into the character's feelings of frustration and fear. This culminates in the scene when we watch James Stewart watching his girlfriend who is trapped in the salesman's apartment, and we wonder whether he will now witness her murder.

The film sustains its timeless qualities further by being more than just an exciting thriller. It is not only the salesman that Stewart is spying on, it is also the newly wed couple, the songwriter and Miss Lonely Hearts, the sad old spinster. We too watch their stories unfold and question the moral dilemma of the nature of privacy in respect of both Stewart and ourselves.

Rear Window is enduring in its ability both to entertain through the power of suspense and to provoke thought in its exploration of more serious issues. Its originality places it high up the list of classic psychological thrillers and it is likely to remain there for some time to come, entertaining young people of each generation.

- general introduction, and reiteration of writer's opinion in the conclusion
- question answered by summarising plot and giving specific examples of why it will be enjoyed
- present tense used to narrate plot
- appropriate style for a review
- title of film mentioned and highlighted

'For and against' essay (Part one)

Your teacher has asked you to respond to this extract from an article in an English-language magazine. Write an <u>essay</u>, giving <u>arguments for</u> and <u>against</u> the <u>opinions</u> it <u>expresses</u>.

> The number of languages currently spoken in the world is set to decline as a few major languages become increasingly dominant. The inevitable outcome of this will be that lesser-spoken languages will eventually disappear entirely.

Major languages such as English, Spanish and German are becoming increasingly influential and are already threatening the existence of some lesser-spoken languages. It is a matter of concern that if this trend continues, many lesser-spoken languages could completely disappear. However, can a language – the living symbol and expression of a particular culture with its own way of life and structure – be wiped out quite so easily?

In a practical sense fewer languages leads to freer communication, and the demand for this is especially important with big business, trade and commerce as it continues to expand across the globe. However, communicating in another language does not necessarily mean abandoning a first. In Luxembourg, for example, people speak English, French and German fluently with no loss to their native tongue.

The continued expansion of television and other media can also have the effect not only of encouraging uniformity and damaging cultural identity but of diminishing minor languages as programmes are invariably broadcast in one of the dominant languages. In spite of this, in many countries, people continue to celebrate national festivals and traditions and in places where their language is genuinely under threat, such as Wales or Canada, there are strong campaigns to retain it.

Advancements in travel have resulted in almost every part of the world becoming accessible to ordinary people and this presents a further threat to lesser-known languages. Many small countries are forced to ensure that people are able to communicate with their visitors by means of one of the dominant languages. Nonetheless, the practicality and convenience of being understood does not diminish the desire to experience the differences and the variety of a place, including its language.

To sum up, although some lesser-known languages have already disappeared and others are under threat, it is unlikely that the end result will be a loss of all such languages. The desire to maintain and enjoy differences is too strong. It is more likely that for the majority, languages such as English will continue to be a second language rather than a first.

- introduction gives overview of situation
- topic of essay presented in interesting question form
- content responds to input
- appropriate use of linking words
- each paragraph balances one argument for with one argument against the statement
- analysis of a few well-chosen issues
- conclusion sums up and clarifies writer's opinion
- written in an appropriate style for an essay

Proposal

You work for the local council. Your manager has asked you to write a proposal on the best way to develop a stretch of water in your town or area.

PURPOSE OF PROPOSAL

This proposal outlines how Sports and Leisure can take advantage of the influx of new residents to our town by making use of the stretch of river close to the new housing estates.

ANALYSIS OF PRESENT SITUATION

At present, the area from the edge of town to the caravan site is a wasted resource. The water is dirty and full of rubbish including larger items of scrap metal such as shopping trolleys. The land on the opposite side to the estates is overgrown and both unpleasant and unsafe to walk along.

THE OPTIONS

I considered the following options for developing the area:
- a boat club
- a picnic area
- a nature reserve

After carrying out extensive research, which included interviewing representatives of local organisations and a postal survey of 2,000 local residents, I propose the building of a boat club. This is something the town lacks and it could also have a number of other amenities, including a gym and a restaurant with river views, to provide leisure activities for the local people. Such facilities would have the added advantage of attracting members and non-members alike and would go some way towards financing the cost of the proposal. With regard to the river itself, in addition to its use by the boat club, the setting up of boat trips for members of the public could also be considred. This would have the further benefit of attracting to the site people other than those who live in the town.

RECOMMENDATIONS

Further research should now be done in the following areas:
- time needed to prepare the area
- the costing of the project
- locating an exact site for the club

- appropriate layout for a proposal: clearly organised sections with headings
- clear introduction and summary of recommendations
- analysis of proposal and justification given
- written in a neutral style, not unnecessarily formal

Paper 5 Speaking Format

Candidates: In pairs or a group of three if there is an odd number of candidates at the examining session.

Examiners: The Interlocutor, who conducts the test, and the Assessor, who does not join in the conversation.

Format: *Part 1 (3 minutes)*

A conversation between the Interlocutor and each candidate.

The focus is on general interaction and social language. You will be asked about yourself and your opinions. The questions will probably focus on where you live, your work or studies, your interests and hobbies, your plans for the future, etc.

Part 2 (4 minutes)

A conversation between the candidates.

You will be given something to look at (usually photos). The Interlocutor will ask you to discuss some aspect of this visual prompt. You may have to compare, evaluate, give your opinion, speculate, and/or make a decision.

Part 3 (12 minutes)

A 'long turn' by each candidate with follow-up questions, and a discussion related to the long turn. (There is unlikely to be any connection between Part 2 and Part 3.)

You will be given a written question with some prompts. You will talk for 2 minutes, then the Interlocutor will ask the other candidate a related question (1 minute), followed by a related question for both of you (1 minute). Your partner will then talk for 2 minutes on another question, followed by a related question for you (1 minute), and a question for both of you (1 minute).

Finally the Interlocutor will ask both of you to discuss a related topic (4 minutes).

Assessment: You are assessed throughout the test on:

- Grammatical resource (range, flexibility, and accuracy)
- Lexical resource (range and appropriacy)
- Discourse management (coherence, relevance, and appropriate length of contribution)
- Pronunciation (stress and rhythm, intonation, and individual sounds)
- Interactive communication (initiating and responding, turn-taking, and lack of hesitation)
- Global achievement (overall performance)

OXFORD
UNIVERSITY PRESS

Great Clarendon Street, Oxford OX2 6DP

Oxford University Press is a department of the University of Oxford.
It furthers the University's objective of excellence in research, scholarship, and
education by publishing worldwide in

Oxford New York

Athens Auckland Bangkok Bogotá Buenos Aires Cape Town
Chennai Dar es Salaam Delhi Florence Hong Kong Istanbul Karachi
Kolkata Kuala Lumpur Madrid Melbourne Mexico City Mumbai Nairobi Paris
São Paulo Shanghai Singapore Taipei Tokyo Toronto Warsaw

with associated companies in Berlin Ibadan

Oxford and Oxford English are registered trade marks of
Oxford University Press in the UK and in certain other countries

© Oxford University Press 2002

Database right Oxford University Press (maker)

First published 2002

ISBN 0 19 433243 8

Printed in Spain by Gráficas Estella

The authors and publisher are grateful to those who have given permission to
reproduce the following extracts and adaptations of copyright material:

p6 'TV Millionaire thanks to Henry II' by Matt Wells © The Guardian 21 November
2000. Reproduced by permission of Guardian Newspapers Ltd. p7 'Starting and
running a business'. Reproduced by permission of Barclays Bank PLC. p18 'The
young men and the sea' by Richard Kelly Heft from the Independent 18 April
2000. Reproduced by permission of Independent Newspapers (UK) Ltd. p19 'Lake
Mead Cruise' from www.grandcanyontours.com. Reproduced by permission of
Grand Canyon Tour Company. p30 'Extra, Extra, read all about it' by Henry Rupert
© The Guardian 7 October 1998. Reproduced by permission of Guardian
Newspapers Ltd. p38 'Bollywood goes global' by Carla Power and Sundip
Mazumdar, Newsweek 28 February 2000. Reproduced by permission of Newsweek
Inc. All rights reserved. p42 Extracts from Fever Pitch by Nick Hornby (Victor
Gollancz, 1992) Copyright © Nick Hornby. Reproduced by permission of The
Penguin Group (UK). p45 'First kiss beats everything as memory of a lifetime' by
John Harlow © Times Newspapers Ltd 6 June 1999. Reproduced by permission of
Times Newspapers Ltd. p49 'Idolising rock stars can damage your health' by
Glenda Cooper, The Independent 4 April 1997. Reproduced by permission of
Independent Newspapers (UK) Ltd. p54 Extracts from Notes From a Big Country
by Bill Bryson © Bill Bryson 1998, published by Black Swan, a division of
Transworld Publishers. Reproduced by permission. All rights reserved. p66 Extracts
from www.hctravel.com. Reproduced by permission of H-C Travel. p66 'An
introduction to inline skating' from www.inliners.co.uk. Reproduced by permission
of Pacer Leisure Ltd. p74 'Downhill racer' © Alf Alderson 1 July 2000. Reproduced
by permission of Guardian Newspapers Ltd. p78 'Sleepy in a teepee? Checking in
at the weirdest hotels in America' © Helen Foster / Times Newspapers Ltd 10 April
1999. Reproduced by permission of Times Newspapers Ltd. p85 'Turning the
tables' by Tamsin Blanchard © The Observer 27 February 2000. Reproduced by
permission of Guardian Newspapers Ltd. p90 'Why dinosaurs won't go away' by
Robert Matthews, The Guardian 22 October 1999. Reproduced by permission of
Robert Matthews. p101 Extract from The Stations of the Sun: A History of the
Ritual Year in Britain by Ronald Hutton. © Ronald Hutton 1996. Reproduced by
permission of Oxford University Press. p102 Extracts from advertisement for S.A.D
Lightbox. Reproduced by permission of S.A.D Lightbox Co. Ltd. p103 'Madness of

the Winter Myths' by John Illman, The Guardian 17 November 1998. Reproduced
by permission of John Illman. p103 'Woman back from dead after she survives
record low temperatures' by Jeremy Laurance, The Independent 28 January 2000.
Reproduced by permission of Independent Newspapers (UK) Ltd. p114 'You are
what you keep' by Jaye Griffiths from The Guardian 10 November 1998.
Reproduced by permission of Guardian Newspapers Ltd. p117 'Anti-stress room is
a smash hit' by Jonathan Watts 25 November 1996. Reproduced by permission of
Guardian Newspapers Ltd. p126 'How to wrestle an alligator (and practical ways
to deal with those everyday disasters)' by Julian Champkin, The Daily Mail 6 April
2000. Reproduced by permission of Daily Mail / Atlantic Syndication Partners.
p130 'Break for the border' by Tony Wheeler, The Independent 20 February 1999.
Reproduced by permission of Independent Newspapers (UK) Ltd. p133 'A bluffer's
guide to bidding' by Siobhan Gonzalez & Luisa Moffet, The Bulletin 7 December
2000. Reproduced by permission of Ackroyd Publications. p134 'Call of the wild'
by John Vidal © The Guardian 9 June 1999. Reproduced by permission of Guardian
Newspapers Ltd. p135 'A lifetime of risk' by Frank Duckworth, The Royal Statistical
Society News October 1998. Reproduced by permission of Frank Duckworth. p138
'High tech crime of the future will be all mod cons' by Tony Thompson © The
Observer 3 October 1999. Reproduced by permission of Guardian Newspapers
Ltd. p150/157 'Riding on a sunbeam' by Tim Radford © The Guardian 27 July
2000. Reproduced by permission of Guardian Newspapers Ltd.

Although every effort has been made to trace and contact copyright holders
before publication, this has not been possible in some cases. We apologise for any
apparent infringement of copyright and if notified, the publisher will be pleased to
rectify any errors or omissions at the earliest opportunity.

p61 'The Bugging Business' by Richard Norton-Taylor, The Guardian 10/12/99.

The publishers would like to thank the following for their kind permission to
reproduce photographs:
Allsport pp 48 (John Cicmici); The Art Archive p 89 (Galleria Borghese/mosaic);
Ross Abraham Arun p 53 (voice pattern); Associated Press pp 34 (Sayyid
Azim/children), 38 (Teh Eng Koon), 41 (Launette Florian/demonstration, Dave
Martin/football fans), 65 (refugees), 83 Nick UT/traffic, 89 (hippies), 99 (Misha
Japaridze), 106 (Mary Lederhandler), 130 (Srdjan Ilic); Bridgeman Art Library
p 107 (Museo de Arte, Puerto Rica/ Flaming June by Frederic Leighton); Bubbles
Photo Library 131 (Angela Hampton/A); Corbis Images pp 5 (Bettmann/money),
74 (Julie Habel), 77 (David Samuel Robins/yurt), 89 (Bettmann/shops), 119
(Macduff Everton/ping pong), 145 (Nik Wheeler); Ronald Grant Archive pp 50
(Miramax/hall), 61 (Eon Productions); H-C Travel p 66 (Patrick Moffat/
motorcycles); Robert Harding Picture Library p 27 (Michael Busselle); Hutchison
Library pp 65 (Liba Taylor/riding), 101 (May dancing); Image Bank pp 37 (Patrick
Altman), 65 (Archive Holdings/pioneers, Tommy Ewasko/lorry); Impact Photos
pp 83 (Geray Sweeney/exam), 101 (Gerey Sweeney/grape picking), 119 (Mark
Henley/girls), 123 (Simon Shepheard), 131 (Rupert Conaut/B); Jules' Undersea
Lodge p 79 (diver and girl); Katz Pictures p 110 (Adrian Kool); Kobal Collection
pp 50 (Miramax/wedding), 117 (20th Century Fox/Paramount/Merie W Wallace/
Titanic); Chris Moore p 85; Network Photographers pp 30 (Raphe/Hans Silvester),
66 Bilderberg/S Enders/rollerblading, 101 (Minique Jacot/Raphe/ candles), 135
(Fritz Hoffman); Oxford Scientific Films pp 26 (Richard Packwood), 111 (Demi
Bown/seed head), 125 (Stan Osolinski/alligator), 127 (Scot Camazine/swarm,
Daniel J Cox/bear); Press Association pp 6 (Peter Jordon), 46 (Paul Faith), 83
(Samantha Pearce/March), 90 (EPA), 131 (EPA/C), 133 (EPA), 137 (Tim
Ockenden/travellers); Rex Features pp 5 (homeless), 17 (Sipa/Stevens/rafting), 41
(Sipa/Michael/Bottle tops), 47 (Nick Cobbins), 59 (Rav Tang/Davina and Sada,
ZZ/Davina eating, Johnny Boylan/Davina posed), 79 (Agence DPPI) 80, 107
(Today/water shortage), 117 (Sipa/explosion), 126, 131 (Patrick Bath/D); Science
Photo Library pp 25 (Peter Ryan/Scripps), 53 Manfred Kage/fingerprint, Rory
McClengahan/retina, BSIP Estiot/hand, Ken Eward/DNA, 107 (Dr Jeremy
Burgess/bee), 111 (Cordelia Molloy/dandelion) 117 (Nasa/Challenger crew), 137
(Mehan Kulkl/Space colony), 157; Stone pp 5 (Stuart McClymont/women), 34
(Martin Barraud/woman), 62 (John Bradley), 103 (Gerben Opperman), 143 (David
Young Wolff); South Bank Management 114, 115 (Marcus Robinson); Elizabeth
Whiting pp 77 (room with fire, modern room).

Illustrations by:
Paul Daviz/illustrationweb.com pp 11, 12 (party), 36, 57, 84, 121, 1128
Mark Duffin pp 22, 29, 58, 65, 70, 82, 86, 147, 149, 150
John Haslam pp 12 (woman), 48, 72, 95, 96, 113, 144
Stuart Haygarth/Debut Art pp 10, 55
Gavin Reece/New Division pp 14, 44, 60, 69, 93, 97, 125, 139
Nicola Slater/Thorogood Illustration pp 8,9, 33, 105, 116, 120, 140, 141

Commissioned Photography
David Tolley pp 35, 119 (boy with computer)
The photograph on page 42 is reproduced by kind permission of The Orion
Publishing Group.